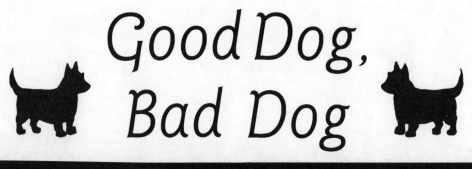

Good Dog, Bad Dog

NEW AND REVISED

Dog Training Made Easy

MORDECAI SIEGAL & MATTHEW MARGOLIS

Photographs By Mordecai Siegal

HENRY HOLT AND COMPANY   NEW YORK

Henry Holt and Company, Inc.
Publishers since 1866
115 West 18th Street
New York, New York 10011

Henry Holt® is a registered trademark
of Henry Holt and Company, Inc.

Library of Congress Cataloging-in-Publication Data
Siegal, Mordecai.
Good dog, bad dog, new and revised: dog training made easy.
Mordecai Siegal and Matthew Margolis.
            p.   cm.
Includes index.
1. Dogs—Training.   2. Dog breeds.   I. Margolis, Matthew.
II. Title.
SF431.S552   1991
636.7'0887—dc20   90-49749
                                                        CIP
ISBN 0-8050-1094-7

FIRST EDITION
Printed in the United States of America
All first editions are printed on acid-free paper. ∞
7   9   10   8

This book is dedicated
to the man who trained the trainers
—Captain Arthur J. Haggerty—
whose far-reaching influence has
helped make dog training a
respected and valued profession.

CONTENTS

II.
AFTER THE OBEDIENCE COURSE

III.
100 DOG BREEDS: A DICTIONARY
OF TRAINING BEHAVIOR
227

ACKNOWLEDGMENTS

Short and sweet—but *very* sweet. The authors are grateful to their families, friends, and supporters for their talents, skills, and much-needed help. We thank you, Vicki Siegal, for your invaluable editorial assistance; TJ, Ida, and Jasper Siegal for staying out of Dad's office during work hours; John Turner for all your generous computer help on the New York end, and for sharing your fax machine; Marla Rosner Johnson, assistant to M. Margolis, for your efficient bicoastal coordination of everything between the Atlantic and the Pacific; Sherry Davis, Executive Director of Training of The National Institute of Dog Training, for your knowledgeable advice and for making the photo sessions in Los Angeles a dream; and to you, Beverly and Jesse Margolis, for making M. Siegal a welcome guest in your home for more than one never-ending visit.

Here's a toast to the wonderful staff of the National Institute of Dog Training in Los Angeles for their enthusiasm and hard work on behalf of this book, especially to Janell Gentile, assistant to the Executive Director of Training; Robert Pirro, trainer; Ashraf Rizk, trainer; Khee Boon (Tony) Beh, student trainer; Anthony Gonzales, master carpenter; Jesse Battle, groundskeeper; and to kennel supervisors Ernie De La Torre, Debbie Schnitger, and Debbie McKean. You were all a joy to work with.

APPLAUSE TO THOSE IN THE PHOTOGRAPHS

The Dogs: Lincoln and Austin Lasorda, Miniature Schnauzers; Mikey Vampotic, Yorkshire Terrier; Quint and Emily Margolis, German Shepherd Dogs; Cappucino Gentile, Cocker Spaniel; Arnold Buckman, Golden Retriever; Bruce and Timmy Davis, Golden Retrievers; Priscilla Suarez, Basset Hound; Duke McKinney, St. Bernard; and Casey Lloyd, Australian Shepherd.

The People: Laura Lasorda, Matthew Margolis, Alan (Armando) Buckman, Marilyn Buckman, Janell Gentile, Ashraf Rizk, and Khee Boon (Tony) Beh.

FOREWORD

Who could have predicted in 1971 that our slender dog training manual would continue its service to pet owners for twenty years and more? We never dreamed that it would become a book club selection or that it would be published in foreign-language editions in France, Italy, Norway, and Israel. Portions of the text appeared in *The Ladies' Home Journal,* and various book chains displayed the book prominently in advertisements and on their best-seller lists. With almost one million copies in print, we have often pondered why this book was so successful. A newspaper reporter suggested that it was the catchy title. But we do not believe that dog owners judge books by their titles.

We have concluded that the original version of *Good Dog, Bad Dog* was successful because it offered a simple dog obedience course that was easy to understand and use. Many pet owners and dog fanciers have used the book with satisfaction. Many have written to us or told us in person how much they enjoyed the book and that they were able to train their dogs with it. They also told us that the training information about individual dog breeds was very helpful and greatly appreciated. Sixty-six dog breeds that Matthew had experience with were discussed in terms of training. If the reader used the book correctly, his or her dog would be trained. In other words, the book kept its promise. Because it did, it has become a time-honored standard that can be found in bookstores and libraries everywhere.

So why revise *Good Dog, Bad Dog*? Can our little best-selling manual be improved? Yes. Since the original version was written, much has been learned about dog behavior and how it influences dog training. Since our book was first published, Matthew has trained or supervised the training of 25,000 dogs, and as a result has refined his original techniques and developed some new ones. Mordecai has researched and written many new pet books over the years in addition to hundreds of magazine columns and articles. Together we have set down the results of a broader understanding of dog ownership, behavior, training techniques, and human/canine relationships.

The most important concept in this revised edition is the idea of bonding with your dog before attempting to train him. Bonding is a simple process designed to develop trust and confidence in the dog, and it is quick and easy to accomplish. It allows a dog, especially a new puppy, to feel safe in his new home and to understand that life is good and his new family is simply that—his new family. We now encourage dog owners to get to know their dogs, love them, and develop a relationship *before* beginning the training course. We feel this is of primary importance.

Another new element is determining your dog's temperament. In Chapter 3 we describe five basic temperament types in detail and ask you to decide which of the five best describes your dog. With that information you will then be able to adjust the teaching/training techniques of the obedience chapters to the requirements of your individual dog. At the end of each training-command chapter you will be offered the opportunity to customize the training techniques for each of the five temperament types.

Because no two dogs are alike, we have abandoned the "one size fits all" approach to dog training. Dogs are either High-energy/Outgoing, Shy, Strong-willed, Calm/Easygoing, or Aggressive. The heart of the new training material is based on this concept. As your own dog trainer, you will have the option of using the standard course (for the average dog) or moving to the back of each chapter and using the customized training adjustments.

We have expanded the breed section from sixty-six to one hundred purebred training entries. In addition to new chapters on bonding and your dog's temperament, we have refined much of the original teaching and added new material to every training command chapter. Oh, yes—the photographs are new and appropriate for the added information. They were taken by Mordecai.

Each year the American Kennel Club (AKC) registers over one million puppies. More than 225,000 are registered by the United Kennel Club (UKC). Although many of these become show dogs, obedience-trial dogs, or field dogs, the greatest percentage are purchased by those who simply want a family pet. This does not include the hundreds of thousands of dogs that are acquired from a veterinarian's bulletin board, over the back fence, found on the streets, or rescued from animal shelters. These new pet owners sooner or later discover their dogs must be trained if they are going to remain in the home. We know for a fact that *Good Dog, Bad Dog* has helped save the homes (and maybe the lives) of thousands of dogs because their owners learned how to train them. Our new and revised book suggests that the days of caveman dog training are over. Getting to know your dog, learning to love him, and *then* training him is the Good Dog way. We wish you well.

Mordecai Siegal and Matthew Margolis

INTRODUCTION

*If you pick up a starving dog and make him pros-
perous, he will not bite you. This is the principal
difference between a dog and a man.*

—Mark Twain

Now that you've made the commitment to own a dog, it is reasonable to want to know how to take care of him. After all, these bundles
of fur are totally dependent crea-
tures and innocently look to their
owners for food, shelter, medical
attention, and love. Everything
connected with their survival depends on the big guys, the humans. And in the human world,
a dog's survival often hinges on
his ability to respond to a direct
command such as "Stay!" "Silver,
come!" "No!" "Down!" "Sit!"
These are not arbitrary orders
shouted from the Gestapo hand-
book. They are scientifically de-

veloped commands given to a trained animal whose correct response may save his life in city traffic or around rural hazards. These commands will also promote a satisfying relationship between dog and human. If a dog is not housebroken, not able to refrain from barking, not able to keep from destroying furniture or property, not able to obey when required, then his survival is in jeopardy. Many people give up their dogs after a few months of frustration, and the future of those animals is then in grave danger. This is why obedience training is not only valuable but necessary.

With the many books on dog training available, one might ask what's special about this one. To begin with, the premise of this book is that the *owner* is being taught how to train the dog. Equal emphasis is given to teaching the owner and to teaching the animal.

Co-author Matthew Margolis is the owner-operator of the National Institute of Dog Training, Inc., in Los Angeles, which has trained over 25,000 dogs *and their owners*. He is one of the pioneers in the techniques of owner-animal training in the home. The benefit of his experience and vast personal knowledge is offered here, along with those of co-author Mordecai Siegal, who is the author of many books and articles concerning pet behavior, nutritional needs, medical care, training, breed descriptions, and human/animal bonding.

This dog-training book attempts to dig beneath the surface of its own method and explain how the technique works. Within these pages is offered a basic obedience training course that has proven itself over and over with thousands of dogs of all breeds. Also offered is a section that describes the behavioral characteristics of approximately one hundred dog breeds, with advice on how to use that information in training. The philosophy of training offered emphasizes affection, kindness, and authority. It is based on the idea that dogs are nice.

I.

The Basic
Obedience Course

1.

SUCCESS

Being a dog is a boring job. Most of his life is spent sleeping or waiting to be fed. Chances are the dog is bored beyond belief. This is especially true if his owner does not know how to communicate with him, to convey what is wanted, or to spend the time necessary to develop a rapport. Dogs are in a foreign country and do not understand the language. This may explain why they often seek the company of other dogs. Dog people are kind and generous. They need only to develop consistent goals and principles to enjoy many years of companionship with a dog.

The difference between a good dog and a bad dog is whether or not he makes his owner's blood pressure rise when things go wrong. As leader of the pack, it is the owner's obligation to offer shelter, nutrition, medical attention, exercise, love, affection, and training. In return, the dog should give you love, loyalty, laughter, and genuine obedience. Although it seems a bit medieval, this is approximately the ideal dog-human relationship. Successful training helps achieve this goal. This course deals exclusively with obedience because it has been proven that the dog-human relationship improves greatly after an effective training course.

THE PROPER FRAME OF MIND

To train a dog successfully, humans must maintain the cool objectivity of a "pro." This means not allowing frustrations to interfere with relating to the dog. Many mistakes are going to be made by the dog as he proceeds from lesson to lesson throughout the course, and your patience will be put to the test over and over again. The dog must not be yelled at or punished in any way. If you have had a trying day, you must either postpone the lesson or stay alert and not abuse the dog because you didn't get that promotion, or the IRS has scheduled you for an audit, or your teenage daughter has shaved the sides of her head and dyed what's left purple. You must exercise patience, kindness, and an understanding of your emotional limitations. Many a kicked dog has been a substitute for the boss, the wife, the husband, the mother-in-law. Before expressing anger at your dog, ask if he really deserves it. There is no place in this obedience course for abuse. Forget the word *punishment*. Replace it with the word *correction*.

WHY TRAIN A DOG?

The answer to this question has to do with why one buys a dog at all. There are many reasons why people keep dogs. Pleasure, companionship, protection, and child education are a few, but the main reason is to enjoy the animal. No living being will love you as completely as a dog will. Training helps remove emotional obstacles that stand between humans and their dogs.

Without training, cute puppy behavior soon develops into annoying adult habits. These annoying habits sometimes become generalized into permanent behavior patterns, creating severe problems. But with a trained dog, you will be able to cope with dog fighting, being dragged down the street, being jumped on, or having

furniture destroyed. Obedience training helps to eliminate stealing food from the table, defecating indoors, throwing up in the car, or the hundreds of other problems that can make it unpleasant to own a pet. If a dog performs any combination of these things he is not necessarily a bad dog. He is merely untrained. This is a correctable situation; it is well within your grasp to change it.

Puppies are like babies. They are helpless and vulnerable. But not all puppies are good dogs. Some inherit poor behavior and have problems early in their lives. Dog behavior is shaped by environmental influences as well as by the genetic characteristics of the dog's bloodline. If a dog is trained properly, he will probably behave well and cause very few problems through his life. A good definition of training is: *Teaching a dog to respond properly to humans and to do what is expected of him when a command is given.* Any dog can be trained.

DISPELLING MYTHS FROM THE DARK AGES

It is important to forget the hearsay methods of dog training that have been handed down through the years like snake oil in a medicine show. Chances are, it was Attila the Hun who first rubbed his dog's nose in his own mess and yelled and screamed at him. Forget that "method." Forget all methods that brutalize and are abusive, such as swatting a dog across the face with a rolled-up newspaper. It teaches the dog nothing except to fear long, cylindrical objects (including your hands) and to run when he sees them. It is merely another form of punishment that accomplishes nothing positive beyond giving you emotional release.

Do you hit your dog? Of course not. But some confused, frustrated owners do. A flinching, cowering, neurotic animal is a giveaway. The owner says in protest ". . . but I really love Tinkle. I only kick her when she's a bad dog." This obedience course shows a better way to make a dog behave and replaces antiquated techniques. Forever resolve not to hit, kick, pinch, punch, gouge, slap, knuckle, tweak, bang, strike, nip, or bite your dog. Please refrain from ever using your hand for anything other than hand signals (used in giving commands) or affectionate praise or love. Never use your hand for threats, violent gestures, or even disciplinary pointing. Pointing your finger at the dog and saying "Naughty, naughty" produces the same negative effect. Pain, fear, and terror retard or prohibit communication, and to inflict them is inhumane.

Imagine entering a taxi in a foreign country. The driver asks, "Where to?" in his native tongue. You stare at him and shrug, not knowing the language. He then goes berserk and smacks you hard on the snout. This would seem painfully unreasonable, to say the least. Yet some dogs face this horror every day of their lives. *If hitting a dog were the least bit useful, why would it have to be done so often?* Your dog can be trained with guaranteed results without being punished. Here is an opportunity to stop feeling guilty and give your dog a punishment-free life. It will also enable you to enjoy your friend, your dog.

Forever resolve not to hit, kick, pinch, punch, gouge, slap, knuckle, tweak, bang, strike, nip, or bite your dog.

WHEN TO BEGIN TRAINING

Training can begin at seven weeks of age for puppies of all breeds. This includes housebreaking, paper training, and all obedience training commands.

WHO SHOULD PARTICIPATE IN THE TRAINING?

Every member of the family should participate in this training course. It is essential that all the family learn about the training commands and how to administer them so that the dog will be obedient with everyone. If the commands are not administered consistently, the dog will become confused. For obvious reasons, only one person should introduce the training to the animal. Then, after the dog has learned each new command, the primary trainer should introduce the techniques to the rest of the family. If everyone participated in the training at the same time, it would become more of a chaotic party than a lesson for the dog, and the session would go out the window. With cross-conversations, inconsistent commands, and general tumult, the dog's attention span fades in a matter of minutes.

It is best to teach the dog a command with no one else present. It may take from one to three sessions for him to respond quickly to the new command. Once he does, do not turn him over to the rest of the family until he has had time to rest and absorb what he has learned. Give him at least five hours before showing the other members of the family. Then take them one at a time and teach them how to execute the new command. This will give you the responsibility of correcting them with patience.

THE BASIC OBEDIENCE COURSE

No training session should last longer than fifteen minutes. Dogs tire and bore very easily. If you work a dog more than fifteen minutes he is going to respond to every distraction imaginable. Obviously, puppies have somewhat different requirements than adult dogs. First, a puppy must learn to adjust to wearing a leash and collar. This is accomplished by attaching a lightweight leash to his collar and allowing him to drag it around the house an hour or two for several days without using it. Second, the length of each training session should depend on his temperament, his age, his willingness to work, and his attention span. Also, a puppy must be corrected in a much gentler manner than an adult dog would be. The length of each training session for an adult dog must also be determined by the dog's temperament, age, willingness to work, and attention span. Each session should last no more than fifteen minutes for the first two weeks. You may gradually increase the time to thirty minutes a session as the dog progresses. Train at least five days a week. You may conduct more than one training session a day, but the sessions must be spaced at least four hours apart. Teach each command until the dog has learned it. Practice all commands that the dog has been taught in each session before teaching the next new command.

Try to be extra patient and understanding during the first few sessions. The dog is going to be denied every impulse that is natural for him. It will be a whole new world of discipline and obedience. You are going to create conditioned responses in his brain that will make it difficult for him to disregard your commands. This represents a major mental chore for the dog and might make him moody and irritable when the first sessions are over. Let him sleep after each session. Sleep is probably what he'll want.

These considerations for the animal come out of an understanding of his immediate problems. Every chapter will contain a section entitled "Beneath the Surface of the Training." For every new command, this section will explain the natural instinct of the dog and how you are going to change or manipulate that instinct. The result should be a greater understanding of the dog in relation to the command. It is important to try to analyze your dog. He is a *student* and, like all students, has his positive and negative qualities. Every dog has a different personality. How does *your* dog react in certain situations?

An important element at the end of each command chapter is "Customized Training." Here you will be advised how best to tailor the training to your dog's temperament type. You can determine how to identify your dog's temperament by following the instructions in Chapter 3, "Your Dog's Temperament."

The best way to train your dog is to take advantage of his good attributes. If he is very affectionate, then that should be the key to getting a good response from him—he will respond to the giving or withholding of affection. With some dogs, too much praise will not bring good results. This type of dog may assume that every time you praise him he can then revert back to doing as he pleases. A withdrawn dog will probably respond better to lavish praise and affection. Determine if your dog is affectionate, stubborn, outgoing, withdrawn, afraid of noises, and so on. Of course, it is safe to assume that any puppy is going to be playful, outgoing, energetic, and generally responsive to affection. They often make the best students. Chapter 3 will undoubtedly be of great help here.

Train your dog in a quiet, secluded area with no one else present.

•   •   •

Pick a suitable area in which to give the training. Inside the home is fine provided there is ample walking space and a minimum of distractions. Outdoors, a quiet, secluded area is best. It is futile to teach a command such as *Sit* where there are eight dogs in heat, ten kids playing baseball, and a group of onlookers.

Your Voice. A puppy does not understand English as such (or any other language). The language skills of a young dog are limited. They're equal to those of a baby. But, you say, "He understands me when I talk to him." What he understands is your tone of voice and a random word or two. It's like a song: It has words and music. Think of your vocal sound as the music. When communicating with a dog, the music is far more important than the words. As a performer, you must act firm, very firm, or pleased and praising through vocal tone and attitude. If you have ever communicated with an infant you will understand this. "Goo-goo" squeaked in a high-pitched voice makes a baby smile. A firmly said "No" makes him let go of your glasses. Because dogs hear much better than humans it sounds to them as if you are talking over a loudspeaker when you correct them verbally. When you yell it frightens them—their ears go down and they cower. The use of your voice has an important effect on the dog. You need a firm tone of voice when administering such verbal commands as *Heel, Sit,* or *Down.* Your voice must become much firmer when correcting the dog verbally with *No.* A third tone of voice must be almost jubilant when praising the dog after he executes each command. The words you say are far less important than is the tone of voice you use. Praise is best given in a higher tone of voice, as though you were talking to a baby. It must be exuberant, happy, and enthusiastic. Matthew uses a high-pitched tone

Your dog is much smaller than you are.

of voice when praising a dog. It always works wonders. Your excited, flattering sounds will motivate your dog. He will work for your praise if you give it generously and with the proper tone of voice.

BODY LANGUAGE

You can best understand the concept of body language by observing dog behavior. For example, at dinner time, many dogs spread out near the table with their chins flat on the floor, following the meat

You are much larger than your dog is. When he looks up at you he sees an overpowering figure with huge, tentacle-like fingers wiggling in a threatening manner, getting ready to pick him up and hug him to death.

platter with their eyes as it is passed from person to person. Planting yourself on the floor in a horizontal position is a way of imposing yourself and pleading for something. The dog is actually begging for food with its body. It is a brilliant performance of nonverbal communication. That is body language.

However, dogs also get physical messages from us. Our bodies are constantly expressing things to them, whether we're aware of it or not. What we do with our bodies communicates messages to our dogs as meaningfully as do the words we use. As a matter of fact, words express only the smallest part of our intent. For this reason it is important to understand our own body language and what it conveys to the dog we're training. When we hold ourselves in too casual a manner, with a loose, noncommittal grip on the leash, this allows an aggressive or strong-willed dog to take control of the situation. The dog then becomes difficult to train properly.

The body language most counterproductive to dog training is the kind that domineers and frightens the average pet. Some dogs cannot respond properly to obedience training when they are overwhelmed and intimidated by humans. Without realizing it, some dog owners overpower their dogs by using their bodies in certain ways that dogs find intimidating. A good working philosophy of body language for dog owners is to be completely nonthreatening to dogs in manner or gesture. This is especially important when dealing with shy, timid, or small dogs. Such dogs not only will remain untrained but may also develop behavior problems such as wetting, chewing, barking, or fear biting. Here is a brief primer of body language for dog owners.

Staring directly into your dog's eyes is not a good idea.

Touching your dog must
develop in him a pleas-
ant, positive associa-
tion, or teaching him
obedience commands
will be very difficult.

YOUR EYES   Harsh stares and staring directly into your dog's eyes
for more than a second or two must be considered carefully. A harsh
or continual stare has a negative effect on any dog. It is unfriendly,
challenging, and threatening, and can erode the bond between you
and your dog. Shy or timid dogs will be made more submissive and
passive than they already are and may even urinate uncontrollably.

When you stare eye to eye at a dog and he does not look away,
you are being defied. Depending on the level of aggressiveness of
the dog, you may also be attacked. Direct eye contact with an
aggressive dog can produce a hostile action from him. Dogs that
stare at each other are making a challenge for dominance and
possibly for territory.

Pointing an accusing finger at your dog while scolding him has a negative effect: It teaches him to fear your hands.

YOUR HANDS   The use of your hands should be a physical expression of the bond you have created with your dog, as described in Chapter 2, "Bonding with Your Dog." They should be used only for teaching, petting, cuddling, hugging, tickling, scratching, and other expressions of affection that support the bond. Touching your dog must have pleasant, positive associations for him, or it will be very difficult to teach him obedience commands. If a dog cringes when human hands come near him, he is *hand-shy*. A hand-shy dog is one who has been hit or abused in some manner. Such dogs must be convinced that they are safe with you and in no danger of physical abuse. You must break through their emotional barriers by patiently touching them with gentle caresses. When touching a hand-shy dog, bring your hand up from the ground, palm up. The first contact should be under the chin. As an alternative, you may offer your knuckles to his nose. Move your hand slowly and gently. These are nonthreatening physical gestures. Never give your dog the impression that your hand is coming down from above in order to hit him.

YOUR POSTURE   Here again, strong-willed dogs and aggressive dogs will take advantage of you if your posture conveys to them

It is wrong to hit your dog—newspapers are for reading only. Striking any dog or standing directly over a small dog will make him fear you.

the feeling that you are not in charge. Holding the leash with an unsure grip while working with a limp, drooping body tells certain dogs that they can do as they please without obeying you. Secure leash control, combined with a confident, upright stride in your walk, gives the dog a positive message.

However, there are dogs who are intimidated by body posture that imposes too much authority, and this will make training them an unsuccessful chore if you use the same methods that work on strong-willed dogs. Small dogs, timid dogs, and shy dogs can be frightened if a person stands too close to them. The average person towers above a small dog, preventing him from seeing the face. This hampers his understanding of your good intentions and warm feelings for him. Small dogs sometimes fear being stepped on or being hit. It's best to stand at least twelve inches away from a small dog's body. This will help alleviate his fears.

Body posture that is overly dominating can be a violation of your relationship, assuming you have bonded in a loving way with your dog. (See Chapter 2.) Do not move with severe, rigid motions. These convey a cold, overbearing message. Put a cheerful stride into your movements and break up each training session by kneeling down to the dog's level and talking to him affectionately. It is easier to make warm, gentle contact with your dog by getting down to eye level with him (unless the dog is aggressive). Your posture must be relaxed, with no sharp edges to it. This will make training much more pleasant both for you and the dog.

Communication is the prime factor in training dogs. Once you have established the lines of communication you are halfway finished with the training. All the rest is simply a matter of teaching your dog what to do. Nothing succeeds like success.

2.

BONDING WITH YOUR DOG

Most of us are familiar with the expressions "My word is my bond"; "the bond of matrimony"; "bond servant"; or "bond slave." There are "Bond, James Bond," and *Of Human Bondage*. So what is a bond? In the financial world a bond is an interest-bearing certificate of debt. In the wonderful world of glue a bond holds things together. What about *bonding*? What is that? In human terms bonding is the creation of close, emotional ties with another person. In animal terms it is the pairing of two individual creatures who develop a long-term attachment to each other as the result of shared experiences. Through the course of their lives they strive never to lose each other.

Bonding can occur between mates, lovers, parent and child, or friends. Bonding can also occur between a human and an animal. *Bonding is the first necessary step toward successfully training your dog.* When a dog is secure in the knowledge that he is accepted as a member of his family, he can respond with confidence to an obedience-training course taught by those who love him. When a dog is aware of being loved, he feels happy. Being happy becomes a habit and is shared with anyone who comes in contact with that dog. Training becomes much easier. Bonding with your dog not only helps the training process, it brings out the best in both of you.

Is there anything that brings more excitement into your home than the arrival of a new dog, especially a puppy? The anticipation is tantalizing, with daydreams of you and the dog running along wet beaches, going out for long walks, rolling around the carpet after dinner, and spending a lifetime together, with thousands of fetched sticks. But the most pleasing daydream of all is the one in which you and the dog become good friends and form a mutual admiration society. These are realities for many dog owners. But they're easy to miss if the dog pee-stains your antique carpet, chews up the arm of a new sofa, and nips your dinner guests on their assets. An obedience-trained dog, however, is not going to upset you with misbehavior and risk losing your affection. When you train your dog you should start by developing a meaningful relationship with him. In other words, the first step is to *bond* with your dog.

To bond with your dog is to learn how to love him. It means creating a personal relationship between you and your pet and developing a very special feeling between you. Dogs who are bonded with their families usually have a strong desire to please, and this is what makes obedience training easier. Bonding with your dog not only satisfies your needs and desires concerning him, it paves the way for easier training by making it more pleasant and effective.

HOW TO BOND WITH YOUR DOG

Often there is no way to know what your new dog has experienced before he came to live with you. He may have been treated well and socialized with other dogs and humans by a knowledgeable breeder or his previous life may have been terrible. In either case you have an opportunity to communicate to your new dog that he is safe, cherished, and respected. *This also applies to a dog you are about to train who has already been living with you for a while. You can change the relationship with your dog for the better, even if he is older.*

The first thing to do with a new dog is to communicate your affection and not worry about training. Of course, paper training or housebreaking must begin immediately. But even here, the underlying philosophy of education must be one of gentle teaching rather than iron-fisted discipline. It is very important to allow your dog, especially if he's a puppy, to explore his home, investigate his new world, and bond with his new family *before* you impose a training program.

The dog's introduction to his new home is critical. Everyone in the family should hold him, hug him, and, by all means, talk to him. Verbal communication is one of the most important aspects of bonding. It is not foolish to talk to your dog. He doesn't understand English, but he *does* respond to the tone of your voice. Your voice is significant. It conveys all that he needs to know about how you feel about him. Observe the parents of a newborn baby. Listen to the things they say to the baby and the manner in which they say them, and then watch the baby's face. The baby may smile or become quiet as it takes in the sounds with wide-eyed fascination. Everything is interesting to a new baby and everything you do or say has an influence on him.

The same is true for a new dog. When you speak to him he listens and then responds. The softer your voice, the sweeter and

Allow your dog, especially a puppy, to explore his home, investigate his new world, and bond with his new family before you impose a training program.

higher in pitch it is, the more loving will be your dog's response to it. The affectionate use of your voice is one of the most important tools you have for bonding with your dog. It will serve both you and your dog for all of his life.

Another meaningful aspect of bonding is the way you touch your dog. You can stroke his fur, pat his head, scratch behind his ears, rub his stomach, squeeze his paws, pull at his lips. Whatever form your physical contact takes, it is helpful if it pleases you as well as the dog. It is always a pleasant surprise to the novice dog owner when her pet walks up to her and places his head under her hand, asking for physical contact. It is the most endearing form of nonverbal communication. Warmth and intimacy are the result of bonding.

Bonding also involves introducing the dog to his environment and teaching him the routines of his new life. Maintain an attitude of teaching without any punishments or corrections. Play with the dog often at established times. Give him several periods of exercise involving tossed toys and rolled balls and ending with small food treats. Establish his feeding place, his sleeping place, and where he can and cannot go. It is important for all of these things to be done in a casual, happy manner. The dog must never be made to

feel that he is being educated or trained at this stage of his life.

Playing with your dog is an important part of bonding. There is a right way to play with your dog that will help the process. Get down on the floor and make yourself reachable. Play with him, roll over with him, and do the sorts of things you would with a crawling baby. These involve play, cuddling, and hugging. And remember, if the dog misbehaves, do not holler, hit, or punish him in any way. You wouldn't do that to a baby and you shouldn't do it to a dog.

Bonding must involve the entire family, and that includes anyone living under the same roof. Each person should be encouraged to develop his or her own separate relationshp with the dog. The more diverse the relationships the better. The person taking care of the dog's needs is going to have a different kind of bond than the others do. He or she will be the nurturing caretaker who feeds the dog, takes him to the vet, and drives him from one place to another. This person will be the substitute mother. Of course, these responsibilities can be shared, and that is another valid approach to nurturing the dog. For example, a different person can feed the dog each day or even at each meal. The same thing applies to walking the dog.

A substitute father may be the one who walks the dog in the early morning and late evening, which may seem more like bondage than bonding. Sharing that responsibility with several people can be good for the dog and the substitute father. The same holds true for exercising the dog. Playing with the dog can be different in style and manner from one person to another, and that has a positive bonding influence. For example, one person may enjoy throwing a ball for the dog, while another person may play hide-and-seek.

One child may relate to the dog as a brother or sister, another will see the dog as a close friend, and some adults may think of the dog as a child. This happens as a result of personality, style, and manner of relating to the dog. Dogs will accept a relationship on any terms without questioning it. Everyone in the household should bond with the dog in his or her own loving way. Individual bonding is the result of your personality and actions. It is helpful to ask yourself what kind of bond or relationship you want to have

Each family member, especially children, should be encouraged to develop his or her own separate relationship with the dog.

with your dog because it will be for a lifetime. Always relate to the dog in a way that is comfortable and natural for you. It will help if you think of a puppy as a three-month-old baby or a grown dog as an older child.

A serious mistake made by the new dog owner and the experienced dog owner alike is to expect too much from a dog all at once. A too-high expectation level is harmful. Whether new pet or old pet, he cannot possibly live up to the burden of expectation that is sometimes placed upon him, and this can create a negative bond or a confused positive/negative bond in the dog. It is not too late for those already living with a dog to create a new and more positive relationship by applying these bonding techniques.

Understanding your dog's temperament will help you form a stronger, healthier bond. For example, if you have a shy dog whom you are housebreaking and he wets on the floor, you would not correct him as you would a dog of another temperament. Punishment here would only destroy the bond. A dog of this temperament is a fear wetter and needs love and affection rather than discipline. You must keep in mind that you are dealing with a fear problem (accompanied by allowing the dog to have too much water), not with a housebreaking problem that involves the dog's unwillingness to learn. By understanding your dog's temperament and adapting your attitude and behavior to it, you will strengthen the bond between you, which, in turn, allows for greater training success. Love and affection strengthen the bond. Discipline and punishment wear it away.

The following activities and the manner in which they are performed help create a strong bond between dogs and their families:

Feeding the dog
Walking the dog
Bathing the dog

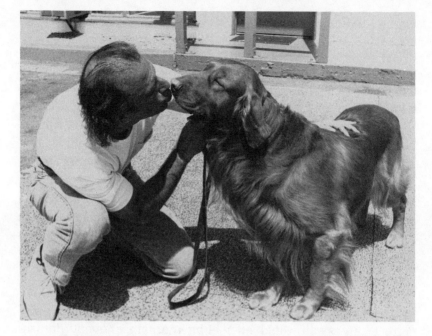

Taking the dog with you on the street or in the car
Allowing the dog to be with you while you are doing chores
Playing with the dog
Exercising the dog
Housebreaking or paper training (without harsh corrections)
Consistent daily routines (for feeding, walking, playing)

When a child is born, the parents are encouraged to bond immediately with the infant. This is accomplished by placing the baby in their arms as soon after delivery as possible. The instant they touch and make eye contact, emotional links are developed for a lifetime. Well, if you think of your dog as a very young child, how can you resist holding it, hugging it, and loving it? When you do that, you are creating a bond with the highest interest rate possible.

3.

YOUR DOG'S TEMPERAMENT

 If you would like to adjust the training methods in *Good Dog, Bad Dog* to your dog's individual character traits, read this chapter carefully. *Customized training* is more effective than the one-size-fits-all approach. It is not difficult or complicated to use the training techniques in a slightly different manner based on your dog's temperament. At the end of each command chapter, such as *"Sit," "Heel,"* or *"Come When Called,"* we describe how to adjust the various training techniques to *your* dog. These adjustments are divided into five temperament categories. Use only those suggestions from the temperament category that matches your dog. This enables you to work like a professional dog trainer. First, determine your dog's temperament by reading the temperament descriptions in this chapter. Once you have a handle on your dog's temperament, you will have the option of customizing the training course instead of using the standard training methods that are offered in each chapter. The standard training methods are best suited for even-tempered dogs.

CUSTOMIZED DOG TRAINING

Even though dog-training techniques differ among professional trainers, they all rely on a basic understanding of dog behavior. Professional trainers know that you cannot handle every dog in the same manner. Because all dogs are different, trainers evaluate each one for temperament before determining how to handle him. For example, a professional would never use a firm correction on a dog with a shy temperament. Nor would he or she be permissive with a dog who has a high-energy temperament. The dog's temperament determines how each aspect of obedience training must be applied.

You can function at nearly the level of a professional dog trainer simply by evaluating your own dog and determining his temperament category. Just about any dog can be trained, or at least improved, with the standard obedience course offered in this book. However, the training can be more appropriate and easier on you and your dog if you understand his temperament and apply the suggested instructions set down in the temperament categories found at the end of each command chapter.

WHAT IS TEMPERAMENT?

Temperament is one of those words that we think we understand until we are called upon to define it. This is especially true when dealing with a dog's temperament. The most common misunderstanding occurs between the words *temperament* and *temperamental*. When the prima donna stalks off the stage of an opera house because the tenor stepped in front of her, she is considered *temperamental*. When your dog hides under the bed when the doorbell rings, it is a matter of *temperament*. Three elements determine a dog's temperament: inherited behavior, the characteristics of its breed, and

environmental influences. The inherited factor is probably the most powerful one: You can always predict a puppy's behavior by observing its sire and dam or grandsire and grandam. If a dog is a true representative of its breed, it will possess some of that breed's temperament qualities. For example, German Shepherd Dogs are traditionally aggressive about protecting their territories, and most terriers are decision makers and difficult to persuade once they've made up their minds about something. The most powerful environmental influences on temperament take place during the first seven weeks of a puppy's life. Its behavior is influenced by its littermates, by its mother, by the external circumstances of its life, and by human handling.

In *Good Dog, Bad Dog*, *temperament* refers to a dog's mental and emotional traits as an individual. We have divided the various temperaments into five general categories: 1. High-Energy/Outgoing, 2. Shy, 3. Strong-Willed, 4. Calm/Easygoing, and 5. Aggressive. Although most dogs possess various combinations of these qualities, there is always one personality trait that is more powerful than the others. For the purpose of effective dog training it is best to focus on the main aspect of your dog's temperament. The following five temperament descriptions are meant to help you understand your dog and train him more effectively. They are based on firsthand experience with thousands of dogs. Read them carefully with *your* dog in mind. They will help you decide which category best describes him. Knowing your dog's temperament category will then help you use the customized training section at the end of each command chapter.

HIGH-ENERGY/OUTGOING

You can always recognize a high-energy/outgoing dog by the owner's arm—the one holding the leash. It will be longer than the other one (from being pulled down the street). Owners of such dogs usually have to change clothing frequently because their pooches jump all over them. These dogs like to hop onto the furniture whenever there are guests in the house, and they enjoy depositing shedding fur and smudgy paws on whomever or whatever they can. When riding in cars they pace back and forth from window to window and may even leap from the backseat to the front seat. If you don't have an accident you will at least get a ticket.

They are like walking milkshakes that never stop vibrating. These dogs become your shadow. They follow you wherever you go, from the living room to the kitchen to the bedroom. High-energy dogs are usually heavy panters and sound like the breather at the other end of an obscene phone call. When they are puppies they turn your house into the Indianapolis 500, running through it, knocking things over like a toddler who has just discovered how to sprint. Every time you come home, these peppy puppies greet you by running back and forth, leaving a trail of pee across the carpeting and on your shoes. They are excitable dogs who bark excessively, making the simplest phone conversation impossible.

You want to holler at them, and when you do, that's when training becomes necessary.

This personality type is more playful than nervous. High-energy/outgoing dogs are pacers and panters who are always on the move. They will jump on you or anyone else, even if they are on-leash. And these are the barkers of the dog world. This is a big problem for those who live in apartment houses. When a passerby is in the hallway of an apartment house, the high-energy dog makes the building sound like the K-9 Corps at an army base. And the barking goes on whether you're home or not. Neighbor then conspires with neighbor and they secretly circulate petitions demanding your eviction.

Dogs of this temperament are easily distracted. They are excitable and responsive to the slightest attention you give them. In extreme examples, they are the closest thing to perpetual motion in nature. At times they work themselves up to a glassy-eyed stare, focusing on nothing at all. It is difficult to get a high-energy/outgoing dog to obey you.

On the other hand, they are fun to be with, spirited, active, playful, and energetic. These are positive qualities even though it is hard to handle such dogs because they do not want to sit still and are all over the place. They are like kids in a candy factory who can't believe all the sights and smells they see. It is hard for them to focus on one thing. Surprisingly, many of the better working dogs are excitable high-energy dogs. They are flashier. They have pizzazz. You must learn to take all that wonderful pent-up energy and channel it into obedience training. When done properly, you get a bright, alert dog who not only responds well to obedience commands but also to his family and friends in all situations.

SHY

Have you ever heard someone defend his dog's behavior by saying, "My dog is never this way at home. He's only shy when he meets a stranger"? Well, the problem here is that we live in a country with 250 million strangers. Shy behavior in the extreme involves running from people, hiding, snarling, and sometimes biting. Such a dog has no social life. But most shy dogs do not exhibit extreme behavior. Some people do not even know they have a shy dog. That is because the dog is rarely shy with them. He may be that way only in certain situations where the owner tends to excuse it. Some shy dogs are like teenagers who are self-conscious about their appearance: outgoing at home but painfully shy everywhere else. This doesn't mean the person will be shy forever. It just takes a while to get over it.

A shy dog is usually comfortable in his own house and is loving with his own family. He is adjusted and secure at home because everyone there is familiar, forgiving, and consoling. He is secure in the routine of his patterned life. But every time a shy dog must cope with a new person or a new situation, his fears and insecurities may come to the surface and create upsetting behavior.

A shy dog may be considered sensitive, timid, reserved, bashful, or even innocent. But he is usually suspicious, distrustful, easily scared away, and at times nasty when sufficiently frightened. He may be shy with certain people and not with others; he may be afraid of confinement; he may react badly to loud noises. Routine conditions that are normal for some dogs may be intolerable for those of this temperament. For example, a shy dog may fear riding in a car or being in a strange place. Another may be nervous with other dogs. Their reactions to the things they dread most range from running away and hiding to snarling and biting. A shy dog may be shy about only one thing. He may be noise-shy, people-shy, hand-shy, or shy about strange environments. Or he may be shy about many things.

When a dog is shy because of abusive experiences or bad handling he may still have the potential to become a more outgoing animal. He must be treated gently and with patience. Owners of shy dogs must avoid excessive or overly firm corrections or too much authority. They must gently coax the animals into obeying commands during the teaching process and never use a harsh tone of voice. The shy temperament requires generosity and kindness along with lavish praise and encouragement. A shy dog can become a responsive dog if he is given gentle care and much loving.

Some breeds of dog are normally more retiring than others. Do not confuse this with a temperament problem. When "shyness" is a breed trait it is in its mildest, most acceptable form and few would want to change it. Such dogs are more reserved than shy and are very lovable. The most extreme characteristics of shyness, on the other hand, are usually inherited from the shy dog's parents, and you must learn how to handle such a dog.

STRONG-WILLED

Strong-willed dogs have interesting personalities and consistently attract attention to their behavior. They are usually intelligent animals and a joy to live with. Training them is the hard part. What really happens between these stubborn dogs and their owners is a battle of wills. The lord of the manor boldly declares, "I'm not going to give this up. I shall prevail." After one week of pulling, yanking, hollering, and begging, the owner runs in a state of near hysteria to an open window and shouts to the world, "I'm fed up and I'm not going to take it anymore!"

Some of the comments trainers hear from the owners of strong-willed dogs are: *My dog pees on the floor just to spite me. I don't understand why after five years he's still not housebroken. The dog knows what he's doing wrong. I think he's trying to get me! Well, it won't work. It's either him or me.* Strong-willed dogs have problems with housebreaking, chewing, barking, and anything that drives their families crazy. However, when they are custom-trained in a manner appropriate for their temperament they become as responsive as any other dog.

Strong-willed dogs are characterized by an unwillingness to obey commands or respond to corrections. They may even growl when their owners attempt to discipline them. A variation is when they *talk back* by barking or yipping after having been given a command. They will stand their ground in the face of threats, yells, and even punishments. And they do not respond to any manner of persuasion such as begging on one knee or bribery. You simply have to know how to train strong-willed dogs.

Eventually, they will meet your expectations, but not without challenging your authority. They are unwilling to please you the first time around—they hold out. Strong-willed dogs are either struggling for dominance or driven by an inherited urge to live on their own terms. They must be handled with assertiveness that establishes you as the leader of the pack. However, this must be accomplished in a nonabusive manner. Proper technique can strengthen the bond between dogs and humans. It is easy to become angry with a strong-willed dog, holler at him, or even hit him, and then confuse your emotional response with training techniques. Abusing your dog does not teach him anything and has the negative effect of shattering the bond between you.

Strong-willed dogs require skillful handling, especially in the teaching process. With persistence, know-how, and patience, dogs of this temperament become highly responsive animals. These are warmhearted, thinking dogs who reward your diligent training efforts with the satisfaction that comes from a job well done. Once you get past the resistance to your authority, you will discover their many fine qualities.

CALM/EASYGOING

When you think about dogs with this personality, you won't have to worry about the commands *Down* and *Stay*, because this type hardly moves anyway. Calm/easygoing dogs always look bored or indifferent no matter what's going on. They should wear tee shirts that say "So What." These dogs are born for the slow lane and are not meant for those who want a dog to jog with. These slow burners will never keep up with you. You can usually find them sleeping by the fireplace. If you don't have a fireplace they'll lie next to a steam pipe and pretend. Calm/easygoing dogs have a mission, and that is to eat well and get as much rest as possible.

To dogs of this temperament love means never having to say anything. These lackadaisical sweethearts are not indifferent to their families—they are merely reserved. Do not mistake their being blasé for disinterest. Their affection is often expressed with a satisfied glance at you or the touch of a lip as you walk past the refrigerator. Sometimes they lay their heads on your lap, asking for an ear scratch. When that happens, all doubts will surely disappear. Their feelings *are* present, but they are expressed without bounce and circumstance.

These cool canines have all of the common behavior problems of puppyhood. They too will nip, chew, jump, and bark. But the good news is that this problem behavior is not as bad as in dogs of other temperaments. Although they train well, because of their casual manner and low energy level, they appear to resist being taught the various commands. They are quiet, inactive, sedate dogs with a desire to stay put. They appear to have great composure and dignity. Obedience training is something of an imposition for dogs of this temperament.

AGGRESSIVE

Aggressive is a term that is sometimes attributed to a dog that is exuberant, curious, and somewhat pushy. That is different from our definition of the aggressive temperament. When we refer to the aggressive temperament in *Good Dog, Bad Dog* we are speaking of an undesirable personality type whose behavior extends from bully to biter. Dogs with an aggressive temperament demand total control over all situations and will do anything to get it. The aggressive dog chases, pushes, growls, barks, and sometimes bites people and other animals. Not even children are exempt from this dangerous behavior.

There are many signs of an aggressive temperament. Body language reveals several of them. Look for a dog who stares directly at you without flinching; raises his hackles on occasion while standing in a stiff, erect posture; displays raised ears, a curled upper lip, and a tail that is straight up or down. The aggressive bully may run at his victim and block his path with a menacing stance. He may even push or slam up against him, holding him hostage with his shoulders or hips. In addition, an aggressive dog may chase, spring, pounce, or jump on his victims.

An aggressive temperament can also be determined by a dog's vocal behavior. Growling, snarling, and threatening barks are clear indications of an aggressive temperament. The tone of a dog's bark is a clue. It is not difficult to tell a friendly or playful bark from one that is menacing. Another clue to the dog's temperament is if the dog barks at you after you have given him a command. In the course of barking, a dog who bares his teeth at people sends an aggressive warning that cannot be misinterpreted.

When a puppy snaps, nips, or growls on a frequent basis it is exhibiting an aggressive temperament. Puppies (also grown dogs) who will not allow you to handle their food bowls or favorite possessions have an aggressive temperament. Aggressive behavior in puppies seems playful and even entertaining. But the behavior that is cute in dogs five months old is upsetting and becomes frightening with maturity. As the dog moves along in years its aggressive behavior becomes more and more dangerous. Aggressive behavior must be dealt with as soon as it is discovered, even if the dog is a puppy.

Aggressive dogs are either *dominant/aggressive* or *fear/aggressive*. The *fear/aggressive* dog is an anxious animal burdened with fright and panic about anyone or anything. His body language reveals his fear when you observe his ears flattened, his head drooped, and his tail tucked between his legs. Add to this menacing vocal sounds and sudden aggressive physical gestures.

The *dominant/aggressive* dog is one who considers himself the pack leader and defender of his territory. He is a bully with a need to control all those around him and will attack any stranger that enters his space.

Some people want these aggressive qualities so their dogs will protect their families and homes. They believe they are creating a watchdog by encouraging this behavior. But this is a confused and dangerous idea. There is a great difference between a trained guard dog and an aggressive dog. Aggressive dogs recognize no boundaries to their behavior. They do not stop barking, growling, or attacking when ordered to do so by their owners. Aggressive dogs are difficult or impossible to control and inevitably harm innocent people. It always comes as a shock to the owners of aggressive dogs when a neighborhood child, a letter carrier, a meter reader, or a visiting friend gets bitten. If your dog has an aggressive temperament, take it as a significant warning that you live with a potential biter.

It is important to understand that the majority of dog bites come from fear/aggressive dogs. Although dominant/aggressive dogs are more dangerous, they have fewer biting incidents than fear/aggressive dogs.

If an aggressive dog is under ten months of age, his bad behavior can be dealt with simply and effectively. The corrective jerk and other techniques work very well. An obedience training course given at an early age and tailored for the aggressive temperament can produce good results. But if the animal is already mature it may be too late for successful change or home training. An eval-

Because there is a person who is right for every dog, it is safe to say that all dogs are the responsive type.

uation from a professional trainer is necessary before attempting to train a dog with an aggressive temperament.

THE RESPONSIVE DOG

Responsive dogs are the least difficult to handle and the most fun to be with. For the purpose of dog training, the authors do not list the responsive dog as a temperament category. We believe that under the right conditions all dogs can be made responsive to dog training and to their families. All dogs have the potential to become responsive with bonding and proper training, regardless of their temperament category. Dog temperaments often match up well with human personalities, and what would seem undesirable for one person can be very desirable for another. A shy or high-energy dog needs a great deal of patience and loving and will fill a paternal or maternal need in some people. Dogs that are either strong-willed or easygoing types are certain to harmonize with the personalities of many dog lovers. Because there is a person that is right for every dog, it is safe to say that all dogs are the responsive type.

4.

EQUIPMENT

There are enough manufactured dog items to completely fill a supermarket—more than one could use in a lifetime. If you bought them all you could create a do-it-yourself Spanish Inquisition. Cattle prods, throw-chains, and various electrical gadgets are more suitable for counterintelligence interrogations. Very few, however, are useful for training a dog.

A great hindrance to acquiring practical training equipment is the "rhinestone and paisley" syndrome. Several years ago a Park Avenue client contracted for an obedience course for her dog. Her silver-gray poodle was as clipped and manicured as they come. When the rather grand lady was asked for the dog's training equipment, she opened a closet door and revealed over fifty collars and leashes of every color, style, and description. She became self-conscious after the trainer gasped, and explained that she always bought Pipa a new collar and leash whenever she purchased a new clothing ensemble for herself. She and her Pipa were at all times fashion-coordinated. However, she did not have the very few items necessary to properly control the dog. Unless one is interested in making Best-Dressed Dog of the Year, there are few items needed to train a dog.

THINGS THAT WON'T BE NEEDED

A SPIKED COLLAR   A spiked or pronged collar is a metal training collar with bent prongs on the underside, the ends of which dig into the animal's neck when the collar is pulled on its slip device. These prongs, though blunted, make dozens of tiny impressions around the throat and effectively restrict the dog's movement when jerked into operation. It is true that these collars can be useful when used properly by a professional trainer, but the chance of misuse and serious injury to your dog is great. One jerk with a pronged collar is worth fifteen jerks with a regular training collar. However, inexperienced dog owners tend to overdo it and could harm the dog.

A LEASH MADE OF CHAIN   No matter how long or short, it is almost impossible to tell ahead of time when these leashes will snap. If it should break while in city traffic the dog might bolt, run out in the street, and the rest is too unpleasant to think about. One can see where a leather leash is wearing thin or losing its stitching—this is not possible with a chain leash.

THICK, SHORT LEASHES   They are useless for training purposes. They may look very masculine with a Doberman Pinscher or German Shepherd Dog on the end of them, but they are ineffective for training.

LEATHER OR NYLON BUCKLED COLLARS   For reasons that will become clear, they work against the training technique. Exceptions are made for long-haired breeds such as Afghan Hounds and Old English Sheepdogs. For dogs with long fur a leather or nylon collar is preferable because it will not rub the fur away or create permanent ring marks or bald spots.

THINGS THAT WILL BE NEEDED

A SIX-FOOT LEATHER LEASH   This is used in every command except where otherwise indicated. It will allow the proper distance for control when teaching the dog to sit. Six feet of leash will also allow you to walk behind him while still exercising control. A leather leash, by the way, will not hurt your hand or the dog's chest when employed in various training techniques.

Leashes come in various widths. The size of your dog should

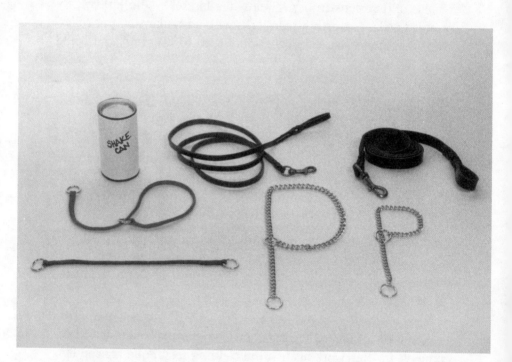

Top row, left to right: shake can, ¼-inch-wide, 6-foot leather leash, ⅝-inch-wide, 6-foot leather leash; *middle row, left to right:* nylon training collar in proper working position; *bottom row, left to right:* stretched-out nylon training collar, large-size jeweled training collar, small-size jeweled training collar. The jeweled training collars are displayed in their correct working positions.

guide you in choosing the proper width, although five-eighths of an inch is recommended as the most comfortable width, and won't sacrifice strength. Toy breeds require a narrower width, such as half-inch or less. The key to buying this equipment is strength and comfort. A fancy multicolored nylon leash may look beautiful, but it might break.

A JEWELED TRAINING COLLAR   A jeweled training collar is one that has small metal links that are welded close together. This is the strongest type and releases the grip around the dog's neck quickly and smoothly. The wide-linked training collar sometimes jams when one link catches in another.

When the collar is properly placed around the dog's neck, it should form the letter P, with one free ring hanging from the right side of the neck. When it is placed incorrectly around the dog's neck, it forms the number 9, with the free ring hanging from the left side of the dog's neck. For correct threading of the jeweled training collar, see the photos on page 78.

This equipment is often referred to as a "choke collar." The term is inappropriate. The collar does not choke the dog unless it is placed on the neck incorrectly. It "corrects" the dog by tightening around his neck when the leash is pulled. If the collar is placed around the dog's neck properly it will release quickly, thus avoiding any pain or choking. (See photos on page 81.) *Do not use a metal training collar for toy breeds and small puppies*. These dogs are too fragile for this equipment. Use a thin leather or nylon collar.

A SHAKE CAN   Similar to a New Year's Eve noisemaker, this is used to startle a dog and get his immediate attention. Take an empty soda can and slip fifteen pennies into it, taping the opening closed. By rattling it up and down you get a demanding sound. This is used primarily for puppy problems such as housebreaking, chewing, jumping, going into the garbage, chasing the baby, and so on.

Shake the can and say "No" in a firm voice. The noise becomes associated with the word "No" and stops the puppy from continuing his indiscretion. The manner in which the shake can is used depends on the dog's temperament. Do not use a shake can if your dog is shy.

DOG CRATE   A dog crate resembles a cage but is really a form of indoor doghouse or container for transporting your pet. It is rectangular in shape and is made of strong metal wire with a solid floor. It can be purchased from a pet-supply store or mail-order catalog in a size suitable for each breed. If used properly it ties in directly with your dog's instincts to have a den as the core area of his territory. A dog crate is a sanctuary for your dog. But it is also a training tool.

It is useful for paper training or housebreaking as a means of confining your dog when you cannot watch him for mistakes. Whether your dog is a puppy or an adult his instinct is to avoid soiling his den, and using a crate during housebreaking helps your puppy learn control.

A crate is also valuable if your pet has a chewing problem because it prevents household damage by confining the dog when you cannot watch him. This valuable piece of equipment can be

A dog crate. Make it as comfortable as possible; place a cozy blanket or cushion inside, along with your dog's favorite toys or chews.

used as part of the overall obedience-training program, or simply as a way of confining the animal when his behavior is annoying. It can prevent him from getting into trouble whether someone is at home or not.

After your dog is obedience trained, the crate becomes an indoor doghouse if the wire door is kept open. Place a cushion or blanket inside and it becomes a comfortable place for your dog to sleep and get away from it all.

The crate should be long enough to permit your grown dog to stretch out and high enough for him to sit up without hitting his head. You can construct a partition in a large crate for your puppy so there is just room for him to lie down or sit up. It must never offer more space than necessary or it loses its denlike quality. As the puppy grows, increase the space by moving the partition back.

When you travel with your dog, the crate becomes a portable den providing security, comfort, and safety in a strange place. Depending upon the size, it can fit into the back seat of a sedan or station wagon. Confined in the crate, your dog cannot stick his head out the window or distract the driver. Don't leave home without it.

PUPPY GATE   When you do not wish to use a dog crate, restrict a dog's access indoors with a puppy gate. This is a common device found in most hardware stores. Although designed for puppies, this wonderful piece of training equipment can be used effectively for a dog of any age or type when you wish to confine him to one room. The see-through aspect of the gate eliminates the need to put your pet in a room with a closed door, which can be harmful to the dog's personality. The best puppy gates are made of wood and thick plastic wire, and are wedged within a door frame. Most dog owners prefer to confine their dogs in the kitchen. It is an effective alternative to a dog crate and less expensive. The puppy gate has its most important use in paper training or housebreaking.

A puppy gate. The best puppy gates are made of wood and thick plastic wire, and are wedged within a door frame.

This is all the equipment one needs to complete the obedience course successfully. The outlay of money is small. These items are standard and available in any pet-supply store or mail-order catalog. With the exception of the shake can, please resist the temptation to substitute with homemade, inadequate versions or expensive, overly complex versions. Purchase exactly what is suggested. This equipment is uncomplicated, inexpensive, and highly functional. Once the equipment is obtained you are ready to begin the course. Good luck.

5.

PAPER TRAINING

In the world of dogs, "pouring" over the Sunday papers has an entirely different connotation. Next to reporting the news, the greatest service rendered to the public by newspapers is to provide an inexhaustible supply of paper-training equipment.

Although most dogs should be fully housebroken, paper training is a workable alternative in some instances, especially if you live in an apartment. The convenience of not having to use the streets at all hours of the day and night speaks for itself. If you have a restrictive work schedule, paper training may be your only option. Elderly persons and others who have difficulty leaving their homes can benefit from this substitute technique, particularly in extreme weather or late at night. However, paper training is only feasible if you own a small dog or a female dog. Large dogs eliminate in large quantities, making it difficult to maintain good hygiene and sanitation. Male dogs lift their legs to urinate and will stain walls and furniture.

DEFINITION OF PAPER TRAINING

This means a dog will urinate and defecate on paper in your house or apartment, in an area of your choice at a time that you designate.

BENEATH THE SURFACE OF THE TRAINING

The main reason a dog likes to urinate on paper is because the urine disappears by absorption. That you remove the papers after he uses them is soon understood. No animal wants to be around his own body waste. Another reason paper training works so well is that dogs prefer to eliminate on the same spot they used previously. It has to do with the territorial instinct for claiming specific areas as their own. Because of a dog's highly developed sense of smell, he is capable of detecting scents of which we are completely unaware. Consequently, after he has soiled one spot, he is drawn back to the same place simply because he can smell it. Only a powerful odor neutralizer can prevent his smelling it.

Paper training is most successful when introduced to the animal as a puppy. If the choice is made to paper train, you must not change over to housebreaking. Too often a pup is taken away from his litter before seven weeks and cannot be taken outside for housebreaking. The owner uses newspapers, indoors, as a temporary measure. It is a mistake to then take the puppy away from his paper procedure. This offers nothing but confusion to the little dog. As a result, the dog starts having one accident after another in his attempts to interpret your wishes. These accidents often occur on an expensive carpet or in a corner of your bedroom during the night. The dog is then punished or shamed because the owner suffers from frustration and rage. This is the beginning of neurotic behavior in many animals.

The rule should be that you do not take a puppy into your house before he is seven weeks old unless you are firm in your resolution to paper train him. In the case of dogs that have already been housebroken, it is only fair to say that the changeover will be difficult and will demand a great deal of patience.

PROCEDURE AND TECHNIQUE FOR PAPER TRAINING

There are four steps to paper training:

1. Confining the dog
2. Proper diet and scheduling
3. Using an odor neutralizer
4. Proper correction

These steps are meant primarily for puppies, although they can be used for older dogs if you take a little more time and exercise greater patience. What should be done first is to pick an area in the house that is convenient for this purpose. Designate it as the permanent paper place for the dog. Here is where he will always relieve himself and feel confident that you will not be angry when he uses it. This will be where you *paper* the dog. Some of the more convenient places to use are the bathroom, the kitchen, the pantry, the basement, or any place where you're least likely to be offended when the dog uses it. Do not, however, pick a place that is inaccessible to him. The easier it is for him to get there, the more success you will have.

CONFINING THE DOG

From the first moment you start this program, after selecting the proper place, lay newspaper over the entire room in a three-to-five-sheet thickness. Do not miss a spot. This must be done for the first five days. If the dog is placed on an area that is completely covered with paper he has no choice but to do the right thing. Immediately after he uses the paper, pick it up, but save one sheet that is soiled and place it underneath the fresh sheets the next time around. If the dog is a very young puppy he may use the paper nine or ten times a day. He will sniff, circle around, or let you know in some way that he wants to use the paper. Learn his signals. As he gets older he will go at less frequent intervals.

After the fifth day, start narrowing the amount of space you cover with the newspaper. Pick up the soiled paper but replace it with less and less paper, until after several days you are laying down only as much paper as he needs. By this time he will probably have confined himself to one favored spot in the room. Of course, if in the first five days you notice that he has already started using one small area, then that is the time to start using less paper. In any event, this process should not take more than two days after the first five days of totally covering the room with paper.

Every pet owner is sooner or later faced with the problem of leaving the untrained dog alone. It is a nagging dilemma for any pet owner, but more so for the novice. One usually comes home to a house littered with urine and fecal matter. If the dog has been yelled at for his indiscretions, he will wait until left alone to do his worst. This is why confining the dog is important. Do not interpret this to mean that you should tie the dog down. Select a small, convenient area where the dog cannot stray and confine him in it. *This area must be where he uses his papers.* The area of confinement must not be so restrictive that the animal has no room to walk around. That would be like punishment and cause him to bark and try to escape the confinement. It is extremely unpleasant for a dog to relieve himself in the same area where he must remain. It is for this reason that confinement acts as an aid in this training. Most people use their kitchen area. Purchase a see-through puppy gate from a pet-supply outlet. If his papers are available he'll use them and walk to the other portion of his area to spend the time. This too helps the training process. A dog crate can be successfully employed here as a means of confinement *for short periods of time.*

To avoid making the puppy's life oppressive, allow him to run around loose when you are home. This is desirable, *provided you watch him.* Always be prepared to correct him if he begins to relieve himself off the papers. If he is never let loose to run around the house it becomes too much like punishment for him, and that will work against this training method.

PROPER DIET AND SCHEDULING

Feed, water, and paper the dog properly. He needs a stable, well-balanced diet consisting of correct amounts of fat, protein, carbohydrates, vitamins, and minerals. The ideal dog food is meat, chicken, or fish mixed with some form of cereal. Consult a veterinarian for the nutritional needs of your dog. It is not advisable, however, to make sudden dietary changes. Because of intestinal sensitivity, this will cause diarrhea. You can avoid this problem by combining the new food mixture with the old one. Phase the old one out over a three-day period.

Feed, water, and walk the dog at the same times each day to achieve favorable results. Consistency is the key to this method. By timing an animal's food intake, you can determine when he will relieve himself. It usually takes food from six to eight hours to pass through his system, depending on the dog's age and size.

PUTTING YOUR DOG ON A PROPER SCHEDULE

The dog must be given the opportunity to use the paper a minimum of four times a day. He is to be fed, watered, and papered—*in that order.*

Seven-week to six-month-old puppy: seven in the morning—paper the dog; seven-thirty in the morning—feed, water, and paper him; eleven-thirty in the morning—feed, water, and paper him; four-thirty in the afternoon—feed, water, and paper him; eight-thirty in the evening—water only and paper; eleven-thirty in the evening—just paper.

Six months to one year old: seven in the morning—paper the dog; seven-thirty in the morning—feed, water, and paper; twelve-thirty in the afternoon—water and paper; four-thirty in the afternoon—feed, water, and paper; seven-thirty in the evening—water and paper (last water of the day); eleven in the evening—paper the dog.

One year old and older: seven in the morning—paper the dog; seven-thirty in the morning—feed, water, and paper; four-thirty in the afternoon—water and paper; seven-thirty in the evening—water and paper (last water of the day); eleven in the evening—paper the dog.

At feeding time allow fifteen minutes for the dog to complete his meal and then take it away, no matter how much he has left in the bowl. He is not to be given food or water except at the scheduled times during the training period. If necessary, a dish of ice cubes will limit the dog's water intake yet quench his thirst. The more you restrict the time for food and water, the closer you come to scheduling his bodily functions.

The minute the dog is fed and watered he is to be allowed to use the paper. Praise him each time he urinates or defecates on the paper and then remove him to another room. He will quickly understand what the paper is for.

Even though you are paper training your dog, he should still be taken out for walks. All dogs require exercise, fresh air, and the benefits of socializing with new people, other dogs, and a variety of environments. We suggest that walks take place any time after the dog has used his papers according to his schedule.

Schedule for nine-to-five working people: Take the dog to the paper immediately after waking up and allow him to use it. Once he does, you may immediately feed, water, and paper him once again so that the routine is established. He is then to be confined in one area with the newspaper laid out for him. You are now able to leave the house for work. On coming home, clean the soiled papers and replace them. Do not correct the dog for this. Repeat the process: feed, water, and paper. Before bedtime place him on the paper one last time without a feeding or watering. Because a small puppy cannot hold his water for eight or nine hours, it is advisable not to give him the run of the house. Confine him to one small area.

If the dog does not use the papers at the scheduled time, try sprinkling a little water on the paper to encourage him to use it. Another technique is to save one sheet of previously soiled paper to place underneath the new sheets. The smell will give him the idea of what is wanted. After he relieves himself, give him a great deal of praise so that he knows using the paper pleases you. This is essentially what he wants to do.

USING AN ODOR NEUTRALIZER

When the dog makes a mistake and relieves himself in the house in a place that is not covered with newspaper, there are two things that must be done. First, there is the correction that will be explained in the "Proper Correction" section that follows. The second thing is to get rid of the odor quickly. This is important. Even when the spot is washed, the smell is discernible to the animal. That is why ordinary cleaning products are useless for this purpose. Products containing ammonia should be avoided because they intensify the odor of urine and consequently become attractive to dogs. Bleach, detergents, and various household sprays do not work. Only a strong liquid odor neutralizer actually eliminates the scent. Place ten drops of neutralizer into one quart of hot water. Mop all soiled areas with this mixture.

A dog cannot help himself once he gets the scent of urine or defecation. Even though we cannot smell it ourselves, he does, and is inevitably drawn to it. Dogs mark their territory by urinating on key parts of it. Other dogs come along and mark the same spot. When walking your dog, you can observe that he is smelling for his or another dog's odor. That is why you should neutralize the odor of all indoor areas where the dog has relieved himself. By removing the scent of his own waste you will prevent him from being tempted to repeat his indiscretion on the same spot.

PROPER CORRECTION

Under no circumstances should a dog be punished for relieving himself off the paper. He can only be corrected. *Unless you are actually there to stop the dog as he begins to relieve himself, it is useless to correct him.* No punishments, not even mild corrections, have any effect in the dog's mind if a few minutes have elapsed between his act and your correction. His mental processes appear to be quite limited in this respect.

This brings us to the meaning of "correction" as the word is used throughout this training program. To *correct* the animal is to communicate to him that he has displeased you. In paper training, as in housebreaking, the technique of correction involves use of the word "No," which must be said in a firm tone of voice. The objective is to startle the dog and thereby impress upon him your displeasure. However, this can only be communicated to him if he is in the middle of his wrongdoing. If one's voice is too mild or if the dog does not respond to the firm "No," it can be accompanied with the noise of the shake can. (See Chapter 4, "Equipment.")

As the dog is relieving himself off the papers, rattle the can behind your back vigorously and simultaneously say "No" firmly. That much noise will have to stop the dog. It is precisely at that moment that he should be taken to his papers. Praise him for having stopped what he was doing at your command. Allow him to finish his act on the papers. Then give him a great deal of praise. *This is the only way you can show the dog what to do.* It is, quite literally, a teaching process.

Paper training, like housebreaking, should not be approached from a negative perspective. If it is, the dog will only understand half the training. He will understand when he has *displeased* you, but he must be made to understand what he has to do to *please* you. Communicating to him what you expect is the objective of all dog training. Keeping the dog off the carpets and the city streets is the objective of paper training.

6.

HOUSEBREAKING

One of the great agonies for dog owners is house-breaking. Here is a method to solve that problem. From the beginning you must make a decision whether to housebreak or paper train your dog. If you housebreak your dog, you must not paper train him. If you paper train him, then you must not housebreak him. To use both techniques creates a great deal of confusion for the dog. When you paper train your dog you are, in effect, teaching him that relieving himself indoors, on the floor, is acceptable. Many dogs return to the place on the floor to eliminate whether the paper is there or not. Bear in mind that the dog doesn't really care where he is trained to relieve himself. Only you care.

If you live in an apartment and want to housebreak your new puppy you may find yourself in a dilemma. Many veterinarians insist that their clients not take their puppies out onto the city streets until they are between twelve and sixteen weeks old or until they have achieved full immunity from their vaccinations.

Although you should either housebreak *or* paper train to avoid confusing the puppy, you may have to temporarily paper train him until he is allowed to use the street. At that time you may then switch to housebreaking. But it is important to understand that this will make housebreaking your puppy more difficult. It will eventually be accomplished, but the transition from paper training to housebreaking could prolong the process.

The confusion stems from the fact that paper training communicates to the dog that it is correct to relieve himself in a designated area of your apartment. Some of the confusion can be avoided if you paper your puppy on a patio, a balcony, a basement area, or even in an exit stairway of the building. You could begin housebreaking immediately by using your rooftop, if it is available to you. Some veterinarians do not object if you carry your young puppy to a clean area of the street and then carry him home.

There are many reasons why a dog may not be housebroken, but the prime cause is the inability of his owner to communicate what is wanted from him. Most new dog owners are extremely inhibited and embarrassed by the whole subject of housebreaking. If dealing with the functions of the animal body is too embarrassing, how can one teach the animal to control those functions? Some dog owners behave like six-year-old children making "toidy" jokes in a Gilbert and Sullivan operetta. "Muff-Muff make do-do." "Princess made ta-ta." Nothing is worse than hearing a grown person say of his 185-pound Mastiff, "Horace makes tinkle on the bed." The worst ever recorded was, "Poofie makes chocolates in the house!" It is desirable to avoid such euphemisms as *surprises, plops, wee-wee, ca-ca, eh-eh, gifts (!), presents, numbers one and two, and others*. A dog defecates. A dog urinates. Let's be brave about it.

DEFINITION OF HOUSEBREAKING

This is, simply, teaching your dog to relieve himself, outside, on a schedule convenient for you.

BENEATH THE SURFACE OF THE TRAINING

There is no such thing as a partly housebroken dog. Many an owner has said something like, "Fang is completely housebroken . . . except he dumps on the bed after we change the linen." Either he is housebroken or he isn't. Some people say their dog is housebroken when they mean he's paper trained. There is a considerable difference between the two. When a dog is housebroken he never, but *never*, uses the house for his toilet, on or off the newspaper.

Many people do not understand why their dog does not know what to do when taken outside. Merely taking him outside does not mean that he knows what he's there for. The biggest problem between dog and owner is that the dog would love to please but doesn't know how, and the owner would love to teach the dog what he wants but doesn't know how to communicate it. This method solves that problem. There is nothing worse than a dog who is not housebroken. It is the first and most important phase of domesticating an animal. Many a dog and owner have parted company at this stage of their relationship. Many a good and loving dog has been saved from being given away or destroyed after the owner was introduced to this housebreaking method.

PROCEDURE AND TECHNIQUE FOR HOUSEBREAKING

This technique is the most humane ever devised. It causes no confusion for the animal. Each phase has its importance and should be followed the way it is outlined. There are four major steps:

1. Confining the dog
2. Proper correction (not punishment)
3. Using an odor neutralizer
4. Proper diet and scheduling

This method is ideal for dogs between the ages of seven weeks and three years. However, good results have been achieved with dogs as old as twelve years. Of course you will not get the same results with a twelve-year-old dog as with a puppy, but the method does work. The ideal age to start housebreaking your dog is when he is approximately eight weeks old. Consult a veterinarian about your puppy's immunization and being allowed outdoors. The method could take two to four weeks or two to four months, depending on the dog and his environment. You should find a great improvement in the first week. If the dog does not respond, it is possible that he has a medical problem and should be examined by a veterinarian. If you have been paper training your dog, pick up the papers and forget that technique. Otherwise the animal will become totally confused.

CONFINING THE DOG

An extremely important phase of housebreaking is *watching* and *confining* the dog. When you are home the dog should be allowed to run around loose, *provided you watch him*. If he is going to relieve himself, be in a position to correct him immediately. Confining is done because the dog will not mess in his own area if he can help it; however, if he is never let loose to run around the house it becomes too much like punishment, and that will work against this method.

For whatever reason, there are many times when the dog must be left alone in the house. This, very often, is precisely when he chooses to relieve himself. It is rare that he will attempt it before your eyes after the first experience with your scorn. Therefore, confine the dog when he is left alone. Confinement, however, does not mean tying him up. He is simply contained in a small area where he cannot stray and make housebreaking mistakes. Dogs do not want to defecate in an area where they must remain. Their normal inclination is to go as far away as possible, relieve themselves, and then go back to their original area. The area of confinement must be large enough to walk around in without feeling punished. Otherwise, many dogs will bark and try to get out. They must not feel imprisoned.

The area of confinement should be where the dog eats, sleeps, or does both, such as the kitchen or bathroom. The doorway should be blocked with a see-through puppy gate rather than a closed door. This is important for socializing the dog. Your pet must never be given the impression that he is being punished. He must be able to see other parts of the house and family activities. Puppy gates are available at pet-supply shops, through pet-supply mail-order catalogs, and in hardware stores.

Another useful tool for confining your dog during the housebreaking period is the dog crate, a rectangular wire cage with a door and a solid floor. It can be purchased in a size suitable for each dog. Dog crates are often recommended by breeders, trainers, and other professionals. It is important to understand that dog crates must be used appropriately. Do not imprison your dog for eight to ten hours in a crate simply because it is convenient for you. Puppies should not be left alone for great lengths of time. A dog crate can be a valuable training tool, but using it improperly can be psychologically damaging and inhumane. When a crate is used as a detention place for long periods, it creates socialization problems. It is important to use this highly effective piece of equipment for training purposes only, and to use it in a kind and balanced manner.

PROPER CORRECTION

Proper correction is an essential step in housebreaking. It is where many dog owners go wrong. Under no circumstances should a dog

borne out by observing him outdoors. He sniffs around for a very specific spot before he performs.

It is important to note that no ordinary cleaning product neutralizes these odors. Products containing ammonia intensify the odor of urine and attract the dog rather than repel him. Bleach and detergents of every kind fail because they are not designed for this purpose. Consequently, the dog's odor remains long after the mess has been cleaned away. A liquid odor neutralizer does its job every time. If your dog urinates in the house, your first step toward success is to odor-neutralize the spot immediately. This process should be repeated each and every time the dog has an accident in order to prevent him from returning to the scene of the crime.

PROPER DIET AND SCHEDULING

Feed, water, and walk your dog properly. He needs a stable, well-balanced diet consisting of correct amounts of fat, proteins, carbohydrates, vitamins, and minerals. The ideal dog food is meat, chicken, or fish added to some form of cereal. Canned meat products mixed with commercial cereal are adequate. Commercial dog food has all the vitamins and minerals essential for your dog's well-being and is recommended. Table scraps are a hit-or-miss affair. When changing the dog's diet, do not do it all at once. Gradually mix the two diets over a three-day period so that the change is not sudden. Otherwise it may cause diarrhea. A dog's stomach is very sensitive to changes in food.

Feed, water, and walk the dog at the same times each day to achieve favorable results. Consistency is the key to this method. The following rules must be followed during the housebreaking period:

1. Do not vary your dog's diet.
2. Snacks or between-meal treats are forbidden.

PUTTING YOUR DOG ON A PROPER SCHEDULE

The following schedules should be adhered to as closely as possible. By imposing a schedule with consistency, your dog's body will adjust itself to eating, drinking, walking, and eliminating at specific times every day. This, in turn, has the positive effect of creating self-control so that eventually your dog can go reasonable periods of time without needing to eliminate.

Bear in mind that these schedules (for eating, drinking, walking, and eliminating) should be imposed only during the housebreaking period, which could last anywhere between two to four weeks or two to four months, depending on the dog and his environment. Once the dog has his bodily functions under control and only eliminates outdoors you may alter his schedule so that it is more adaptive to your life-style. An adult dog is usually fed once a day and walked two, sometimes three, times a day. Some dogs live in a house with a front or backyard and have no need for a walking schedule (once housebreaking is completed).

The times given in the following housebreaking schedules are general suggestions and can be altered to some degree. If your dog wakes at a time earlier than seven in the morning, then that is the time to begin the first walk. The same is true if the dog wakes later. Simply adjust the remainder of the schedule accordingly.

Seven-week to six-month-old puppy: seven in the morning—walk the dog; seven-thirty in the morning—feed, water, and walk him; eleven-thirty in the morning—feed, water, and walk him; four-thirty in the afternoon—feed, water, and walk him; eight-thirty in the evening—water only and a walk; eleven-thirty in the evening—just a walk.

Six months to one year old: seven in the morning—walk the dog; seven-thirty in the morning—feed, water, and walk; twelve-thirty in the afternoon—water and walk; four-thirty in the afternoon—feed, water, and walk; seven-thirty in the evening—water and walk (last water of the day); eleven in the evening—walk the dog.

One year old and older: seven in the morning—walk the dog; seven-thirty in the morning—feed, water, and walk; four-thirty in the afternoon—water and walk; seven-thirty in the evening—water and walk (last water of the day); eleven in the evening—walk the dog.

At feeding time, allow fifteen minutes for the dog to complete his meal and then take it away, no matter how much he has left in the bowl. Allow him a few minutes to drink water. *He is not to be given food or water except at the scheduled times.* (This dietary schedule is for the duration of the housebreaking period only.) Please consult a veterinarian on all matters pertaining to your dog's diet and water intake.

The more you restrict the time for food and water during the training period, the closer you come to scheduling the dog's bodily functions. A dish with four or five ice cubes may substitute for a bowl of water, thus satisfying the dog's thirst while reducing his water intake. Once again, we advise you to consult a veterinarian about the specific needs of your dog.

The minute the dog is fed and watered, take him out for his walk. Once he has relieved himself, praise him and take him inside immediately. He will soon begin to understand why he is being taken out.

The length of time a dog should be walked for purposes of elimination must not exceed fifteen or twenty minutes. If taken on a long walk before or after he has performed his bodily functions, the impact of *why* he is being taken out will have been diminished and the method will not work. This is why most dogs do not know what is expected of them when they are taken outside.

Schedule for nine-to-five working people: Take the dog out immediately after waking up. Bring him back inside, feed and water him, and then walk him once again so that the routine is established. When you come home from work, repeat the process. Take him out, back in for feeding and watering, and then out for another walk immediately. It would be good for the dog if you could arrange for someone to repeat this cycle at lunch time. Before going to bed, walk him one last time without a feeding. Because a small puppy cannot hold his water for eight or nine hours, it is advisable to confine him at night to an area that he can urinate in without causing any household damage. It is inevitable that a young puppy will have many accidents throughout this training period. He will eventually gain control.

If the dog has a favorite outdoor area, let him go there to sniff around. Many dogs develop a favorite spot and this should not be discouraged.

When this program is first begun, do not be frustrated if the dog does not relieve himself for the first two or three rounds of feeding, watering, and walking. He may hold out for as long as twenty hours. Bear in mind that he is being forced to break his old habits and do something new for the first time. If the dog has been paper trained previously, take some paper outdoors. Place several clean sheets on top of one that has been soiled with the dog's urine. This will help him establish a toilet area outdoors. If he holds out for more than 24 hours, insert a glycerin baby suppository in his anus after his feeding and watering. Take him outside. You will definitely get results. After he relieves himself, praise him so that he knows that going outside pleases you. These are temporary measures until the dog is completely housebroken.

. . .

Many methods of housebreaking are negative in approach. Consequently, the dog only half understands. He knows he's done something wrong, but he gets little or no instruction for what he should be doing. The emphasis of this method is on prevention and instruction. This was once illustrated to a client who called the trainer at home at three in the morning. A frantic voice asked, "Mr. Margolis?"

"Yes," he mumbled.

"This is Mrs. Baxter. You're training my little Filbert."

"Yes," he answered, "but it's three in the morning. What do you want?"

"You told me to call you if Filbert had an accident. Well, he made do-do on the rug. What should I do?"

"Clean it up," he said as he hung up the phone.

That's instruction.

7.

PROPER USE OF *NO* AND *OKAY*

Spoken words are vocalized symbols that are used to communicate information, emotion, or combinations of the two. But for the purposes of dog training, words are tools for manipulating behavior. In this context we weigh our words carefully when training a dog to submit to our will. Two very valuable words are "No" and "Okay." These tools should not be used in a wasteful and unproductive manner, to wit, "Sidney, *no*, get your head out of the garbage." Or, "*Okay*, Sidney, what did you do? Now you're gonna get it." In dog training the words "No" and "Okay" are used for very specific purposes and do their jobs well. The trick is to use these words *only* to accomplish their designated tasks.

DEFINITION OF *NO*

The command *No* is applied to stop the dog from doing anything that is considered undesirable. It is never accompanied by other words or phrases.

BENEATH THE SURFACE OF THE TRAINING

The most common cause of a dog's confusion is inconsistency in the commands given by his owner. When you want the dog to refrain from jumping on the furniture, stealing food from the table, messing on the floor, or any other bad habit, use only one corrective word: "No." Too often an owner will use ten different corrective words in the course of one day. Words such as Stop! Don't! Please! Bad dog! Shame! only communicate anger or defeat.

No is the most authoritative and negative sound in the language. It is almost impossible to say this word in a positive way. The most timid personality can get the idea across to the animal with "No." If used consistently, the dog will always associate "No" with a bad thing and stop what he's doing instantly. The objective is to create an instant response in the animal to the word "No."

It is important that "No" never be associated with the dog's name. If it is, he will associate his name with a bad thing. The consequences are great. For instance, in all action commands, the dog's name is used before giving the actual command: "*Silver*, heel"; "Pete, come." But if the dog associates his name with a bad thing, he will never come to you on command or do anything associated with his name except slink away in fear. With a little practice you will discover that "No" used as a correction without any other word will do the job perfectly.

One other point is necessary with this correction. Do not use "No" more than once with each correction. Correct the dog with precision rather than with a display of emotion. Most dogs respond badly to hyperemotionalism and pick it up as part of their own behavior. If you shout "No, no, no" in a shrill voice you might create a nervous, high-strung, and very neurotic animal. The way to make the correction is with a firm, authoritative vocal sound that comes from the diaphragm. This is accomplished by taking in a deep breath and allowing the stomach to expand with air. Say the word "No" as you release the air. With practice, your tone will resonate and become deeper. One deep "No" will get the job done without inflicting emotional damage on the dog. Your voice should indicate a no-nonsense attitude rather than anger or worse. The point of the command is to get his attention and mildly startle him. Don't make him collapse with fear and urinate uncontrollably in the wake of thundering wrath. "No" should only get his attention and indicate to him that he is doing something wrong.

The reverse of this problem is using the correction in too mild a manner. Do not take on the tone and style of a doting grandmother with whining, nagging phrases like, "Ohhh, what did you do now, Wolfgang?" Well, sly little Wolfgang knows he has a sucker and can get away with just about anything. It is quite common for an owner to avoid exerting authority in his corrections for fear of losing the animal's love and attention. The truth of the matter is that the animal is grateful to know, once and for all, what he can and cannot do. His respect and love grow in leaps and bounds when he knows *exactly* how to please his master. The dog wants to get along and be accepted with love and affection. If given praise for what he does properly and authoritative corrections when he is behaving badly, he will work consistently for the praise. Dogs, like children, have a keen appreciation for the security of consistency and justice.

PROCEDURE AND TECHNIQUE FOR *NO*

With a firm, authoritative voice, give the command *No* in any situation when you want the dog to stop what he is doing. Never use his name in this connection. Give him time to respond to the command. Some dogs obey immediately, while others take a second or two before complying. Depending on the breed and temperament of the individual dog, obeying will take between one and five seconds. One "No" is all you should say. Once the dog has obeyed, praise him for it. This is the beginning of making him work for praise. Remember that it's not the word itself that gets the results. It's the *way* you say it. The sound must come from deep within the stomach and indicate cool authority rather than uncontrolled anger. You should not have to repeat the correction or something is wrong. Try using more firmness in your voice. Under no circumstances hit the dog. The word "No" is a key factor in correcting the dog during all training sessions.

The correction *No* is also used with a shake can, which was explained in detail in Chapter 4, "Equipment." When the dog misbehaves and doesn't respond to "No" as well as he should, shake the can behind your back and then deliver the vocal correction. Dog training is the rare exception where "No" accentuates the positive.

DEFINITION OF *OKAY*

This word is used in several ways. It is used when calling your dog as an affirmative prefix to his name. *Okay* is also your dog's release from training sessions and a release from walking by your side when he has to use the street to relieve himself.

BENEATH THE SURFACE OF THE TRAINING

Okay is a positive command. It should represent a pleasant experience for the dog. The word is essentially a release from discipline. But it is more than that—it is an important word when calling the dog *to* you. When the dog is far away, you must raise your voice to be heard. This could sound like a reprimand and would tend to make the dog hesitate. It implies, "You'd better get here or else." But when you prefix the command with a cheerful "Okay"—"*Okay,*

Pete, come," it automatically assures the dog of a happy reception. It is almost impossible to say "Okay" negatively. It seems to make its own cheerful sound because it forces the tone of voice to go higher. Since all the dog wants is love and affection, the use of "Okay" will indicate that everything is fine.

PROCEDURE AND TECHNIQUE FOR *OKAY*

If one uses the word "Okay," then everything *should* be okay. Do not use the word in any negative context or you will render it useless as a training tool. The word is still considered a command, even though it is a light, breezy one. It should make the dog aware that something pleasant is going to happen.

AS A RELEASE Assuming he is housebroken, a good dog walks by his owner's left side when on his way to the area in which he relieves himself. He is only allowed three feet of the leash, and the rest is gathered up in the owner's hand. This prevents him from leaving the owner's side. When they arrive at the designated place, the owner says "Okay" in a pleasant tone of voice and allows the extra length of leash to slip through his hand. The dog should then be led off the sidewalk and into the street. He will soon begin to understand what is expected of him if he is *consistently* made to walk by his owner's side until he arrives at the designated area. "Okay" will become a very important word for him. (If the dog's need is urgent, stand clear. It has happened that an owner was forced to change her slacks after releasing the dog.)

"Okay" is also used when a training session is finished. "Okay, Pete; that's all" should bring a joyful response, unless the dog is exhausted from his lesson, which is often the case. Even so, "Okay" will be a welcome sound. This should be true throughout the dog's life.

8.

THE CORRECTIVE JERK

The "corrective jerk" has nothing to do with the latest dance step or the neighborhood chiropractor. A dog does not speak any language known to man, but there are two basic things he does respond to: your pleasure and your displeasure. The very first thing he must learn is that there is only one way to perform—your way. Therefore, it is important to learn how to communicate your displeasure when he does not perform correctly. Hollering at him or hitting him may get across the idea that he was bad, but then his mind is in no condition to go to the next step, which is knowing what he *should* have been doing. What has he learned from a smack other than to fear you and your hands? Your hands should represent to your dog the physical extension of your love.

The most effective communication technique is the corrective jerk. *It is the primary corrective action in this obedience course and will be used over and over again.* Its importance cannot be stressed enough. Once this technique is learned, you will have a valuable teaching and corrective tool for as long as you have a dog.

DEFINITION OF THE CORRECTIVE JERK

The six-foot training leash is attached to a training collar that hangs loosely around the dog's neck. The leash is held in both hands as the dog sits or stands on the left side of the owner. Both are facing the same direction. Approximately three feet of the leash dangle from the collar, across the owner's knees, while the rest is gathered in *both* of the owner's hands.

The leash is jerked to the right, sideways and slightly upwards, away from the owner's right thigh. The word "No" is said in a firm tone of voice when the jerk is administered. The jerk should be made quickly, so that the hands return to their original positions in a fraction of a second. As the jerk is performed, the training collar tightens slightly around the dog's neck, giving a mild tightening sensation. As the owner's hands return to their original position, the training collar is automatically released and once again hangs loosely from the dog's neck. The jerk must always be firm but gentle. It must never be done abusively.

BENEATH THE SURFACE OF THE TRAINING

This technique will be disturbing and a bit of a shock to the dog when done for the first time. Although it does not hurt, it does startle him. The firm "No" reinforces the jerk and leaves no doubt in the dog's mind that he has displeased you. This is how he will learn right from wrong. Whenever the dog refuses to execute a command or indulges a bad habit, give him a corrective jerk. Dog trainers refer to this as a correction. *However, immediately following each corrective jerk, it is essential that you praise your dog and tell him how good he is.* Every time you correct your dog you must follow the correction with praise. This tells the dog you are still friends and rewards him for obeying you. It is a very important part of the teaching process.

It is better to give the dog one firm jerk properly than many jerks that are too mild and ineffective. In the end, ten or fifteen niggling tugs will not only irritate and exhaust the animal but will also produce poor obedience. Excessive use of this technique will make any dog "jerk shy." If a firm "No" is said with every corrective jerk, eventually the spoken correction "No," without the jerk, will suffice. This will be the beginning of a conditioned reflex to which the dog will respond properly for the rest of his life.

PROCEDURE AND TECHNIQUE FOR THE CORRECTIVE JERK

PUTTING ON THE TRAINING COLLAR   Place the collar around the dog's neck in the proper way (as described in the accompanying photos) and then attach the leash to the collar. A training collar is baffling to anyone looking at it for the first time. However, it is not as difficult to place around the dog as it may seem.

Simply hold either end of the collar by its ring with your left hand. Allow the chain to dangle vertically. Hold the ring hanging at the bottom with your right hand. Work the chain through the bottom ring so that it begins to form a loop. The weight of the chain will force it to drop into itself, forming a larger loop. Place the dog's head through the loop so that the collar slides down around the dog's neck. If it is placed correctly, the collar will form the letter P, with one free ring hanging from the dog's right side. If it is incorrect, it will form the number 9, with the free ring hanging from the dog's left side. When the collar is applied properly, it tightens around the dog's neck when it is jerked and instantly loosens when the leash is relaxed. Be sure you've put the collar on correctly before you add the leash.

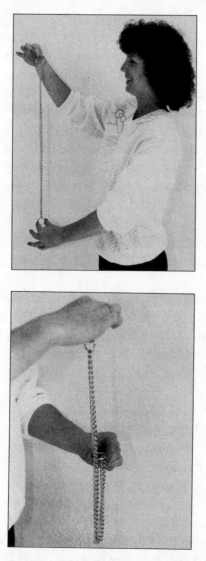

Top: Extend the collar to its full length. *Bottom:* Work the chain through the bottom ring so that it begins to form a loop.

Now attach the leash by its clip to the dangling ring of the training collar.

HOLDING THE LEASH PROPERLY   The six-foot training leash is held in the right hand as it connects to the training collar. The dog stands at your left side and you and your dog face in the same direction.

With your right arm hanging straight down, hook the sewn loop, which is at the top of the leash, over the thumb of your right hand, as pictured on page 83. As the leash hangs from your right thumb, grab the middle of the leash with your left hand and fold it over your right thumb, creating a second loop. In effect, you will have four straps of leather across the palm of your right hand. Close the fingers of your right hand around the four straps with your fingernails facing you. Adjust the length of the leash so that it crosses no more than the width of your body, allowing just a few inches of slack.

For added security, grip the folded leash with your left hand as well. Place your left hand directly under the right so that both hands are holding the leash like a baseball bat. The fingers of your left hand will be pointing away from your body. Both hands hold the leash, but in opposite directions. This gives you the most secure grip possible while allowing you to administer a proper corrective jerk.

Depending upon your height, only two or three feet of the leash should be traveling from the dog's collar across the front of your knees. The remainder of the leash dangles from your hands, barely touching the outer right thigh. You now have a firm hold and absolute control. If the dog should bolt, your thumb will hold the leash firmly in your hand.

Once the length of the leash is correct for both you and your dog, draw a line with a felt marker on the middle portion of the leash where it loops over your thumb. This will help you find the

Correct.

Incorrect.

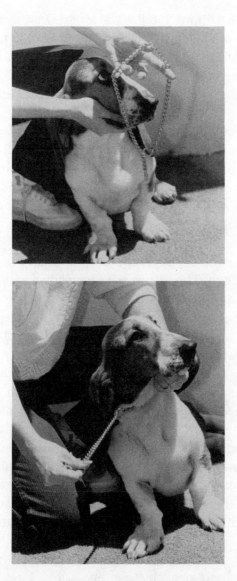

Top: If the training collar is placed correctly around the dog's neck, it will form the letter P.
Bottom: Test the collar. It should tighten and release quickly and smoothly.

right location each time you use the leash. Draw a second line on the sewn loop at the top of the leash to remind you to hook it onto your thumb. Draw additional lines for each person that uses the leash and place their initials next to their line. The coded lines will help them adjust the leash according to their size and height.

PROPERLY EXECUTING THE CORRECTIVE JERK   Start by facing in the same direction as the dog. He is standing at your left side with the leash attached to his training collar. Hold the leash as described above, with your arms slightly curved and your hands resting just below your waist. Relax your body so that you do not communicate tension to the dog.

To perform the correction, the leash is quickly jerked toward your right side and slightly upward, away from the outer portion of your right thigh. This is always accompanied with a firm verbal command, "No." The tone and loudness of your voice depends on the sensitivity of your dog and the quality of his response to your corrections. This is different for each dog and must be determined by the dog's personality.

Move your arms as if they were springs. Only your wrists and forearms should be used as your hands return to their original positions immediately after the jerk. The training collar will have tightened around the dog's neck for a split second and then returned to its loose position. The action is a jerk and then a quick release. The entire movement should take no longer than one second. Any longer than that may hurt or injure the animal. For an instant the dog will hear the snapping sound of the metal collar as it moves and feel it tighten and release. Although it is a negative sensation, and a bit of a surprise, he should feel no pain.

WHEN JERKING THE DOG   It is not necessary to jerk the leash too hard. Under no circumstances should the correction force the dog's legs to leave the ground or cause the slightest pain. That would be

HOLDING THE LEASH PROPERLY

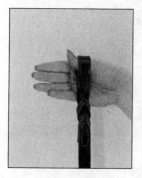

Hook the sewn loop over the thumb of your right hand.

Close your fingers around the loop.

Extend the leash and grab it in the middle with your left hand.

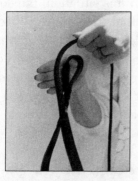

Fold the middle portion over your right thumb, creating a second loop.

For added security, grip the folded leash with both hands. You should be holding four straps of the leash leather.

When executing the corrective jerk, start by facing in the same direction as the dog.

punishment rather than correction. The corrective jerk is a teaching method. The object is to communicate to the dog that he performed incorrectly. The leash should be a means of communication much like the reins used on a horse.

The dog may whine or cry out after the first few corrections. Do not be upset by this. The sensation of the training collar is a startling surprise for most dogs. In this situation, the dog's whimpering is more like a complaint rather than an expression of pain. Your dog may be trying to manipulate you into letting him maintain control over the situation. Some dogs are criers and will emit a shrill squeal to force you to stop making them do what they don't want to do. This is a ploy and does not indicate that the dog is experiencing the slightest bit of pain. Maintain a firm attitude and never let the dog control the situation.

PRAISE Immediately following the corrective jerk, give the dog a great deal of enthusiastic praise. Compliments such as "Good girl," "Good dog," "Atta boy," are very effective. Make the praise verbal and do not pet the dog—a pat on the head often indicates to a dog that the lesson is over and he can relax. Verbal congratulations are

To perform the correction, the leash is quickly jerked toward your right side and slightly upward.

his reward and he needs them in order to know that he has pleased you. Many people go wrong in this aspect of training. It seems embarrassing to walk down the street talking to your dog, but it is the best thing for a successful training program. Do not be inhibited in expressing affection and enthusiasm for a job well done. Talking to an animal is not as eccentric as it may seem. One talks to an infant knowing he doesn't understand one word. What one is communicating is approval through the tone of voice. Humans and domestic animals respond to it. Vocal praise produces greater results than most head pats and body rubs. In this way you are expressing approval without sacrificing disciplinary demands.

When teaching yourself how to execute the corrective jerk, do not practice on the dog. It will exhaust him and create confusion. The correction is merely a tool to be used when teaching the other commands. It is not an end in itself. It would make a lot more sense to practice on a broom handle or stairway banister until you have learned to execute the maneuver correctly.

Do not correct the dog for something he didn't do. Always go *to* the dog to correct him. Never call the dog to you so that you can administer a negative message. This is counterproductive and un-

86

Return to the original position. The action
is to jerk and then quickly release.

fair. If you do this the dog will never come to you when you call
him. The corrective jerk is a technique—not a person.

CUSTOMIZED TRAINING

FOR THE HIGH-ENERGY/OUTGOING TEMPERAMENT

VOICE CORRECTIONS   Use a firm, authoritative tone of voice.

LEASH CORRECTIONS   Use a strong correction with the leash. Do
not scare the dog, simply be authoritative.

FOR THE SHY TEMPERAMENT

VOICE CORRECTIONS   Use a soft tone of voice, as though you were
speaking to a child.

LEASH CORRECTIONS   When correcting the dog, tug on the leash
in a very gentle manner.

FOR THE STRONG-WILLED TEMPERAMENT

VOICE CORRECTIONS   Use a firm tone of voice. Be authoritative and demanding. If that is difficult for you, think of this as a dramatic performance and act like a no-nonsense dog trainer. You may play this role much better if you imagine your untrained dog chewing up your furniture, soiling your good carpet, or running in the street.

LEASH CORRECTIONS   Think of the degree of firmness of the corrective jerk on a scale from 1 to 10, 1 being very mild and 10 being the firmest. A dog with a strong-willed temperament should be corrected in the 7 to 10 range. Administer the corrective jerk in a firm, quick manner. Be authoritative when executing a no-nonsense type of correction. However, do not upset your dog with fear tactics. Even a strong-willed dog may simply not understand the basics of the command. Give him the benefit of the doubt and repeat the teaching portion of the command.

FOR THE CALM/EASYGOING TEMPERAMENT

VOICE CORRECTIONS   Use a demanding yet encouraging tone of voice. Try to be slightly authoritative without hurting the dog's feelings.

LEASH CORRECTIONS   When correcting the dog, administer a firm jerk, hard enough to get his attention, yet soft enough to avoid hurting his feelings . . . or his neck. On a scale of 1 to 10, correct the dog with a 3.

FOR THE AGGRESSIVE TEMPERAMENT

VOICE CORRECTIONS   If your dog is dominant/aggressive, adjust the intensity of your voice correction to the size, age, and degree of aggressiveness of the dog. A dog with a dominant/aggressive temperament might snap or bite if the tone of your voice is too harsh or challenging. Be firm and authoritative without scaring the dog. If your dominant/aggressive dog is a puppy between seven weeks and six months of age, use a firm tone of voice. If your dominant/ aggressive dog is between six months and ten months of age, use a *very* firm tone of voice. Without actually shouting or hollering, make sure the dog understands that you mean business by the sound of your voice. A dog with this temperament who is more than ten months old should be evaluated by a professional dog trainer, animal behaviorist, or veterinarian, depending on the degree of dominant/aggressive behavior.

If your dog is fear/aggressive, voice corrections are important. Fear/aggressive dogs are, in a sense, shy, and behave aggressively against those who frighten them. This behavior is purely defensive in nature. The improper use of your voice could cause such a dog to bite. A seven-week to six-month-old puppy requires gentler handling. He must be allowed to be a puppy, although corrections are essential. Give him firm but not harsh voice corrections. If the dog is six months to ten months old, use your voice in a firm, authoritative manner. A fear/aggressive dog that is older than ten months of age may be too difficult to handle. Have the dog evaluated by a professional dog trainer, animal behaviorist, or veterinarian.

LEASH CORRECTIONS   If your dog is dominant/aggressive, use the leash accordingly. For puppies between the ages of seven weeks and six months, execute firm leash corrections. They should be administered in a manner that establishes you as the dominant figure. You must "win" in each situation where the young dog challenges your authority, although not at the expense of the dog's well-being. The corrective jerk is not meant to be abusive in any way. The idea is to teach the dog his behavioral boundaries, not to punish him. For young dogs between the ages of six months and ten months, use *very* firm and authoritative leash corrections. Do not back down in any leash correction situation unless the dog is becoming super-aggressive. In that event, seek professional help. Once the dog is past ten months of age, you must have him evaluated by a professional before attempting to train him.

The fear/aggressive dog must be handled in a slightly different manner. You must take into account the shy, frightened aspect of his temperament. A seven-week to six-month-old puppy requires leash corrections that are not severe. Be firm, but use a softer touch when jerking the leash. If the dog is six months to ten months old, use a firm, authoritative tug of the leash when administering a corrective jerk. A fear/aggressive dog who is older than ten months of age is difficult to handle. Have the dog evaluated by a professional dog trainer, animal behaviorist, or veterinarian.

9.
SIT

Have you ever seen a dog ignore his owner when given a command? It is painful to watch the person's face redden and the voice progress from one octave to another as he or she yells, Sit... *Sit*... SIT... SIT!!! Perhaps you've been that person. You have no idea how to communicate with your dog and you don't know what to communicate. Commands should be precise and consistent. For that reason, each command is defined at the beginning of every command chapter. The same command should not be given with a different expectation each time. The command *Sit* is incorrect if used to stop a dog from barking, from running, or from urinating on your friend's leg. None of these have a single thing to do with the command *Sit*.

DEFINITION OF *SIT*

On command, the dog sits erect with all his weight on his haunches. His body is upright and his front legs are straight and slant inward slightly at the top.

BENEATH THE SURFACE OF THE TRAINING

Sitting is a natural position for a dog. But having your dog sit on command requires patient training and a good understanding of why and when you want him to sit. His inclination to sit occurs when he is curious and wants to observe. The *Sit* command is one of the best techniques to gain quick control of his behavior when something is exciting him or distracting him from your purposes. If the doorbell rings, for example, he may start barking or running frantically to the door. In order to control this burst of energy and avoid scaring your caller half to death, undercut the dog's reaction by controlling his behavior. Having him sit would accomplish this if the dog could respond to that command in the middle of his mischief. But he cannot. He must be made to stop what he's doing first, and then he can be commanded to do something else. Therefore, give him the command "No" first, and "Sit" immediately afterward. If the dog were to get loose while on the street, it would be a lifesaver to be able to trigger the mechanism in his brain that makes him sit at your command. If trained properly, he cannot refuse your command unless he is running at top speed or is involved in an intense dog fight. But even then you will have some control.

From this chapter to the end of the obedience course it is important that you not feed the dog before beginning training sessions. Otherwise he may be too sluggish to respond properly. Starting with *Sit*, every command taught thereafter will require every ounce of concentration the dog possesses. If his stomach is full he will not want to learn. It is also important to allow the dog to relieve himself if the session is being conducted outdoors.

PROCEDURES AND TECHNIQUES FOR *SIT*

Whenever teaching this or any other command, you must have absolute control and attention. The main tools for exercising this control are the six-foot leash and the training collar. Nothing can be accomplished without them.

Since this will be the first command the dog will be taught, try to make it as easy as possible by giving him the benefit of little or no distraction at all. Take him to a quiet, out-of-the-way place in your neighborhood or to a secluded room indoors. There should be no audience—it will be less inhibiting for both you and the dog. If the lesson is being conducted outdoors, allow the dog to relieve himself before beginning. Otherwise he will not be able to concentrate.

Like most commands, *Sit* requires that you *not* use the dog's name before giving the command. Use his name only before commands that involve forward motion. The two forward or action commands in this course are *Heel* and *Come When Called*.

THE LEASH   Because the leash and the training collar are of primary importance, their use will be described once again. The six-foot training leash is connected to the training collar, which should be properly placed around the dog's neck (when it forms the letter P, it is on correctly, and when it forms the number 9, it is on incorrectly).

Hold the leash in your right hand with the sewn loop hooked over your thumb. Take the middle of the leash with your left hand, create a loop, and drape it over your right thumb so that you have four straps of leather in your right palm. Close your fingers tightly around the four straps. With your right arm hanging straight down, the leash goes across your body diagonally to the dog's collar. Only two or three feet of the leash should be hanging across the front of your knees from your right hand to the dog's collar. Adjust the length of the leash from the collar to your right hand if necessary. It is easier to maintain control when teaching *Sit* with a shorter length of leash.

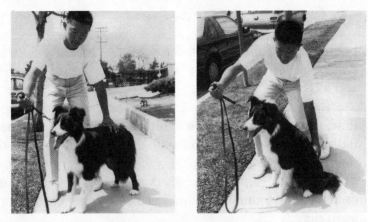

The Pushing Technique. *Left:* Find the hip joints or hip sockets of your dog's hindquarters with the fingers of your left hand. *Right:* As you say the command "Sit," push down with your left hand and pull the leash up with your right hand at the same time.

1. *The Pushing Technique.* With the leash in your right hand, position yourself and the dog to face in the same direction with the dog at your left side. With the fingers of your left hand, find the hip joints or hip sockets of your dog's hindquarters, which are located near the base of the spine, on the dog's back. Run your fingers from the dog's shoulder blades down the spine until you come to the end. You will feel two indentations. Hold them with a firm, gentle squeeze. As you say "Sit," push down with your left hand and pull the leash up with your right hand at the same time. Stretch the sound of the word "Sit" until the dog is actually sitting. If this is done too hard or too fast it will startle him and he will jump up and move around. Give the command with gentle authority and push on his hip joints slowly. When the dog reaches the proper sitting position praise him.

    Try not to use your hands when giving praise. If your dog is a puppy, he may nip. An older dog may take an affectionate stroke or pat on the head as a sign that the lesson is over. Develop an enthusiastic, happy tone of voice that suggests praise and satisfaction with the dog's performance. Relate to the dog as you would a baby taking its first steps, falsetto voice and all.

Repeat the process until the dog responds properly every time. Once you accomplish this, try teaching the command *without* using your left hand on the hip joints to push the dog into a sitting position. Simply say "Sit," and slowly pull up on the leash with your right hand. Don't forget to praise the dog each and every time. It will not take very long for the dog to learn this.

When the dog consistently obeys the command with ease, eliminate the pull-up with the leash. Say "Sit," with no other action on your part. Praise the dog for obeying the command.

That is the teaching process. It is very important that no correction be given during the teaching process. Correcting a dog for something he has not yet learned is pointless and counterproductive.

Once the dog has learned to obey the command, if he *then* fails to do so, the corrective jerk is used. In this first session, repeat the teaching process ten or fifteen times and give your dog a rest. Do not give him reason to believe it is play time. Just stop and walk around a little, but do not release him from the session. After the break, go back to the command and repeat it again another ten or fifteen times. Both halves of the session should not last more than fifteen or twenty minutes. It is quite possible that he will have learned the command in the first session. If not, give him another session, but wait at least four hours. You may give two sessions a day.

USING THE CORRECTIVE JERK   If the dog is still having problems learning the command after several sessions, employ the corrective jerk. With the dog close to your side, take up all but two or three feet of the leash. Give the command *Sit*, and gently jerk the leash with your right hand as you push him down by the hip joints, as described above. Once he is in the sitting position, praise him. This is vital. Repeat the command; pull him up with the right hand, lower him with the left. As he sits, give him his praise. Repeat this process until he sits immediately after your command. Do not give him time to consider the command once it is given and never say the command more than once without making him respond properly.

The basic formula for this training course is: *Command, Correction*, and *Praise*. It applies to the teaching of every command. Assuming the dog has been taught the command and he knows it, apply the corrective jerk whenever he does not respond properly. If he ignores you or simply doesn't obey when you say "Sit," snap the leash to the right and firmly say "No!" He will sit because he has been reminded to do so. Remember the formula: Command, Correction, and Praise. *If he responds to your command, do not correct the dog, go right to the praise.* If he does not, execute a corrective jerk and *then* give him his praise. The secret of successful dog training is immediate praise after every correction or command. The dog knows he has pleased you and begins to work for your approval. Verbal praise will spare you the futility of fifteen years of bribery.

2. *The Placing Technique.* This method teaches the command *Sit* without applying downward pressure. As in most training techniques, this one assumes that the dog is friendly and not aggressive. *It is recommended for dogs who are sensitive to being held or touched at the lower end of the body.* This includes dogs who have been hit on the rump, dogs who are rear shy, and dogs who cannot cope with the Pushing Technique. It is ideal for frightened dogs because you will not be standing over

them but, rather, placing yourself at eye level. This method is also kinder for dogs who have arthritis or hip dysplasia. The Pushing Technique applies pressure on the hindquarters, which forces the dog into a sitting position; the Placing Technique does not.

Follow *all* of the instructions given in the Pushing Technique, with the following exceptions:

Stand, bend over, or kneel next to the dog. The size of the dog will determine this. Instead of placing your left hand on the dog's hip joints (as in the Pushing Technique), gently but firmly place it behind the dog's rear legs at the first joint beneath the rump (the equivalent of the human knee). These joints bend forward naturally when the dog sits. The palm of your hand should face upward as though the dog were going to sit on it.

As you give the command *Sit*, bend the dog's rear legs forward at the joint with the edge of your left hand. The effect is to make them collapse forward. As you do this, pull upward on the leash with your right hand. This gets the dog into a sitting position. When giving the verbal command, stretch the sound of the word "Sit" until the dog is actually sitting. Don't forget to praise the dog after each command. Repeat the process until he responds properly every time.

3. *The Food Technique.* Follow *all* of the previous instructions given in the Pushing Technique, with the following exceptions: Use food as an inducement for dogs who are aggressive or very frightened and do not like anyone to go near them.

Hold the leash as previously described in the Pushing Technique. Have the dog's favorite food treat in your left hand, show it to him, slowly bring it up toward his nose, and then past his eyes. When you do this, give the command *Sit* and smoothly pull up on the leash. As the dog looks up at the

The Food Technique. Slowly bring the food treat up toward the dog's nose and then past his eyes. Say the command "Sit," and smoothly pull up on the leash. Praise him lavishly when he sits, and give him the food treat.

food, the pressure of the leash gets him into a sitting position. Praise him lavishly when he sits, and give him the food treat. Repeat this process until the dog responds properly every time. Once you have accomplished this, try teaching the command *without* the use of food. Simply say "Sit," and slowly pull up on the leash with your right hand. Never forget to praise the dog after each successful execution of the command. Remember the formula, Command, Correction, Praise. Never correct the dog until you are convinced the dog has learned the command.

4.   *The Small Dog Technique.* Small dogs are often frightened or intimidated when humans tower over them during training. This technique avoids potential behavior problems created by fear of training. Follow *all* of the previous instructions given in the Pushing Technique, with the following exceptions: Do not stand over the dog. You may bend over or kneel next to the dog during the teaching process or you may place the dog on a table. This keeps the dog and the trainer at an acceptable height difference. Then use either the Pushing Technique or the Placing Technique for teaching your small dog the command *Sit*.

CUSTOMIZED TRAINING

FOR THE HIGH-ENERGY/OUTGOING TEMPERAMENT

OWNER'S FRAME OF MIND   Try to understand your dog in positive terms. Think of him as a lovable lunatic or an outboard motor on high. He is energy in motion. Everything interests him all the time, every time. Think back when you were a kid and became excited about something, like a surprise birthday party or the last day of

The Small Dog Technique. Small dogs can be taught *Sit* on a tabletop, using the Placing Technique (see page 95). Place your left hand gently but firmly behind the dog's rear legs. As you say "Sit," bend the dog's rear legs forward at the joint with the edge of your hand.

school. As adults we still get excited but we're usually able to control it. Bear in mind that the high-energy dog will keep on dancing unless we calm him down. Your goal is to channel all that wonderful energy properly. Think of your dog as a child who can't sit still when trying to do his homework. Maybe twenty minutes of running around and playing ball will calm him down. Always try to turn a negative into a positive.

BODY LANGUAGE   An excited dog will jump all over the place and not be able to concentrate when taken out for a training lesson. Start each session with some form of exercise. That will help spend some of his energy and relax him. Next, go to the nearest wall or barrier and stand beside it with the dog. Work the dog there, in a confined space. Do not give him enough room to run, jump, and hop all over the place.

TONE OF VOICE   Firm, authoritative, no-nonsense. Your voice should communicate to the dog that playtime is over and it's now time to learn.

VOICE CORRECTION   Your voice should be firm, consistent, and de-manding but not intimidating or scary. In the beginning use leash corrections (the corrective jerk) with your voice corrections in order to be more effective. Use one-word commands.

LEASH CORRECTIONS   The nature of the leash correction must be determined by the size, age, breed, and tolerance of the dog. For example, a three-month-old Toy Poodle would require a much gen-tler tug of the leash than would a three-month-old Golden Retriever. Remember, the leash is not a weapon, it is a tool of instruction. A very quick jerk and release is the most effective leash correction for dogs with high-energy/outgoing temperaments.

WHERE TO TRAIN It is essential to use a secluded, quiet area where there are no distractions. Do not allow anyone to be there besides you and your charge of energy.

FOR THE SHY TEMPERAMENT

OWNER'S FRAME OF MIND Try to see the situation from the shy dog's frame of mind. Being taught the command *Sit* could be nerve-wracking. How would you want to be taught or treated in a situation where you are frightened? Be patient and understanding.

BODY LANGUAGE Standing over a shy dog or a puppy or a small dog may be frightening for the dog. From the dog's point of view, you tower over him like a six-story building. Kneel down when relating to the dog. For a small dog, consider putting him on a table to give him the comfort of relating to you at eye level.

TONE OF VOICE Soothing, loving, and very assuring. Use a high tone as you would with a baby. Try to imagine that you are talking to a frightened child and adjust your voice accordingly.

VOICE CORRECTION None or very little, depending on the degree of shyness. Remember, the idea is to teach and correct, not to punish.

LEASH CORRECTION Hold the leash very loosely, keep the dog in place with gentle pressure. Don't pull it. Use the Placing Technique when teaching *Sit* to dogs with a shy temperament.

WHERE TO TRAIN Use a quiet area such as a backyard or someplace indoors where there are no distractions. You may want to use some type of a barrier or wall to keep the dog in place in case he is very frightened.

FOR THE STRONG-WILLED TEMPERAMENT

OWNER'S FRAME OF MIND   Strong-willed dogs behave in a very stubborn manner. It may help you to understand that stubbornness reflects independence—not necessarily a bad quality. Strong-willed dogs require your time, patience, knowledge, and staying power. In order to teach this command effectively to dogs of this temperament, you must maintain a positive attitude. Do not get discouraged, and be assured that you will succeed, even if it takes a little longer than expected.

BODY LANGUAGE   Exercise before each lesson is useful for strong-willed dogs as well as for high-energy dogs. If you help him spend his excess energy, he will obey just for the rest. Your posture must reflect firmness but not aggressiveness. Kneeling down and using the Placing Technique will get the dog to respond very quickly. Or use the Pushing Technique, but quickly, while you are standing.

TONE OF VOICE   Use a tone of voice that is firm enough to get your point across without being harsh. Do not yell at the dog or intimidate him with your vocal quality.

VOICE CORRECTION   It should be an attention getter. The objective is to get the dog's undivided attention, so that he believes you mean business. However, do not be excessive. Try not to scare him into listening. Just convey the idea that when you say "Sit," it means now, not later.

LEASH CORRECTION   Be firm with your leash corrections, but don't overdo it. You can always increase the intensity of the corrective jerk if the dog does not respond properly. Start soft, go to medium, then to very firm, if necessary. Sometimes a quick jerk will work, and sometimes just pulling up slowly and forcing the dog to sit works well.

WHERE TO TRAIN   Use a quiet area with no distractions and no spectators. Choose a place where you and the dog are comfortable.

FOR THE CALM/EASYGOING TEMPERAMENT

OWNER'S FRAME OF MIND   Try to understand your dog's temperament and sympathize with it. Think of him as a couch potato and accept him the way he is. Imagine what it must be like to be an easygoing, sedate dog. He cannot be rushed. If you put a calm/easygoing dog in a race, he'll probably finish last, but he *will* finish. You must tolerate the dog's slower pace.

BODY LANGUAGE   How to relate to the dog physically depends on his size. If he is a small dog, kneel down and be very loving, playful, and exuberant. Stand up with a big dog and give him big hugs and kisses. Whether you kneel or stand, use your hands and touch the dog a lot; be affectionate and praise him lavishly. He may, at some point, lie down in the middle of the lesson. If he does, pick him up very gently, move him around to reenergize him, and then try to refocus his attention on the lesson.

TONE OF VOICE   Very exuberant with high energy. Change the pitch of your voice as often as you can to keep your dog's interest up and to motivate him. Make funny sounds, whistle, whine like a puppy. Do anything to get his attention. Just make sure your family or friends don't hear you. They'll probably think you need the training more than the dog does.

VOICE CORRECTION   Use a soft tone when needed. Change to a high-energy or firm tone of voice, depending on how the dog responds. Be flexible.

LEASH CORRECTION   Some easygoing dogs may take longer to teach, and that depends on their size and how easygoing they are. Accept slow responses in the beginning. But gradually increase your demand for better responses to your commands and corrections. At first, jerk the leash in a soft manner. Gradually change to a medium degree of intensity. When you feel the dog is accustomed to leash corrections, tug it firmly when necessary. Never use the leash harshly. Do not confuse lack of motivation or aloofness for not understanding or refusing to learn.

WHERE TO TRAIN   Go anywhere that you will have undivided attention and be free from noise and distractions.

FOR THE AGGRESSIVE TEMPERAMENT

OWNER'S FRAME OF MIND   When training a dog with an aggressive temperament, it is necessary to stay aware of his potentially dangerous reactions. Be cautious. This is especially the case when dealing with a dog that has already indicated a tendency to bite.

BODY LANGUAGE   Do not stand over your dog, making direct eye contact. In dog behavior, a direct stare into the eyes is taken as a challenge to the animal's position of dominance. This is very important to remember with an aggressive dog.

When using your hands to push the dog into the *sit* position, consider how he responds to them. If the dog was hit with the hands or with a rolled-up newspaper held by hands, he may bite any hand that comes near him. Be cautious and very slow-moving with the body and especially the hands. You can recondition the dog to respond differently to the hands by stroking him gently, lovingly, and speaking in a soothing tone of voice at the same time. This should be done at every possible opportunity, whether training or not.

TONE OF VOICE   The tone of your voice depends on the dog's age and if he is dominant/aggressive or fear/aggressive. A dominant/ aggressive puppy between the ages of seven weeks to six months requires a firm (but not harsh) tone of voice. For dominant/ aggressive dogs between six and ten months, use a very authoritative, demanding tone of voice. A fear/aggressive puppy between the ages of seven weeks and six months requires that you use a soft tone of voice that is still firm enough to correct him. For fear/ aggressive dogs between six and ten months, use a firm (but not harsh) tone of voice. Get professional help for all aggressive dogs past ten months of age.

VOICE CORRECTION   May not be effective unless accompanied by a leash correction at the same time. Some dogs are so aggressive that a voice correction is not effective at all. For this reason, always have your aggressive dog on a leash at training sessions. All corrections should be followed with praise for acceptance of the correction.

LEASH CORRECTION   You must consider the dog's age, size, and level of aggressiveness when administering leash corrections. Is the dog a bully? Does he growl, snarl, or curl his lip? Puppies between seven weeks and six months old should be corrected with quick, firm jerks that are not too hard. For dogs between six and ten months, correct with quick, firm jerks. However, you might need to administer slightly harder jerks at that age, depending on the dog's level of aggressiveness.

When your dog behaves aggressively, correct him quickly. Repeat the corrections until he stops behaving aggressively. Unless he is severely aggressive, you should be able to obtain at least ninety percent satisfactory results this way. Bear in mind that it is only safe to correct an aggressive dog until the age of ten months. After that he will be too dangerous for nonprofessional handling. Have the dog evaluated by a professional dog trainer, animal behaviorist, veterinarian, or all three.

WHERE TO TRAIN   Take advantage of the privacy of your home or your backyard. Do not allow any distractions, such as dogs, kids, or neighbors, to interfere with the training sessions.

10.

THE *HEEL* AND *AUTOMATIC SIT*

If a human being is referred to as a "heel," it is accepted that he is a bounder, a rotter, one who will take advantage of anyone and double-cross his friends. If he is "well heeled," he has money. But a well-heeled dog is quite another matter. This refers to a dog who *walks in heel*, which is to say, a dog who does not pull his master down the street like an Alaskan sled. The bounding energy of a dog out for his first walk offers little pleasure unless he is trained to heel, especially if he is the size of a small horse.

DEFINITION OF *HEEL*

Heeling is having the dog walk on your left side with his head next to your thigh. He walks when you walk and stops when you do. When executed properly, the dog never leaves your side.

BENEATH THE SURFACE OF THE TRAINING

Don't throw this book across the room and say, "I'll never get Killheart to do that for me." Although it sounds like a great deal to

Does this scene look familiar? If your dog does not heel properly you may be yanked down the street.

accomplish, it's not as hard as it seems. The alternatives are unpleasant. If the dog does not heel properly, you will either be yanked down the street like a Brahman bull rider at the rodeo or you will be dragging him along the sidewalk as you wear away the lining of your stomach. Heeling is not a trick and is not too difficult to teach, but it does not conform to the natural instincts of the dog, so he must be taught to do this with patience, diligence, and repetition.

As in every lesson, do not feed your dog before beginning a training session. Otherwise he will be too sluggish to respond properly. If the session is conducted outdoors, allow the dog to relieve himself. Otherwise he's in no condition to learn something new. Find a quiet outdoor area with a minimum of distraction. The dog's first response to the outside will be to run ahead, straining at the leash as he pulls you down the street.

Everything out of doors is new and intriguing, especially to a young puppy, and the street holds a thousand adventures in sight and smell. In his excitement he becomes an absolute ingrate and forgets all you've done for him. Thus it becomes important to teach him that you are the most important factor when out for a walk or a training session.

The dog's spirit is going to be high as he is walked to the training place. You don't want him to dread each session, so try not to discourage his pleasant, happy feeling.

In order to succeed in training your dog, you must learn to communicate. There is a kind of language you need to develop. Dogs are like babies that never grow up. An infant responds to the tone, volume, and pitch of the voice speaking to it. Dogs respond in much the same way. The word "no" delivered in a firm tone will stop most dogs in their tracks.

Gaining the dog's attention without a correction is accomplished by pitching the voice high and speaking as you would to a baby: "That's a *good* boy!" Affection and praise are given softly and sincerely. If the dog is trained to sit on command, he will do it properly if you say "liver." It is all in the voice.

PROCEDURE AND TECHNIQUE FOR THE *HEEL*

Limit each session to fifteen minutes and conduct no more than two sessions a day, spaced at least four hours apart.

PROPER POSITION   The first step in teaching the *Heel* is to put your dog in the proper position. Place him in the *sit* position on your left side. (Choosing the left side is merely traditional. It began as a safety factor for hunters who carried their weapons with their right arms while the dog walked astride on the left.)

Using the six-foot leash, hold it with both hands as if you were going to execute the corrective jerk. Both arms should hang loose and unbent. Always allow two or three feet of slackened leash to drape across your knees. Do not hold your hands chest-high. They must be by your side to do the corrective jerk properly.

USING HIS NAME   Once you and the dog are in the correct position and ready to go, give the command: "Timmy, *heel!*" Use his name this time because *Heel* is an action command and it alerts him to move into a forward position. Saying his name first gets his attention. Once his name is said, the dog's focus should be on you. He should be ready to move. At the command "Timmy, *heel,*" begin walking, starting with your left foot. The reason one starts with the left foot is because it is closer to the dog's eyes and he will move when it does. In this way you will move together. Remember, the objective is to have the dog walk at your side.

IF THE DOG RUNS AHEAD   The first problem you will probably encounter is the dog's desire to run ahead. The best way to solve this

The first step in teaching the *Heel* command is putting your dog in the proper position.

is to allow him to run to the end of the six-foot training leash. As he reaches the end of it, turn right quickly and make a complete U-turn. At the moment of impact say "Heel" in a loud, authoritative voice. Walk briskly in the opposite direction. The dog will have been startled and forcibly turned in the direction you are walking. Praise the dog as he catches up with you. Once again his primitive instincts will have been totally thwarted by your will.

Keep walking at a brisk clip and the dog will catch up. When he does, adjust the leash to the length at which you started. If the dog shoots ahead of you again, repeat the procedure. Turn right quickly and make a complete U-turn. At the moment of impact, say "Heel" in a loud, authoritative voice. Walk briskly in the opposite direction. This business of turning in the opposite direction is hard on the dog, therefore he must be praised lavishly as he catches up. The praise will help teach him what walking in *Heel* means. Praise is the way you communicate to him what is expected. It tells him he is good if he walks by your side. It also keeps his attention on you, which prepares him for any stops or turns. *The technique for*

At the command "Timmy, *heel*," start walking with your left foot. The reason one starts with the left foot is because it is closer to the dog's eyes, causing him to move when you do.

The first problem you will probably encounter is the dog's desire to run ahead. Allow him to run to the end of the six-foot leash. As he reaches the end of it, turn right quickly and make a complete U-turn. Say "Heel," and walk in the opposite direction.

praising the dog varies from dog to dog, based on temperament. Either give immediate praise after the sudden turn or withhold it for a few seconds. Some dogs need immediate approval, while others take it to mean they are released from the lesson. You will quickly discover how and when to praise your own dog.

LAGGING BEHIND   The dog's tendency to run ahead will diminish with each fifteen-minute lesson. Once he is no longer running ahead, be prepared to cope with the problem of his lagging behind. This problem is easily solved by extending verbal encouragement if the dog fails to keep up with you. Tell him what a good dog he is, and literally entice him to catch up. A lavish invitation to walk by your side will keep his attention fixed on you and will probably solve the problem. If the dog does not respond properly, you may gently snap the leash with a slight jerk or pull. What is desirable is to help the dog develop the habit of keeping his attention on you whenever he is taken for a walk.

WALKING BY YOUR SIDE   After three or four lessons it will be time to teach the dog a more exact position when walking with you. Up to this point he will have been keeping one or two lengths ahead, which is all right. But now he must learn always to walk with his head lined up to your left thigh, no farther ahead or behind.

As before, start with the dog in the *sit* position. Give him the command "Timmy, *heel.*" Start walking, leading with your left foot. Every time the dog's head moves beyond your thigh, execute a corrective jerk, and firmly say "No." Turn right quickly and make a complete U-turn. Say, "Timmy, *heel,*" and continue to walk in the opposite direction. Praise him. This procedure should be repeated again and again until the dog is walking in the prescribed position. It is possible for a dog to learn this in a single fifteen-minute session. However, keep repeating the technique for as long as it takes him to learn it. Do not work the dog for more than fifteen

When the dog lags behind, tell him what a good dog he is, and literally entice him to catch up. Pat the side of your thigh with your hand as you talk to the dog.

minutes at a time and give him four hours rest between lessons. Only two lessons a day are recommended.

TOO SHY TO WALK   Occasionally a dog is either too shy or too frightened to walk at all on his first encounter with the outside. This is usually the case with puppies. He will cower with fear and probably duck under your legs or look for the protection of the nearest wall. The objective is to rid the dog of his fear. Too much authority will tend only to reinforce his terror and uncertainty. First, try to start him out on the *Heel* command. If he will not walk, step in front of him and go down on your knees. Gently call him with affectionate entreaties and playful tones. Get him to come. Do this about three or four times until he comes every time you bend down. Once he is doing that, start backing away as he comes. Keep lengthening the distance he has to go.

Once he is on his feet and walking, stand up, turn, and walk together. If he is a particularly stubborn dog and freezes at this point, keep walking, pulling him along until he gives in. Be careful not to scrape his paw pads too hard along the sidewalk or any other hard surface. The pads are sensitive and will bleed easily. This could create a trauma that will make the problem of training acute. If the struggle continues, take him to a park. If the dog again freezes, keep walking as you pull him along the grass. This will prevent traumatic injury and force the dog to walk with you.

Part of the problem could be the leash. Many dogs, especially puppies, have a difficult time adjusting to the idea of a leash. You may need to deal with the problem of leash rejection first.

LEASH REJECTION   Many puppies and some adult dogs twist, turn, push, pull, and bite the leash to escape being controlled in any way. Dogs do not understand that a leash can save their lives and also functions as an important means of communication. *Rejection of the leash is unacceptable. It is a lifeline between humans and dogs.*

To get your dog to accept a leash, put a buckled collar and lightweight leash (three or four feet long) on your dog as soon as you can. You may even use a short piece of clothesline. The idea is to accustom the dog to the feel and the weight of the leash and collar. Be certain the collar fits well and is comfortable. Allow the dog or the puppy to drag the leash around the house or yard all day, but *the dog should never be left alone with the leash or clothesline attached.*

Be exuberant and make a happy fuss as you attach the leash, creating a pleasant association with it in the puppy's mind. Because puppies are unaccustomed to having anything hang from their necks, heavy leashes bother them. If the leash stays attached much of the time for approximately seven days, the puppy will adjust to it. When he does, you can switch to a conventional six-foot, five-eighths-of-an-inch-wide leather leash. If the dog rejects the standard leash by biting it or pawing it, correct him by saying "No" in a firm tone of voice. Pull the leash out of the dog's mouth after the correction and then praise him. Grown dogs require more patience. They must not be left alone when wearing the lightweight leash around the house. Puppies or adult dogs may try to chew or bite the leash. It is important to correct them when they do this.

Throughout the course of the seven leash-training days, pick up the leash many times during the day. Be casual. Place no tension on it, whether it is a lightweight or normal leash. If you notice the dog happily dragging the leash behind, pick it up and walk with him around the house. If the dog seems happy enough with this arrangement, try walking him outside on a soft, grassy surface. He will lag behind you if he still resists the leash. But a leash-broken puppy or dog will either walk close to you or try to pull ahead. Allow the dog to pull ahead for a while. This can be corrected once you begin teaching *Heel.*

Until the dog is ready to be taught the *Heel* command, allow him to pull you and take care not to use the leash in a negative manner. If the dog continues to reject the leash, it may be necessary to consult a professional dog trainer.

JUMPING   If your dog is overexuberant and continually jumps on people on the street during his training session, employ the corrective jerk at the moment of his infraction and firmly say "No!" It is important to note that if the dog is corrected for jumping on people, then it must be consistently enforced both indoors and outdoors.

WALKING OUT OF THE COMMAND   If the dog is overly affectionate, he is probably wrapping himself around your legs. It could be insecurity or acute sensitivity. Obviously, this creates an absurd situation. This is the only instance where one uses the left hand while walking in *Heel*. Place the dog in the proper position as you walk, all the while giving him encouragement. His head must always be lined up with your left thigh. If he continues to wrap around your legs, walk and hold him in place with the left hand, employing the corrective jerk less frequently than usual and manipulating the dog more with a soothing tone of voice. In the beginning it is more important to stress the proper position than the other aspects of heeling. Never use excessive authority with a nervous or frightened dog. Affection and gentleness are the only techniques that will rid him of his fear.

WALKING INWARD   Another problem is when the dog begins to turn inward while heeling, causing owner and dog to step into each other's paths. The problem may have stemmed from too many turns to the right (patterned training) while teaching the *Heel*. Correct the dog and vary the turns. Make many left turns and right turns during each training session. As the dog walks into your path, execute a corrective jerk. At the same time firmly say "No!" Then make a left or right turn, depending on how far inward he has gotten. As you turn, your knee will gently force him to turn with you. Praise him. Then say, "Timmy, *heel.*" Continue walking. Praise him. Do this every time he gets underfoot.

Whenever the dog becomes distracted, tries to wander off, or turns the session into play, give the corrective jerk. Firmly say "No!" Then say, "Timmy, *heel.*" Continue to walk. Praise him.

CUSTOMIZED TRAINING

FOR THE HIGH-ENERGY/OUTGOING TEMPERAMENT

OWNER'S FRAME OF MIND   Do not lose sight of your objective, which is to teach the dog to walk alongside you. He will pull ahead, to each side, stop, go, run backwards. It will be a battle. Bear in mind that

When your dog wraps himself around your legs and tangles himself up with you, try holding him in place by extending the leash away from you with your left hand.

he doesn't care where he walks, only you do. It's not natural for him to walk on your left side, so your job is to teach him, not choke him into submission. Be patient and think of yourself as a teacher.

BODY LANGUAGE Be flexible in your moves, but do not be predictable. The dog will be like an outfielder waiting for the ball to be hit, not sure where to go but always ready for anything.

TONE OF VOICE Sound happy and outgoing when teaching the command and practicing. When the dog does not respond properly, use a reserved tone of voice.

VOICE CORRECTION Be firm, consistent, and demanding.

LEASH CORRECTION Use moderate to firm corrections as needed.

WHERE TO TRAIN The privacy of your yard or your home is essential. Do not allow any distractions to interfere with the

If your dog walks inward when you are teaching him the *Heel* command, correct the dog each time he gets too close by turning left or right and continuing to walk. Vary the direction of the turns.

dog's concentration. Spectators will prevent the dog from learning.

FOR THE SHY TEMPERAMENT

OWNER'S FRAME OF MIND   A shy dog might not walk. He may need to be leash-broken. Your patience will be taxed to the limit, as will your ability to avoid being frustrated. Going outdoors could frighten your dog to the point where he becomes too scared to move, too scared of noise, and too scared of people. He may hug your leg. Stay calm, gently methodical, and sympathetic. Try to understand the dog's fear. Your shy dog may follow a second dog around, if you have one. (Another dog could help the leash-breaking process, as well.) A kind, patient frame of mind is essential. Do not pull or choke the dog with the leash. Allow him to drag it around. Some shy dogs react to a leash the way some horses react to being saddled for the first time.

BODY LANGUAGE   If your shy dog is too frightened to walk with you when you first teach this command, turn to face him and position yourself close to the ground. Your physical presence should not pose any threat to the dog. Try kneeling, crawling, or even lying down and facing him. Do not allow your body to frighten the dog.

TONE OF VOICE   Very soft, loving, and reassuring.

VOICE CORRECTIONS   None.

LEASH CORRECTIONS   None. Use the leash delicately, as if it were a silk thread.

WHERE TO TRAIN   Conduct the lesson in a quiet, secluded location. A cement or asphalt surface may hurt the dog's feet if he strenuously resists the leash. Grass, carpet, linoleum, or some other smooth surface will be easier on the dog.

FOR THE STRONG-WILLED TEMPERAMENT

OWNER'S FRAME OF MIND   A strong-willed dog may insist on going left, right, in front of you, or behind you. He may challenge your authority. Be prepared for a struggle. Do not lose your cool. Learn the techniques for teaching the command and know what to do when the dog tries to go his own way. Stay in control by anticipating the dog's stubborn moves.

BODY LANGUAGE   Be consistent. Make the dog keep up with you by walking in the same direction you started with. Be as rigid as a lamppost and get the dog to stay next to you. A strong-willed dog may run in many directions, but you can win out by walking in a consistently straight line.

TONE OF VOICE   Firm, clear, and authoritative.

VOICE CORRECTION   Be firm and demanding. State your commands with a no-nonsense attitude. Do not *ask* the dog to heel. *Tell* him.

LEASH CORRECTION   Use well-defined, firm corrections, depending on the size and the age of the dog. If you're going to correct him, employ one firm correction instead of many mild ones. An excessive number of corrections is not the answer.

WHERE TO TRAIN   Conduct training lessons in a quiet, secluded location where there are no distractions.

FOR THE CALM/EASYGOING TEMPERAMENT

OWNER'S FRAME OF MIND   Be patient and very encouraging. Do not jerk the leash; give the dog lots of praise for responding properly. Dogs with calm/easygoing temperaments are usually slower than other dogs. Do not confuse this with resistance. Teaching *Heel* to a slow-moving dog can be irritating. It's not a bad idea to put yourself in a calm state of mind to match the dog's.

BODY LANGUAGE   Use lots of body movement. Walk swiftly, run, walk slowly; keep changing your pace. The idea is to keep the dog guessing without giving him time to anticipate your next move. This will motivate him to pay attention and keep his eyes on you.

TONE OF VOICE   Speak energetically, using many different tones of voice. Keep talking to the dog. Give him a great deal of encouragement.

VOICE CORRECTION   None. Use lots of praise.

LEASH CORRECTION   None. Use the leash as a tool for guiding the dog to the right position.

WHERE TO TRAIN   Outdoors or indoors. The more distractions the better.

FOR THE AGGRESSIVE TEMPERAMENT

OWNER'S FRAME OF MIND   When training a dog with an aggressive temperament, it is necessary to stay aware of his potentially dangerous reactions. Be cautious.

BODY LANGUAGE　Do not make direct eye contact. In dog behavior, a direct stare into the eyes is taken as a challenge to the animal's position of dominance.

When using your hands, consider how the dog responds to them. If he was ever hit with bare hands or with a rolled-up newspaper, he may bite any hand that comes near him. Be cautious and very slow-moving. You can recondition the dog to respond normally to your hands by stroking him gently and lovingly, and speaking in a soothing tone of voice at the same time. This should be done at every possible opportunity, whether training or not.

TONE OF VOICE　The tone of your voice depends on the dog's age and if he is dominant/aggressive or fear/aggressive. A dominant/aggressive puppy between the ages of seven weeks to six months requires a firm (but not harsh) tone of voice. For dominant/aggressive dogs between six and ten months, use a very authoritative, demanding tone of voice. A fear/aggressive puppy between the ages of seven weeks and six months requires a soft tone of voice that is still firm enough to correct him. For fear/aggressive dogs between six and ten months, use a firm (but not harsh) tone of voice. Get professional help for all aggressive dogs past ten months of age.

VOICE CORRECTION　May not be effective, unless accompanied with a leash correction at the same time. Some dogs are so aggressive that a voice correction is not effective at all. For this reason, always have your aggressive dog on a leash during the training sessions. All corrections should be followed with praise for acceptance of the correction.

LEASH CORRECTION　Be on guard when you jerk a dog of this temperament. He may try to jump on you or bite your hand. In starting the *Heel,* let the dog run ahead, then jerk him as outlined in "Procedure and Technique for the *Heel," but do not turn around.* Do not turn your back on him. Let him go to the end of the leash as you stand facing him, then jerk him. He may try to bite the leash or hold it down with his paws. Leave some slack in the leash and praise him if it calms him down. Be very verbal in your praise and avoid petting him. Begin a turn in the opposite direction and go into the *Heel* command. It is important to establish firm control over the dog and command his respect without hurting him. Always maintain control and authority and never back down. If the dog frightens you, do not let him know it.

You must consider the dog's age, size, and level of aggressiveness when administering leash corrections. Is the dog a bully? Does he growl, snarl, or curl his lip? Puppies between seven weeks and six months should be corrected with quick, firm jerks that are not too hard. For dogs between six and ten months, correct with quick, firm jerks. However, you might need to administer slightly harder jerks at that age, depending on the dog's level of aggressiveness.

When your dog behaves aggressively, correct him quickly. Repeat the corrections until he stops behaving aggressively. Unless he is severely aggressive, you should be able to obtain at least ninety percent satisfactory results this way. Bear in mind that it is only safe to correct an aggressive dog until the age of ten months. After that he will be too dangerous for nonprofessional handling. Have the dog evaluated by a professional dog trainer, animal behaviorist, veterinarian, or all three.

WHERE TO TRAIN   Train him in a private area with no distractions. One should consider having this type of dog trained by a professional.

THE *AUTOMATIC SIT:* DEFINITION

When the dog is walking in *Heel,* he must stop when you do and sit without being given a command. He then waits until he is given the next command, which is usually *Heel.*

PROCEDURE AND TECHNIQUE FOR THE *AUTOMATIC SIT*

This is accomplished by letting the dog know that you are going to stop. By simply slowing down, he will be alerted to a change of some kind. Because he watches you most of the time, he will slow down, too. Here are some suggested ways of letting the dog know that you are slowing down: 1. scuff your feet and make a noise; 2. add tension to the leash by pulling it up a bit; 3. say his name; 4. make a verbal sound, such as clicking your tongue or squeaking your lips; or 5. snap your fingers. Do anything that will signal that you are slowing down. It is necessary to get the dog's attention.

As you come to a full stop, give the command *Sit.* Do not use the dog's name on this command. *The verbal command is used during the teaching process only.* Slowly pull the leash upward as you force the dog to sit by pushing his haunches down with your left hand. Repeat this as often as necessary until he learns it. If the dog fails to sit, use the corrective jerk accompanied by a firm "Sit" as a reminder. Do not forget to praise him after he successfully obeys each command, even if he did so after a correction.

If he does not sit: Do not give the command more than once. This should be a firm rule throughout the training. You cannot stand in the street saying "Sit, Sit, Sit, Sit, Sit" *ad nauseam* until he finally obeys. Use the corrective jerk and in a sharp voice say, "No!" The dog will understand this and sit for you. Praise him for obeying.

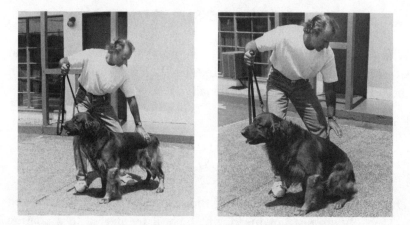

Left: When teaching the *Automatic Sit,* use the Pushing Technique as described in Chapter 9. Find the hip joints of your dog's hindquarters and gently squeeze them as you push down with your left hand. *Right:* Pull the leash up with your right hand until the dog is actually sitting.

To reiterate, slow your pace and gradually come to a full stop. If the dog does not sit, give the command to sit. If he does not respond, give him a corrective jerk and repeat the word "Sit!" If he responds properly, praise him with enthusiasm, even though he was corrected. This is his motivation. In that rare instance when the dog does not even respond to the corrective jerk accompanied by the "No," give him another corrective jerk and the command *Sit.* One usually never gives the command word with the corrective jerk. It causes the dog to associate a negative reinforcement with that particular command. However, in this extreme instance it becomes necessary. If you give the corrective jerk properly, you can avoid this problem. One or two firm jerks will save much time and frustration for you and the dog. He must know that you mean what you say. It will be useful to remember that the word "Sit" is a command and the word "No" is a correction. The commands are given with authority. But the corrections should be given with a stronger tone of voice.

Because every training session should end on a high note, the lesson ought to be terminated when the dog has completed his task successfully for the first time. Obviously, he is not going to be perfect in his execution of your commands for several weeks. Therefore, the instant he performs his new command correctly, end the lesson and extend lavish praise. This will help him to remember what he has just learned and to look forward to performing properly the next time. Try to instill in him the idea that training is fun.

If the dog does not sit, give the command "Sit." If he still does not respond, give him a corrective jerk and repeat the verbal command. If he responds properly, praise him with enthusiasm.

CUSTOMIZED TRAINING

The customized training for the *Automatic Sit* is the same as that for *Sit*. See Chapter 9.

11.

SIT-STAY

Now that you have taught your dog to sit and to automatically sit after walking in heel, the next command is perfectly logical. You want him to stay in his sitting position. But it's not as simple as it sounds. Dogs take you at your word, quite literally. If given the command *Sit*, a trained dog will sit—for an instant—and then move on to whatever interests him. His obligation has been fulfilled, from his point of view. If expected to remain in a sitting position for any length of time, he must be commanded to do so.

DEFINITION OF *SIT-STAY*

On command, the dog sits erect with all his weight on his haunches. He remains in this position until released from the command, no matter what!

BENEATH THE SURFACE OF THE TRAINING

This command is used when you do not want the dog to move. When leaving your home, if the dog follows you to the door, you know he'll dash out the minute it is open. Give the command *Sit* and he'll obey. But as soon as you start to leave, he'll be out of the house too. Therefore, give the next command, *Stay.* As you close the door release the dog from the command by saying, "Okay." Be sure the dog cannot run out the door when you release him.

This command goes against every instinctual impulse the animal has. Most dogs, especially puppies, will follow you to the edge of the earth, and then jump off if you do. The dog wants to go where you go and do what you do, then he'll be happy. The pattern is set in the first months of ownership. The dog grows up following you wherever you go, often underfoot—into the kitchen, onto the couch, and into bed. By now he is so used to being with you he looks up at you as if you are a lunatic when first given the command *Stay.* He will completely disregard the command and race you to wherever you're going.

After the dog has been taught the command *Stay,* there will still be times when it will be almost impossible for him to obey. For instance, if there is a party going on in your house, he may have a nervous breakdown trying to comply with your command and to ignore his own impulse to join the fun. Either remove him from the scene or invite him in to be admired and ogled. The same applies if you're cooking a steak in front of his nose. Also, don't expect him to remain in a stay position for eternity. If he will remain in position from three to five minutes, he has been well trained.

The command *Sit-Stay* as taught in this book is not designed for off-leash discipline. If such a foolish thing is attempted, one might well be considered an executioner. The free-roaming dog may obey perfectly outside for six months off the leash. But it only takes one mistake for him to chase another dog or a pigeon and lose his life to an oncoming automobile.

Sit-Stay can be taught indoors with a six-foot leash or outdoors (in a fenced-in backyard) with a six-foot leash. Learning the command is so demanding that there must be no distractions during the training sessions.

PROCEDURE AND TECHNIQUE FOR *SIT-STAY*

Teaching this command involves three elements: a voice command, a hand signal, and a pivoting technique using your left foot.

THE VOICE COMMAND AND HAND SIGNAL   Place the dog in the *sit* position on your left side. Both dog and owner should be facing in the same direction. Give the command *Stay* in a firm voice. Because this is not an action command, do not preface it with the dog's name. The leash is held in the right hand. Upon giving the command, flatten your left hand with all fingers closed together (as for a salute) and place it in front of the dog's eyes, four inches away. Do not touch his eyes—simply block his vision. The hand signal is given simultaneously with the voice command. As the right hand holds the leash, the left hand extends in front of the dog's face four inches and then moves left to block the dog's vision. The hand signal is a deliberate but quick gesture. Return your left hand to your side two or three seconds after having blocked the dog's vision. Eventually, the dog will respond to this hand signal without the vocal command.

THE PIVOTING TECHNIQUE ON THE BALL OF YOUR LEFT FOOT   You and the dog are facing in the same direction. The objective now is to make one deliberate turn without moving the dog, so that you will be facing him. Do not step off with your left foot as you normally would in the *Heel*. Step off with your right foot and turn toward the dog. The left foot is used as a pivot and revolves in place. It is all right if the left foot must move a very short distance. Once your body is turned and facing the dog, bring the left foot back to where the right foot has landed so that both feet are together. If you move your left foot before facing the dog, he is going to assume it's time to heel and start walking.

THE SECRET OF TEACHING STAY   As you pivot in front of your dog, hold eighteen inches of the leash straight up so that the leash and

Both dog and owner should be facing in the same direction.

collar are high on his neck. The remainder of the leash dangles in a slackened loop from the bottom of your right hand. In this position the dog cannot move as you turn to face him. What you are doing is holding him in a fixed position with the extended leash. If the

Upon giving the command, flatten your left hand with all fingers closed together (as for a salute) and place it in front of the dog's eyes, four inches away.

The Pivoting Technique. Turn without causing the dog to move, so that you will be facing him. Step off with your right foot and turn toward the dog. Pivot on your left foot until you are facing the dog. Finally, bring both feet together.

leash is held properly, there will be eighteen inches of taut leash extended upward. Do not hold the leash too tightly or he may choke or become frightened and struggle.

It is this strict leash control during the pivotal turn that com-

Hold the leash in a fixed position above the dog's head. Strict leash control during the pivotal turn communicates the idea of *Stay.*

municiates the idea of *Stay*. The entire movement should be accomplished with dispatch so that your dog does not have time to think about turning or walking. Keep him in position and get in front of him without wasting a motion. It is going to take ten or fifteen tries before he gets the idea. Do not forget to give the dog praise once you have made the turn and he has remained in position, even though he had to be held there with the leash. (Do not use his name when giving the praise. If you do, he will try to move.) Once you are in front of the dog, remain still for ten or fifteen seconds, leash still held high, so that he begins to absorb what's expected of him. This technique of stepping in front of the dog is only used in training. If you are training a puppy, do not be too strict.

BACKING AWAY AS THE DOG REMAINS IN STAY   Once the dog accepts the leash control as you stand in front of him, it is then time to back away as he remains in *Stay*. While still holding the leash above the dog's head, transfer it to the left hand, placing the thumb inside the loop at the very top. With the right hand, grasp the leash eighteen inches above the collar and hold it loosely. The leash must be able to slide through the right hand once you start to move away from the dog. The technique will eliminate any slack from developing as you move away. This is important. If the leash slackens, you will be unable to force the dog to remain in *Sit-Stay*.

Using the right hand as a guide for the leash to slide through, begin to back away slowly. If the dog starts to move forward—and he will—give the command *Stay*. As you do, step in toward the dog, pull the leash through the right hand, and hold it eighteen inches over the dog's head. Keep the leash tight so that it forces the dog to sit. (When stepping in, try to pull the leash slightly to the side as you extend it upward, so you will avoid hitting the dog on the chin with the metal clip.) The correction will stop the dog from moving. As he repositions himself, give him praise for stopping. Wait a few seconds and then continue to back away. As you do this you may gently repeat the command *Stay*. Slowly continue to slide the leash through your right hand as you move. You will probably be able to go a little farther back this time before he begins to move again. The instant the dog moves forward repeat the procedure: Give the command *Stay*. Step in toward the dog and hold the leash tightly over his head. Praise him for stopping after he repositions himself. Continue to back away until you reach the end of the six-foot leash. Reinforce this instruction by repeating the entire process ten times.

WALKING AROUND BOTH SIDES OF THE DOG AS HE REMAINS IN STAY It is now time to condition the dog so that you can walk

When teaching *Sit-Stay* from a distance, continue to back away until you reach the end of the six feet of leash.

around him or to either side without his violating the *Stay* command. Usually, when you walk to the dog's side or behind him while he is in *Stay*, he will turn his head to watch and then turn his entire body to face you. This is a violation of the command. If he is allowed to move that much, it will soon become permissible to move away completely. He must remain in the same position in which he was originally placed. A certain amount of head turning is inevitable, but that is all.

Once again, standing in front of the dog, hold the leash tightly with your right hand eighteen inches above his head. Take one or two steps to the right without loosening up on the leash, and then return. Do the same thing again, but move to the left. This will condition the dog to your side movements while he is still held in place. Repeat this ten times. Return to the original sit position with the dog at your left side and repeat the entire lesson to this point five times.

WALKING BEHIND THE DOG AS HE REMAINS IN STAY   Once again, hold the leash with your left hand. Stand in front of the dog, slide your right hand in on the leash, and extend it over the dog's head about eighteen inches. As you hold the dog in place, begin a brisk but deliberate circular walk around him. If he starts to move, tighten up on the leash and repeat the command *Stay*. When walking around the dog, take large steps. The command should be given in a low, soothing voice that reassures. However, it is the subtle use of the leash that is your line of communication.

The leash is comparable to the reins of a horse. Although it is extended upward, it does not tighten unless the dog tries to move. The moment he stops moving, you loosen up a bit. A horse respects a rider the minute he is mounted if the rider knows how to handle the reins. The same applies to a dog. If an owner is in control with the use of the leash and collar, the dog will respect him and submit to his authority. The minute he observes a lack of consistent control, he is likely to disobey. In turn, the owner will get frustrated and angry and the lesson will be shot.

Because *Stay* is difficult for your dog to learn, do not attempt to teach it all in one training session. Give him a chance to learn it slowly. Sometimes it takes several sessions for the dog to get accustomed to your pivot. When teaching more than one phase of this command in one day, rest one hour between each phase. Do not teach more than two sessions a day. Dogs tire and bore easily and after a point lose their ability to pay attention. It is more important that the dog learn well and eventually obey when given a command than learn quickly and forget the command two days later.

Another aspect of *Stay* has to do with placing a dog in that position and leaving the room. It can be useful and convenient from time to time. Place the dog in the sit position. Hook the six-foot leash to his collar and let it drop to the floor. Start out by placing him in stay and leaving the room. Do not forget to use the hand signal. Return in five seconds. If he did not move, praise him. Do this ten times. The next step is to leave the room for ten seconds, return, and praise him for his good performance. This reassures him that you are not really leaving. Gradually increase the length of time out of the room until he will stay by himself for at least five minutes. Once again, do not do this off the leash until it is certain that he will stay without moving. The leash, even though it is not being held, represents the line of authority between you and the dog. He knows and respects it. A good way to practice this command is to put it in operation right away during everyday household situations. If he approaches the garbage can when the lid is off, put him in *Sit-Stay* until it is covered. The same applies when the doorbell rings or a visitor enters the house. This kind of practice plus his regular lessons will help round off his schooling perfectly.

Once the dog has completely learned the meaning of the command *Stay*, you can, with confidence, leave him in a room alone, or talk with visitors while he sits still. This command will also keep him out of intimate situations that do not concern him. Every dog is a born voyeur and the command *Stay* could save your marriage. Work hard on this one!

CUSTOMIZED TRAINING

FOR THE HIGH-ENERGY/OUTGOING TEMPERAMENT

OWNER'S FRAME OF MIND   It is natural for the dog to leave his position constantly and walk away. He wants to be with you. Your task is to keep him relaxed in the *stay* position. That's the scenario. Patience, consistency, and a cool head should prevail. Think of your dog as "having ants in his pants." A good way to calm him down before each training session is to exercise him. Run, play ball, throw a Frisbee, anything. Get him to use all his excessive energy and then begin the session. Be willing to understand his problem.

BODY LANGUAGE   Move in a slow manner, offsetting your dog's high energy level. Make your moves precise and keep absolute control of the leash. Do not move away or go long distances too quickly. Use your body to block the dog's extraneous movements.

TONE OF VOICE   Your voice should sound firm and authoritative. Say the commands in a precise manner and with a moderate, subdued amount of praise. Otherwise, the dog may lose his concentration and energetically try to play with you.

VOICE CORRECTION   Quick, authoritative, no-nonsense. Give the dog praise after each correction, but in a moderate, subdued manner.

LEASH CORRECTION   Use the leash with a quick, firm snap. The tug of the leash should go right to the point of the correction and match your voice correction.

WHERE TO TRAIN   It is important to train the dog in the privacy of your home, yard, or apartment *until the command has been mastered.* It is then equally important to practice the command while exposed to normal daily distractions.

FOR THE SHY TEMPERAMENT

OWNER'S FRAME OF MIND   Consider the dog's form of shyness. Is he shy of noise, shy of new environments, shy of people? And then consider how difficult it may be for your pet to *sit-stay.* The most important thing you can do is put yourself in your dog's position and try to understand his shyness. Through understanding comes compassion, patience, and a more methodical approach to dog training.

BODY LANGUAGE   You must not be overbearing or make quick, sudden moves. Standing close and towering over a shy dog is body language that is too dominating. Be aware of your hand movements in case he is hand-shy. Do not move quickly at the start of each lesson so that the dog will not try to follow you or move away from you. Make sure you stay in front of him for a while, then move side to side and then slowly behind him as described in the training procedures.

TONE OF VOICE   Use a very soft and reassuring tone. Constantly use lavish praise as a form of encouragement. Spend most of your time teaching, not correcting. Do not use any harsh tones at all.

VOICE CORRECTION   Be gentle when you say "No." Follow each voice correction with loving praise. Harsh corrections will add to your dog's shyness.

LEASH CORRECTION   No firm or harsh corrections are needed. As a matter of fact, they can be detrimental to the training. Keep the leash taut, but do not allow the training collar to tighten too much around the dog's neck. The tension of the leash must not be too great. The more you use the leash to hold the dog in place, the easier the command will be to teach.

WHERE TO TRAIN   Work in your home or backyard with no spectators present. If your dog is sound-shy, work in a very quiet area at first, which will make it easier for him to learn, and then gradually move to a busy area with more distractions.

FOR THE STRONG-WILLED TEMPERAMENT

OWNER'S FRAME OF MIND   Understand that your dog will not want to sit still and stay. He is going to try anything and everything to keep from doing this at first. Your job is to teach him *Sit-Stay* without losing your cool. Patience and technique are the keys to success when an irresistible force meets an immovable object.

BODY LANGUAGE   Be authoritative in your physical presence without being overbearing. Do not allow yourself to show anger at the dog and do not overpower him. That will entrench him even further in his stubborn (or sometimes aggressive or shy) behavior. See the situation from the dog's point of view. Would you want to be totally dominated? How would *you* feel?

TONE OF VOICE   Firm, authoritative, no-nonsense, but not harsh or angry.

VOICE CORRECTION   The dog must be made to realize that you are the teacher and he is the student. In terms of dog behavior you are a pack leader. In human terms, you are the boss. An effective boss gets the job done by commanding with a firm, but not frightening, tone of voice. It is harmful to the human-animal bond to intimidate a dog with harsh voice corrections. Your goal should be simply to teach the command and get the dog to obey it. Constant verbal repetition of the command is the way to accomplish that.

LEASH CORRECTION   Maintain firm leash control with medium to firm corrections. One firm jerk is better than three or four that are too mild and ineffective. Too many corrective jerks are irritating and intimidating.

WHERE TO TRAIN   It is important to train the dog in the privacy of your home, yard, or apartment, with no spectators, *until the command has been mastered.* It is then equally important to practice the command while exposing the dog to normal daily distractions.

FOR THE CALM/EASYGOING TEMPERAMENT

OWNER'S FRAME OF MIND   Think of your dog as a sweet, lovable animal who lies on the floor watching you walk around saying "Stay." He must wonder what all your movement is about because his thoughts are not about moving. Never confuse a calm/easygoing temperament with a lack of intelligence or stubbornness.

BODY LANGUAGE   It really doesn't matter what your body does. Dogs with this temperament simply do not care.

TONE OF VOICE   In most situations use an easygoing, soft tone. There are time when you must use a lively, louder sound or a calm/

easygoing dog may fall asleep. At those times you must energize him and yourself.

VOICE CORRECTION   Softer voice corrections are usually the rule. You can also be firm, but not harsh, if he's too lethargic.

LEASH CORRECTION   Keep the leash taut if the dog has a tendency to lie down. Several of the giant breeds, such as the St. Bernard, Newfoundland, and Mastiff are calm/easygoing. If your dog is one of these breeds, you may pass on *Sit-Stay* and go right to *Down-Stay*. Such dogs are so heavy that *Sit-Stay* is too much of a chore for them.

WHERE TO TRAIN   Doesn't really matter—inside, outside, with or without distractions.

FOR THE AGGRESSIVE TEMPERAMENT

OWNER'S FRAME OF MIND   It's what's going to set him off with this command that you need to be aware of. Will it be your voice and leash corrections? Body language? Teaching methods? Ask yourself what would trigger an aggressive response in you if you were being taught this command. When training a dog with an aggressive temperament it is necessary to stay aware of his potentially dangerous reactions. Be cautious. This is the case especially when dealing with a dog who has already indicated a tendency to bite.

BODY LANGUAGE   Do not stand over your dog, making direct eye contact. In dog behavior, a direct stare into the eyes is taken as a challenge to the animal's position of dominance. This is very important. Do not overpower your dog by leaning over him too much or by making him feel cornered. Be careful when giving hand commands.

When using your hands to push the dog into position, consider how he responds to them. If the dog has at some time been hit with a bare hand or with a rolled-up newspaper, he may bite any hand that comes near him. Be cautious and very slow-moving with the body and especially the hands. You can recondition a dog to respond differently to hands by stroking him gently, lovingly, and speaking in a soothing tone of voice at the same time. This should be done at every possible opportunity, whether training or not.

If he has been jerked by a leash too much, he may react badly to you. Stay aware of what you're doing, especially with your teaching technique, and try not to be dominant with him. Be patient when he feels trapped.

TONE OF VOICE The tone of your voice depends on the dog's age and if he is dominant/aggressive or fear/aggressive. A dominant/ aggressive puppy between the ages of seven weeks and six months requires a firm, but not harsh, tone of voice. For dominant/aggressive dogs between six and ten months, use a very authoritative, demanding tone of voice. A fear/aggressive puppy between seven weeks and six months requires a soft tone of voice that is still firm enough to correct him. For fear/aggressive dogs between six and ten months, use a firm, but not harsh, tone of voice. Get professional help for all aggressive dogs past ten months of age.

VOICE CORRECTION A determined attitude with a sharp and firm "No" is usually effective, but always praise the dog immediately afterward. With some dogs, a voice correction may not be effective unless accompanied with a leash correction at the same time. A voice correction is not effective at all for such dogs. For this reason, have your aggressive dog on a leash during all training sessions. Follow all corrections with great praise for acceptance of the correction.

LEASH CORRECTION   Many dog owners are taken by surprise when their dogs growl, snap, or bite them after a correction. The cause may have been corrections that were administered too harshly or too frequently. You must consider the dog's age, size, and level of aggressiveness when administering leash corrections. Is the dog a bully? Does he growl, snarl, or curl his lip? Puppies between seven weeks and six months of age should be corrected with quick, firm jerks that are not too hard. For dogs between six and ten months, correct with quick, firm jerks. However, you might need to administer slightly harder jerks at that age, depending on the dog's level of aggressiveness.

Bear in mind that it is safe to correct an aggressive dog only until he is ten months. After that he may be too dangerous for nonprofessional handling. Have the dog evaluated by a professional dog trainer, animal behaviorist, veterinarian, or all three.

WHERE TO TRAIN   Take advantage of the privacy of your home or your backyard. Do not allow any distractions such as dogs, kids, or neighbors to interfere with the training sessions.

12.

DOWN AND DOWN-STAY

Professional dog trainers often are confronted with seemingly difficult problems that are easily solved. One client, a musician with a magnificent Basset Hound named Cat, had a problem. (In the language of contemporary musicians, "cat" is a compliment; the name gathers no blue ribbons in Dogdom, however.) Cat couldn't sit like a dog. Owing to his long, heavy body and his short legs, it was impossible for him to *sit-stay* for more than a few seconds. His *sit* was sloped at a ten-degree angle. He looked like a jacked-up car with a flat tire. Too much weight rested on those short front legs and Cat had to get off his dogs quickly. It was then that the *Down* and *Down-Stay* were taught.

Even though you may not own a Basset Hound, your dog may have Cat's problem to some degree. The *sit-stay* position is a temporary one and is used for short periods of time. But if the dog is to stay in his corner while guests are being entertained, employ the *Down* and *Down-Stay*. It's more comfortable for the dog and dictates a longer staying time to him. It was a great relief for Cat and will be for your dog, too. Does all this seem confusing? Well, think of poor Cat, the dog!

DEFINITION OF *DOWN*

The dog is on the ground, head erect, eyes looking forward. The front legs are extended and the hind legs relaxed with the rear weight resting on both haunches. The hind legs should be equally tucked under in a straight parallel.

BENEATH THE SURFACE OF THE TRAINING

The *down* position is probably the most comfortable one for the dog. But it may take the longest time to teach. Sitting and walking are natural movements for a dog and are assimilated as commands quite easily. But going down on command is unnatural for most dogs, even though they sleep and rest in that position. Quite often the command *Down* is given as a remedy for undesirable behavior. *Down* should be used only as a command. As outlined in Chapter 11, "*Sit-Stay,*" you cannot go directly into a command when the dog is misbehaving until a correction has been made first.

Consider how many times you have used the word "down" when you didn't mean *lie* down. We tend to say "Down" when we mean "Don't jump on me," or "Get off the furniture." Your dog needs to understand exactly what you mean when you use a one-word command such as *Down*. It is natural for dogs to lie down, but not necessarily when you order them to do it.

In "Procedures and Techniques for *Down*," which follows, you will see that a hand signal is used to help the dog perform properly. The hand signal entails using your unbent extended arm in a slow downward sweep with the flattened palm of the hand facing the ground. The hand signal may be a problem if the dog has been hit in the past. When he sees that hand come down, his first reaction will be fear. Naturally, he will think he is about to be hit again.

The dog probably will have the same reaction when someone reaches out to pet him. He will either run away, flinch, or literally bite the hand that feeds him. If he has this condition he is called *hand-shy*.

If your dog is hand-shy, you must stop hitting him. It is now time to convince him that hands reaching out to him or commanding him mean something good rather than the smack on the snout they too often represented in the past. If the dog has been hit over a long period of time, or has been hit severely, then it is too late. He will never be taught this command with a hand signal. You will have to rely on a voice command only. You may try extending your hand while lavishing him with praise and affection. If applied long enough, and consistently enough, this may possibly recondition the dog's reaction. Refrain from ever using your hand for anything other than hand signals or affectionate praise or love. This rule also applies to the use of the hand for threats, violent gestures, or even disciplinary pointing. Pointing your finger at the dog and saying "Naughty, naughty" produces the same negative effect.

There are many occasions when the *Down* and *Down-Stay* are useful and make life more comfortable. When you're having guests for dinner, it is extremely difficult for Gusman to keep his nose out of things. In the *down* and *down-stay* positions, he is able to participate in the festivities without getting into trouble. These commands are extremely useful outdoors if, for example, you want to sit on a park bench without being disturbed by a dog pulling on his leash. The main reason this position works so well is that it is comfortable and relaxing for the dog.

Because of the difficulty involved in teaching this command, it is important to be alone with the animal. Do not expect him to learn it in one session. Take as long as is necessary. Maintain only two sessions a day, spaced at least four hours apart. Each session must be confined to fifteen minutes. Before starting each session, work the dog in his other commands in order to get him in the proper frame of mind. Teach only as much in one day as the dog can absorb. It is interesting to note that the dog will learn *Down* and *Down-Stay* better than any other command he has been taught. The reason is that more time and diligence are required in teaching it than for any other part of this course. You will also be using these commands more often than any other during a single day. These sessions will prove to be the most rewarding. There is nothing more gratifying than raising your hand in the air when the dog is five or ten feet away and watching him go down as you lower your hand.

PROCEDURES AND TECHNIQUES FOR *DOWN*

There are many different techniques for teaching the first step of this command. They are offered to you here, numbered from 1 to 8. Please choose one of them. Read the beginning of each technique for help in making your selection. The variations are offered so that you can select the one technique that is most appropriate for you and your dog.

After completing one of the eight methods, you must then continue with ALL the teaching procedures that follow.

1. THE PAWS TECHNIQUE

Most dogs can be taught with this technique, which is the standard *Down* method. It is best for dogs of the shy and calm/easygoing temperaments. Never use this technique for the high-energy/outgoing or the aggressive dog.

The Paws Technique requires that you stand by the dog's right side as in the *Heel*, holding the leash in the right hand. You and the dog face in the same direction. Place the dog in *Sit-Stay*. Kneel down on your left knee. In a firm voice give the command "Down," (see "How to Say the Command *Down*," page 162) and with your left hand lift his two front paws slightly and pull them forward so that he has no choice but to ease himself to the ground. This is best accomplished by placing your index finger between his paws so that you can grip both of them with one hand. The reason for separating his paws with your finger is so they will not be crushed together.

Always praise the dog after each repetition (see "Praise," page 163). Repeat this procedure ten or fifteen times, until the dog offers no resistance when he is placed in the proper position. If you're very lucky he may begin to go down without being placed in the *down* position.

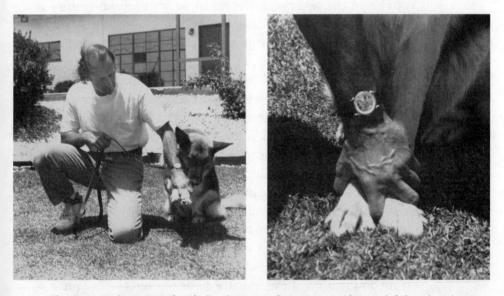

The Paws Technique. *Left:* Lift the dog's two front paws with your left hand and pull them forward so that he has no choice but to ease himself into the proper position for *Down. Right:* Place your index finger between the dog's paws so that they can be gripped with one hand. Use another of the eight teaching techniques if the paws are too wide and you cannot grip both with one hand.

You are now ready to move on to the basic teaching techniques. Go directly to "How to Say the Command *Down*," page 162).

2. THE LEG TECHNIQUE

The Leg Technique is extremely useful for large dogs or if your dog's paws are too thick to hold with one hand. This method uses the leg instead of the paws for placement of the dog in the *down* position. It is best for dogs of the high-energy/outgoing, shy, strong-willed, and calm/easygoing temperaments.

The Leg Technique requires that you stand by the dog's right side, as in the *Heel*, holding the leash in the left hand. Both you and the dog face in the same direction. Place the dog in a *sit-stay* position to begin the session. Kneel down on your left knee. In a firm voice give the command "Down" (see "How to Say the Command *Down*," page 162) and with your right hand put the dog in the *down* position by slightly lifting the right or left front leg and placing it forward, as pictured on page 151. Whether to lift the right front leg or the left front leg forward depends on the dog. If he tends to place most of his weight on his right side, then lift his right front leg forward. Lift his left front leg forward if that is where he puts his weight. Always praise the dog after each repetition (see "Praise," page 163). Repeat this procedure ten or fifteen times, until the dog offers no resistance to being placed in the *down* position. It is possible that he will begin to go down without being placed in the *down* position. That would be excellent progress. (If you are training a very large dog you may have to *stand* by his side throughout the teaching process.)

You are now ready to move on to the basic teaching techniques. Go directly to "How to Say the Command *Down*" on page 162.

3. THE SWEEP TECHNIQUE

The Sweep Technique is an important option if it is too difficult to get your large dog to respond properly to the first two methods. It is recommended for dogs who have the shy, strong-willed, and calm/easygoing temperaments.

The Sweep Technique requires that you stand by the dog's right side as in the *Heel,* holding the leash in the left hand. Both you and the dog face in the same direction. Place the dog in a *sit-stay* position to begin the session. Kneel down while continuing to hold the leash with your left hand.

The Leg Technique. Kneel next to the dog and put him in the *down* position by lifting the right or left leg and pulling it forward. Always praise the dog after he moves into the proper position.

Place your right hand behind the dog's front legs or under his belly, whichever is easier for you. In a firm voice, give the command "Down" (see "How to Say the Command *Down*," page 162). At the same time, hold the leash taut with your left hand, keeping the dog in position. (See the photos on page 153.)

Slide your right hand forward, under the dog's belly, pushing his legs forward so that he lowers gently into the *down* position. The effect is to lift his front legs off the ground and push them forward. Keep your right hand extended forward until the dog is placed in the proper position. Always praise the dog after each

The Leg Technique when the trainer is standing next to the dog.

The Sweep Technique. *Top:* Place your right hand behind the dog's front legs or under his belly, whichever is easier for you. *Middle:* Slide your right hand forward, pushing the dog's legs forward. *Bottom:* Keep extending your right hand forward until the dog is placed in the proper *down* position.

repetition (see "Praise," page 163). Repeat this procedure ten or fifteen times, until the dog offers no resistance to being placed in the *down* position. He may begin to go down without being placed in position at the end of this teaching step.

You are now ready to move on to the basic teaching techniques. Go directly to "How to Say the Command *Down*," on page 162.

4. THE PRESSURE TECHNIQUE

This technique emphasizes pushing the dog into the proper *down* position instead of lifting and lowering him there. The Pressure Technique is an effective alternative. It is best for dogs of the high-energy/outgoing, shy, strong-willed, calm/easygoing, or aggressive (if under ten months) temperaments.

The Pressure Technique requires that you stand by the dog's right side as in the *Heel,* holding the leash with your right hand. You and the dog face in the same direction. Place the dog in a *sit-stay* position to begin the session. Kneel down on your left knee or bend over the dog while still facing forward. In a firm voice give the command "Down" (see "How to Say the Command *Down*," page 162).

Keep the leash taut, with your right hand about twelve inches above the dog's head. With the thumb and middle finger of your left hand, grip the dog's shoulder blades as pictured and push down. This action takes place as you give the verbal command "Down," so that the dog will eventually learn to move into the proper *down* position without being placed in it. Always praise the dog after each repetition (see "Praise," page 163). Repeat this procedure ten or fifteen times, until the dog offers no resistance when he is placed in the proper position. If you're very lucky he may begin to go down without being placed in the *down* position.

Some dogs may require a combination of techniques that includes the Pressure Technique. For example, the Pressure Tech-

The Pressure Technique. *Top:* With the thumb and middle finger of your left hand, grip the dog's shoulder blades and push down. *Middle:* This action takes place as you give the verbal command "Down." *Bottom:* Praise the dog lavishly once he is in the proper *down* position.

nique works quite well in combination with the Leg Technique because pressure on the shoulders may not be sufficient to get the dog into the *down* position.

You are now ready to move on to the basic teaching techniques. Skip the remainder of the placement techniques and continue with the other training procedures. Go directly to "How to Say the Command *Down*," page 162.

5. THE SLIDING LEASH TECHNIQUE

This technique should only be used on dogs with the strong-willed, calm/easygoing, or aggressive (if under ten months) temperaments. It is a useful method for oversized dogs with whom the other techniques may be awkward or difficult to use.

The Sliding Leash Technique requires that you stand by the dog's right side as in the *Heel*. You and the dog face in the same direction. Place the dog in a *sit-stay* position to begin the session. Remain standing. Hold the leash with both hands. Allow just enough slack so that part of the leash touches the ground. Place your left shoe on top of the leash so that the leash is located in the space between the heel and ball of the foot. Give the dog the verbal command "Down" in the elongated, descending tone of voice (see "How to Say the Command *Down*," page 162).

As you give the verbal command, pull up on the leash with all your strength in one smooth, continuous hoist, allowing the leash to slide through the arch of your shoe. This will result in the dog's being forced to move into the *down* position (as pictured). Praise the dog when he reaches the ground (see "Praise," page 163). Repeat this procedure ten or fifteen times, until the dog offers no resistance to being placed in the *down* position. He may begin to go down without being placed in position at the end of this teaching step.

You are now ready to move on to the basic teaching techniques.

The Sliding Leash Technique. *Top:* Place your left shoe on top of the leash so that the leash is located in the space between the heel and ball of the foot. *Middle:* As you give the verbal command, pull up on the leash with all your strength in one smooth, continuous hoist, allowing the leash to slide through the arch of your shoe. *Bottom:* This will force the dog into the *down* position. Praise him each time he goes into the proper position.

Skip the balance of the placement techniques and continue with the remainder of the training procedures. Go directly to "How to Say the Command *Down*," page 162.

6. THE FOOT-LEASH TECHNIQUE

This technique should be used only on dogs of the strong-willed or calm/easygoing temperament.

The Foot-Leash Technique requires that you stand by the dog's right side as in the *Heel*. You and the dog face in the same direction. Place the dog in a *sit-stay* position to begin the session. Remain standing. Hold the leash with both hands. Allow only a small amount of slack in the leash. Give the dog the verbal command "Down," with the elongated, descending tone of voice (see "How to Say the Command *Down*," on page 162).

As you give the verbal command, raise your left foot high off the ground and set it on top of the leash where the leash clip connects to the training collar. As your voice goes down in tone, apply pressure to the leash with your left foot. Obviously, this will push the dog into the *down* position. The trick is to pull up on the leash as you press your foot down, allowing the leash to slip around your shoe (as pictured). Give the dog lavish praise when he reaches the ground. Always praise the dog after each repetition (see "Praise," page 163). This technique is often necessary for strong-willed dogs who refuse to learn with any other method. It certainly is the only answer if the strong-willed dog is also very large and powerful. Repeat this procedure ten or fifteen times, until the dog offers no resistance to being placed in the *down* position. In a short time but after much practice, the dog will go into the proper position with the verbal command only.

You are now ready to move on to the basic teaching techniques. Skip the balance of the eight placement techniques and continue

The Foot-Leash Technique. *Top:* As you give the verbal command, raise your left foot high off the ground and set it on top of the leash where the leash clip connects to the training collar. *Middle:* As your voice goes down in tone, apply pressure to the leash with your left foot. *Bottom:* This will push the dog into the proper *down* position. Pull up on the leash as you press your foot down, allowing the leash to slip around your shoe.

with the remainder of the training procedures. Go directly to "How to Say the Command *Down*," page 162.

7. TABLE TECHNIQUE

To small dogs, humans can appear like six-story buildings and completely overwhelm them. The use of a table avoids this. Small dogs may be placed on a table top to make it easier to use one of the other techniques. A dog placed on top of a table does not have a human towering over him. This avoids the problem of overpowering the dog and intimidating or frightening him. It is also more comfortable for the trainer. It is best for dogs of the high-energy/outgoing, shy, strong-willed, or calm/easygoing temperaments.

For dogs who can keep their balance on a smooth table surface, employ the Paws Technique. However, your small dog may become insecure or upset when having his paws pulled forward on a slippery table. In that event, place a rubber mat on the table. If he is still distressed, use the Sweep Technique or the Leg Technique.

8. THE FOOD TECHNIQUE

For a dog who will not respond to any of the other techniques, try enticing him into the *down* position with a food morsel that he finds irresistible. Although this course does not approve of the use of food as a lasting training method, it *can* be a useful aid for this command. This technique can be used with dogs of all temperaments, with the exception of dogs who are aggressive over food.

The Food Technique requires that you stand by the dog's right side as in the *Heel*. You and the dog face in the same direction. Place the dog in a *sit-stay* position to begin the session. Step eighteen inches in front of the dog. Remain standing. Hold the leash with one hand. Allow approximately three feet of slack in the leash.

The Food Technique. *Top:* As you give the verbal command "Down," hold a food treat six to twelve inches in front of the dog's nose. *Middle:* As your voice descends in tone, lower your hand, taking the food to the ground. *Bottom:* The dog should lower himself into the *down* position. If he does, praise him lavishly.

Give the dog the verbal command "Down," with the elongated, descending tone of voice (See "How to Say the Command *Down*," below).

As you give the verbal command, hold the food treat six to twelve inches in front of the dog's nose. As your voice descends in tone, lower your hand, taking the food to the ground. The dog should lower himself into the *down* position. If he does, praise him lavishly (See "Praise," page 163) and give him the food. Raise another morsel of food above his head and give him the command "Sit," and then the command "Stay." Repeat this procedure until the dog willingly moves into the *down* position on command. He may begin to go down without the use of food at the end of this teaching step.

You are now ready to move on to the basic teaching techniques, beginning with "How to Say the Command *Down*."

HOW TO SAY THE COMMAND *DOWN*

For the command *Down*, the vocal intonation is different from all others. The very word must be said in an exaggerated manner so that the sound suggests to the dog a downward motion. The tone of your voice should descend in pitch as the dog obeys the command and goes down. Stretch out the middle part of the word so that you do not finish saying it until the dog has reached the ground. This is done by elongating the "ow" part of "D-ow-n." Somewhere in the middle of the elongated "ow," the voice should descend so that it accompanies the downward action of the dog. It looks like this on paper: "DOWWWWW-wwwn." Dogs do not understand words as well as they understand intonations. "DOWWWWW-wwwn" is a sound they remember all their lives.

USING THE LEASH

Maintain control with the use of the leash. If the dog gets up in the middle of the session, use the leash to place him in the *sit-stay* position again. Simply pull up on the leash as you lower the dog by pushing down on his rump. *Do not give him a corrective jerk or any other kind of correction. That is never done when teaching a new command.* Actually, the leash is used primarily to keep the dog in a sitting position as you slowly give the command and pull his paws forward.

PRAISE

Each time the dog goes down, give him praise and congratulations. At this stage, however, he may roll on his side. Give him his praise anyway. It is for going down on command (even if he was placed in the proper position). The important thing at this stage is that he learn the most fundamental meaning of the command *Down*. He may play or get frisky once he is on the ground. You may allow him to do this, but without encouragement. That can always be corrected later. Place the dog in the *sit* position using the proper command and then go through the proper procedure for *Down*.

TEACHING THE HAND SIGNAL AS YOU KNEEL BY THE DOG'S SIDE

Now that the dog understands the meaning of the voice command, you start introducing the hand signal. To do so, go to the side. Always start out in this position because it makes it easier to control the dog. It offers fewer distractions and allows the hand to manipulate the leash with greater authority. If the dog has ever been hit, or for some unknown dog reason doesn't like this command, he may growl, snap, or even bite when you use the hand signal. Begin the lesson with the side position because it is safer.

You are now in the *heel* position, but with one knee on the ground. Hold the leash with your right hand and leave your left hand free. The leash is extended to the right of the dog, in front of your body. There should be absolutely no slack in the leash. Allow about twelve inches from his collar to your right hand. If the dog tries to jump up on you in a playful manner, simply raise the leash so that he has no room to do anything but sit. Command him to sit, give him a "Good Dog," and return your right hand to its original position.

Stay in a cheerful mood and do not say anything harsh. This is the crucial part of the lesson. Bring your left hand up above the dog's eye level and slightly to the right of his head. Keep it flattened, fingers closed, palm down. With your right hand, make sure that

Teaching the hand signal for *Down* as you kneel by the dog's side. *Left:* Bring your left hand up above the dog's eye level and slightly to the right of his head. With your right hand, make sure that the leash is taut. *Right:* As your hand goes down, it will press on the leash where the metal clip connects with the collar ring. The dog is pushed to the ground by the force of the hand against the leash.

the leash is taut. This is very important. If your left hand is posi-
tioned properly it should be in sight of the dog's peripheral vision.

Give the dog the vocal command "DOWWWWW-wwwn" as
you begin to lower your left hand to the ground. As your hand goes
down, it will press on the leash where the metal clip connects with
the collar ring. The dog is pushed to the ground by the force of the
hand against the leash. *Because the dog sees your flattened hand
push him down, he will always associate that hand gesture with
his cue to go down.* It should not take too many repetitions for him
to offer little or no resistance. The point is that he has already been
taught the meaning of the vocal command "DOWWWWW-wwwn"
and will know what to do. Of course, it took the first two steps to
get to this point. Some dogs require considerable energy to force
them down in this manner. It can be tiring for both dog and trainer.
If the dog resists or offers opposition, just keep pushing down and
don't worry if the collar tightens up; it will loosen when he is down.
Once he's down, lavish him with praise. If he really fights hard on
this lesson, stop immediately, tell him he's a good boy, go into the
Heel and the *Sit,* and then start over. If the dog continues to resist
this portion of the command, go back to the beginning of the technique and begin again.

Exercise patience and the strictest control over your temper.
The dog cannot be intimidated into learning this lesson. He must
be brought around to it with persistence and the reassurance that
it pleases you. Reposition yourself and place the dog in *Sit-Stay.*
Hold the leash tightly in your right hand and kneel down. Place
your flattened left hand on top of the leash near the clip, give the
command "DOWWWWW-wwwn," and push the tightened leash
to the ground. When the dog touches the ground, congratulate him
with a "Good dog" in a cheerful voice. Let him know that you are
very pleased with him. This is very hard work for the dog and it
will tire him quickly. Every ounce of concentration he possesses is
being called upon. Give him at least an hour's rest after this session.

TEACHING THE HAND SIGNAL AS YOU KNEEL IN FRONT OF THE DOG

You are now going to be standing or kneeling eighteen inches in front of the dog. He saw the hand from the side make him go down. Now he is going to see it from the front. It is important that your hand was first seen from the side. It represented no threat to him. It will now be easier for him to accept the hand signal from the front because he is familiar with it.

From *Heel*, place the dog in *Sit-Stay*, then step in front of him. Hold the leash with your left hand, to your left side. This gives you greater control as you push down. Kneel on one knee, raise your right hand, palm down, on top of the leash, and push it to the ground. At the same time give the vocal command "DOWWWWW-wwwn." Once the dog is on the ground he may try to nip playfully at your fingers. As long as it doesn't hurt, this is permissible and can be corrected at a time when he knows the command perfectly. If, however, the dog tends to hide or play between your knees, exercise control with the leash by placing him in *Sit-Stay* and starting all over. Praise the dog lavishly after each repetition. Repeat this entire step until the dog is performing with no resistance. This is as far as you should go in one day. End the session on a happy note and continue the next day. Resist the temptation to show the new command to your friends and relatives until it is absolutely certain the dog has thoroughly printed it in his mind.

TEACHING YOUR DOG TO RESPOND WITHOUT KNEELING

Repeat the training procedures of the previous sessions. The object of this step is to get the dog to respond to *Down* with a vocal command and a hand signal as you stand in front of him without

Teaching the hand signal for *Down* as you kneel in front of the dog. *Top:* It will now be easier for the dog to accept the hand signal from the front because he is familiar with it from the side. Kneel down on one knee and raise your right hand, palm down. *Middle:* Lower your raised hand onto the top of the leash where the clip connects to the training collar and push it (and the dog) to the ground. *Bottom:* Once the dog is in the proper *down* position, praise him lavishly.

kneeling. Stand eighteen inches in front of the dog. Place the dog in the *sit-stay* position. Hold the leash with your left hand. If he tries to get up, step forward quickly and tighten the leash by raising it above his head, and give him the verbal correction "No." *It is acceptable to use the corrective jerk now because the dog is quite familiar with the command.* This will hold him in place. Even if the dog doesn't obey the command properly, he will be forced to sit and wait for you to correct him or reinstruct him. Return to your position in front of him.

For this step, leave half the leash slack (three feet of the six-foot training leash). Raise your right arm and flatten your hand, palm down, as if for a salute. Give the vocal command "DOWWWWW-wwwn." As you say the command, start lowering your arm. Bring the flat of your hand to the top of the slackened leash, which should be held at an angle to your left. The dog should go down without having to be forced by the leash. Give him an enthusiastic "Good boy" and repeat the step ten times.

TEACHING HIM *DOWN* FROM A LONGER DISTANCE

After a short rest, repeat the procedure, but from a longer distance. You were eighteen inches away before; now extend the distance to three feet. You are still at a distance where the dog can be corrected if he gets too playful or does not respond properly to the command. If he starts to move away or come forward, give him a corrective jerk and a firm "No." *It is acceptable to use the corrective jerk now because the dog is quite familiar with the command.* You are no longer teaching the basics of the *Down*, but rather the refinements.

Once again, raise your arm with a flattened hand, as if for a salute. While saying "DOWWWWW-wwwn," bring your arm down with the palm facing the ground. Only this time, the hand goes

Teaching *Down* from a longer distance. *Top:* The final step is to repeat the teaching procedure from the full extent of the six-foot leash. Raise your arm with a flattened hand, as if for a salute. *Middle:* While saying "DOWWWW-wwwn," bring your arm down with the palm facing the ground. This time, the hand goes past the leash without touching it. *Bottom:* At this point, the dog thinks you are going to touch the top of the leash and push him down. He should go into the *down* position in anticipation of being pushed down. Praise him lavishly.

past the leash without touching it. This is the hand signal as it will always look. Visually, it is the lowering of the arm as it returns to its natural position by the side of the body. At this point, the dog thinks you are going to touch the top of the leash and push him down. His response should be to go into the *down* position in anticipation of being pushed down. Praise him lavishly each time he goes into the proper position. Repeat this maneuver fifteen times. The movement will soon become natural for him and will never require anything more than a lowering of your raised arm.

The final step is to repeat the teaching procedure from the full extent of the six-foot leash. Although it is difficult to correct the dog from this distance with the leash, it should be unnecessary. Once the dog has absorbed this much, you will be able to execute the command with the hand signal or with the voice command only. Practice giving the command "DOWWWWW-wwwn" without the hand signal. Repeat the vocal procedure without the hand signal several times and then switch to giving the hand signal only. End the session by using both hand signal and voice command. Remember, generous praise is necessary in this lesson. Lavish the dog with praise every time he performs properly. But never use his name during his praise or he's going to get up and walk toward you.

If the dog acts confused when you give the hand signal without the voice command, repeat the signal several times. If he still does not respond, then go back to giving the hand signal accompanied by the voice command. Immediately afterward, try the hand signal only. This process should reinforce his understanding of what is expected of him. What's important is the consistency between your hand descending and the tone of your voice descending in the elongated command "DOWWWWW-wwwn." Once he executes the command to your satisfaction, stop work. End the lesson on a high note.

CUSTOMIZED TRAINING

FOR THE HIGH-ENERGY/OUTGOING TEMPERAMENT

OWNER'S FRAME OF MIND   Teaching *Down* to a high-energy/outgoing dog is like trying to balance a ball in your hand while riding a roller coaster. Your dog wants to move all over the place. But your objective must be to keep him in one spot so that you can teach him this—the most difficult of all the commands. Exercise the dog before you begin each teaching session in order to wear him out. Run him as much as you can, and then inhibit his movements with two chairs or some kind of furniture arrangement on each side of him. The more you can confine him after the exercise the better. You must be persistent, insistent, and patient.

BODY LANGUAGE   You will need stamina and firm footing when teaching this command. Whether you teach from a standing or kneeling position, execute all motions and movements quickly and firmly.

TONE OF VOICE   Firm, clear, and loud.

VOICE CORRECTION   Firm and demanding, no-nonsense.

LEASH CORRECTION   Strong corrections are necessary. One strong correction is better than four mild ones. Less is better.

WHERE TO TRAIN   Teach this command in a secluded area with no one present but the trainer. It is important to conduct the training sessions in the privacy of your home or backyard with no distractions.

FOR THE SHY TEMPERAMENT

OWNER'S FRAME OF MIND   Be aware of your attitude before each training session in relation to your dog's shyness, timidity, or fear. Try to be as understanding and sympathetic as possible. Think of your shy dog as a very frightened child. Your goal must be to make him as comfortable as possible.

Consider the various types of surfaces available that would make it easier for your dog to lie down when being taught the command *Down*. Grass, linoleum, or carpet are comfortable. A very frightened dog might not be so reluctant to lie down on command if he were on top of his favorite blanket or towel. If you are loving and patient when teaching this command, you will succeed with a shy dog.

BODY LANGUAGE   All physical movements and gestures should be nonthreatening. Always kneel or sit down alongside your dog or in front of him. You could even try lying down next to him. These unorthodox positions are kind, thoughtful, and very comforting to a shy dog having difficulty with this command. They also help get the job done.

TONE OF VOICE   Your tone should be soft, easygoing, and assuring. This is the ideal time and place to express the affection you have for your dog. Be sensitive to the dog's fears and insecurities and reassure him that everything is going to be okay.

VOICE CORRECTION   None. Use all your energies in the teaching process.

LEASH CORRECTION   Very little. When you use the corrective jerk, tug the leash gently. Use the leash more as a guide than as a correction tool. The dog should have as little awareness of the leash as possible.

WHERE TO TRAIN Use a quiet, private area such as your backyard or a room in your home, provided there are no spectators or distractions. Make the dog comfortable. Do not teach this command on a cement surface that is too hard or too cold. And of course, be aware of the time of year in which you train. If it is summer, train the dog in a cool environment. If it is winter, train the dog in a warm place.

FOR THE STRONG-WILLED TEMPERAMENT

OWNER'S FRAME OF MIND It is important not to view your strong-willed dog as an opponent when teaching this command. Otherwise, this could turn into a battle that you never win no matter which *Down* technique you use. The more force you use, the fewer results you'll have. Use the placing techniques that tend to show the dog what to do rather than those that force him into position. Both you and the dog will be happier for it.

BODY LANGUAGE Kneel or bend down to the dog's level. Always start on the side. That will give you greater control and make the teaching process more fun.

TONE OF VOICE Use a firm but not harsh tone, one that indicates you are determined but not forceful. Do not overpower your dog with your voice. Bear in mind that you are expressing a command, not a punishment.

VOICE CORRECTION Your voice correction should be given clearly, quickly, and authoritatively. Say "No" loudly, but do not yell. Your corrections should have a no-nonsense message for your dog.

LEASH CORRECTION   Maintain a firm control of the leash. Administer strong correction when needed. It is more effective and better for the dog to execute one strong correction than four mild ones in a row. Less is better.

WHERE TO TRAIN   Train your strong-willed dog in a quiet area such as your backyard or a room in your home. Privacy is very important.

FOR THE CALM/EASYGOING TEMPERAMENT

OWNER'S FRAME OF MIND   There is no big deal here. A calm/easygoing dog will lie down if you want him to. Note the difference between his learning the command and simply resting because he's bored or tired. Take advantage of the dog's easygoing nature by constantly repeating the commands so that he will lie down when he is ordered to.

BODY LANGUAGE   Kneel down beside the dog. All the rest should follow along easily as you teach the procedures and techniques.

TONE OF VOICE   Use soft tones when the dog is learning properly. Use an energized tone if he becomes uninterested in what is being taught. The same is true if the dog acts bored, lazy, or tired.

VOICE CORRECTION   You may have to be firm if he does not pay attention. It all depends on how easygoing he is.

LEASH CORRECTION   Use it to guide him in the command. He may want to roll over on his back in the beginning. That's okay, but only in the beginning. If he continues to lie down on the job, administer the corrective jerk.

WHERE TO TRAIN   It does not matter where you go to train a calm/ easygoing dog. Use any place that feels comfortable.

FOR THE AGGRESSIVE TEMPERAMENT

OWNER'S FRAME OF MIND   You could easily get bitten when teaching *Down* to an aggressive dog. The age of your dog and which of the *Down* teaching techniques you use are important considerations. Most of the teaching techniques are effective for aggressive dogs under ten months of age. Use only the food technique or the foot technique for dogs over ten months of age. If your dog has ever bitten anyone, seek professional help.

BODY LANGUAGE   Be certain that your gestures and movements are nonthreatening in nature. Do not make direct eye contact with an aggressive dog over ten months old. In dog behavior, a direct stare into the eyes is taken as a challenge to the animal's position of dominance and could instigate an aggressive action. Do not stand over the dog. It is better to kneel down alongside him. Age is the key factor. A dog under ten months old is less dangerous than a dog over ten months of age. You really need to be careful.

TONE OF VOICE   The tone of your voice depends on the dog's age and if he is dominant/aggressive or fear/aggressive. A dominant/ aggressive puppy between the ages of seven weeks and six months requires a firm, but not harsh, tone of voice. For dominant/aggressive dogs between six and ten months of age, use a very authoritative, demanding tone of voice. A fear/aggressive puppy between the ages of seven weeks and six months requires a soft tone of voice that is still firm enough to correct him. For fear/aggressive dogs between six and ten months, use a firm, but not harsh, tone of voice. Get professional help for all aggressive dogs past ten months of age.

VOICE CORRECTION   A voice correction may not be effective unless it is accompanied with a leash correction at the same time. Some dogs are so aggressive that a voice correction is not effective at all. For this reason, always have your aggressive dog on a leash for all training sessions. Every correction should be followed with praise for acceptance of the correction.

LEASH CORRECTION   You must consider the dog's age, size, and level of aggressiveness when administering leash corrections. Is the dog a bully? Does he growl, snarl, or curl his lip? Puppies between seven weeks and six months of age should be corrected with quick, firm jerks that are not too hard. For dogs between six and ten months of age, correct with quick, firm jerks. However, you may need to administer slightly harder jerks at that age, depending on the dog's level of aggressiveness.

When your dog behaves aggressively, correct him quickly. Repeat the corrections until he stops behaving aggressively. Unless he is severely aggressive, you should be able to obtain at least ninety percent satisfactory results this way. Bear in mind that it is safe to correct an aggressive dog only until he reaches the age of ten months. After that he will be too dangerous for nonprofessional handling. At that time have the dog evaluated by a professional dog trainer, animal behaviorist, veterinarian, or all three.

WHERE TO TRAIN   Take advantage of the privacy of your home or your backyard. Do not allow any distractions such as dogs, kids, or spectators to interfere with the training sessions.

DEFINITION OF *DOWN-STAY*

The dog is on the ground, head erect, eyes looking forward. The front legs are extended and the hindquarters relaxed with the rear weight resting on one haunch or the other. If he is to remain in that position for three to five minutes, he must stay alert until he is released by the person who placed him there. If he is placed in *Down-Stay* for a longer period of time, he may make himself comfortable and even go to sleep.

PROCEDURE AND TECHNIQUE FOR THE *DOWN-STAY*

If the dog has learned the *Sit-Stay*, then it is simply a matter of using the same technique for the *Down-Stay*.

After placing him in *Down*, give the command "Stay" in a firm voice. Because it is not an action command, do not use his name before or afterward. Upon giving the command, flatten your left hand with fingers close together as for a salute and place it in front of his eyes. Your hand should be four inches in front of the eyes. The hand signal is given simultaneously with the voice command. It is a deliberate but quick gesture that temporarily blocks the dog's vision. Assuming the animal has been taught the *Sit-Stay*, that's all there is to be done. If he does not respond properly, then review Chapter 11, "*Sit-Stay*," and give the dog a few brush-up lessons.

One last note: The commands *Down* and *Stay* are not corrections. If the dog jumps up on a stranger, the couch, the bed, the dinner table, or into the cat's litter box, do not yell "Down" and expect him to respond properly. He will become confused. A firm "No" is the

Teaching *Down-Stay*

The hand signal. After giving the verbal command "Stay," flatten your left hand with fingers close together and place it in front of the dog's eyes.

The Pivoting Technique. Hold the leash with both hands. As in *Sit-Stay*, make one turn without moving the dog so that you will be facing him. Step off with your right foot and turn toward the dog. Pivot on your left foot until you are facing the dog. Finally, bring both feet together.

Hold the leash with your left hand in a fixed position, keeping the dog in place. Reinforce the command by repeating the hand signal with your right hand. Be ready to correct him if he moves. Leash control during the pivotal turn reinforced with the hand signal communicates the idea of *Stay*. Do not hold the leash too tightly or he may move out of position.

When teaching *Down-Stay* from a distance, continue to back away until you reach the end of the six feet of leash. See Chapter 11, *"Sit-Stay."*

only way to make a correction. From there you can employ any command you wish. *Down* and *Stay* will do very well.

CUSTOMIZED TRAINING

See Chapter 11, "*Sit-Stay*," under "Customized Training," pages 138–144.

13.

COME WHEN CALLED

The dog's name prefixed to the word "Come" is all that's necessary to get the animal to come when called. As pointed out earlier, language is not your dog's forte. Adding "Okay" to "Silver, Come" gives a note of good cheer and reassurance that you're not angry with him. Anything more than that will louse up the command and draw a blank in the dog's mind. "Okay, Silver, Come," is all it really takes, once the dog has been taught the command. More than that adds confusion, uncertainty, and a lack of response.

Whether your dog is a puppy or an adult, whether he lives in the city, suburbs, or a rural area, it is extremely hazardous to allow him off the leash. Therefore, consider it very carefully before using *Come* when outside. It could result in the death of the animal. On the other hand, using the command indoors or in a confined outdoor area is very practical and offers a convenient way to get the dog to where you want him to be. Teaching this command indoors can be easily accomplished in a hallway. If you decide to teach it outdoors, you are urged to use a fenced-off backyard or an out-of-the-way local park.

DEFINITION OF *COME WHEN CALLED*

The dog comes to you when you call him and goes into a *sit* position in front of you, regardless of any distractions.

BENEATH THE SURFACE OF THE TRAINING

This is probably the command that people want most and have the least idea how to execute. It makes the greatest demand on the dog. Most of his life is spent playing and pursuing all distractions that cross his path. Now he is being asked to respond immediately by shifting his focus and using all his concentration to please you. When a dog is indoors there is nothing for him to do but come when you call him. But when he is outside, there are smells, sights, other dogs, children, people, moving objects, and noises that command his attention. To get him to resist all that and obey your command is quite a chore and, to be perfectly frank, it can be dangerous because it is never totally reliable.

The most important rule to remember is that you must *never* call the dog to you in order to reprimand him. If you use his name or the command *Come* and then correct or punish him, he will never come to you again. Avoid statements like "Princess, Come. What did you do? Shame, shame! Don't you ever do that again!" Some people go even further and hit the dog after he has obeyed the command. Each command must be dealt with individually. If the dog obeys a command, praise him. If he comes when called, it is a betrayal to scold him. Besides, using his name for correction will only give him an association of "Uh-oh, here it comes" with the sound of his name. No one in his right mind will run enthusiastically to get hollered at or punished. If the dog needs correction for an infraction of the rules *you must go to him to do it*. In that way his ability to come when called will not be impaired. A dog should feel that coming to you is a good thing. He should always feel confident that it is a pleasant experience. This attitude is achieved by lavishing him with praise every time he obeys. If you are consistent, he will always come to you.

It is important in teaching this command that the dog never get into the habit of hesitating when called. He should respond immediately. His reward for coming is the praise, but it should be established from the beginning that he must come on the first command. His immediate response could be important to his safety. More dogs are killed on city streets and country roads by automobiles than by natural causes. This consideration alone makes the command a very valuable one.

PROCEDURE AND TECHNIQUE FOR *COME WHEN CALLED*—ON-LEASH

Begin indoors or out. An area that offers a few distractions is not objectionable as a training place. Use the six-foot leash. First put the dog through his basic commands: *Heel, Sit, Sit-Stay, Down, Down-Stay*. Then put him in *Sit-Stay*. Begin the lesson facing the dog.

Stand in front of the dog, at a distance slightly less than the full extent of the six-foot leash. Holding the leash with the left hand (thumb in loop as described previously), allow a very slight amount of slack so there is no chance of pulling the dog forward. With the slightest tug the dog will walk toward you, and that is undesirable without a command. Keep the leash hand (the left) slightly above your waist for greater control of the dog.

The next thing to do is to employ the voice command. It is important that the tone of voice indicate to the dog that coming to you is one of the most exciting, fun things he could do. The dog should be happy coming to you because he's going to get a tre-

Put the dog in *Sit-Stay* and place yourself in front of him, at a position slightly less than the full extent of the six-foot leash. Hold the leash with your left hand and allow a very slight amount of slack so there is no chance of pulling him forward.

mendous amount of praise. Because this is an action command, employ the dog's name as a prefix to the command *Come*. However, always say "Okay" before his name. The command, therefore, sounds like this: *"Okay,* Princess, Come!" The "Okay" should be delivered in a very cheerful, upbeat tone of voice. Try to communicate your affection. Never sound harsh or stern. Accentuate the "Okay" and let the "Princess, Come" trail along. The dog should start moving on the "Okay." It is quite possible that in the past the traditional "squeaking" sound was made to get the dog to come. You know the sound, the one that's like a squeezed balloon. Lip squeaking and whistling are poor substitutes for a definite command. Very few of us can whistle or squeak loud enough if the dog is in the middle of the street surrounded by the distraction of traffic or other outdoor noises.

It is quite possible that the dog will come on the first try. If he does, be sure to reward him with lavish praise. It is not important, at this point, that he sit once he gets to you. If he jumps on you the first few times, it's quite understandable. *Do not correct him when he is being taught a new thing.* He may associate coming with the correction, and the command is shot forever. He can always be corrected at another time, after he has learned the command properly.

TUGGING THE LEASH   Once little Waldo starts coming to you freely, extend the leash hand and give a gentle tug on the word "Okay." Always tug the leash on the word "Okay." The sequence is: "Okay," (gently tug the leash) "Waldo, Come." (He comes to you.) "That's a good fella!" As soon as he comes to you give him his praise. Make it very exciting for him. We emphasize the praise in this command because later you will be competing with very great distractions, and the only way to overcome them is to motivate the dog properly. That can only be done with praise.

THE HAND SIGNAL   The next step is to teach the dog the hand signal that accompanies the voice command. This is very useful if the dog is a great distance away. The hand signal is a natural, logical gesture that should feel very comfortable. It is simply a matter of moving your right hand upward from the side of your body and swinging it around toward your left shoulder. (This gesture is used for the same purpose to get people to come to you.) The sequence becomes: "Okay," (tug the leash with your left hand. Swing your right hand around, making a complete gesture) "Melba, Come." Give her a lot of praise when she gets to you.

GOING INTO THE SIT POSITION AFTER COMING WHEN CALLED   After the command is given, pull in the leash—using both hands, one after another—until the entire leash is in and the dog has no choice but to sit when he gets to you. In order to help him along, pull up on the leash once he is at your feet and give the command *Sit*. This sequence is: "Okay," (tug the leash with your left hand. Swing your right hand around, making a complete gesture, *but grab the leash this time*) "Pete, Come." (Pull in the leash, using both hands.) "Good boy, good boy." (By now you have pulled him gently to your feet. Raise the leash with both hands.) "Sit! Good boy. That's a good boy."

• • •

The hand signal. It is simply a matter of moving your right hand upward from the side of your body and swinging it around toward your left shoulder as though you were going to pull in the leash.

The animal is taught to sit when he gets to you for a couple of very practical reasons. First of all, when he responds to the command *Come* he will start running to you. If he is some distance away it is quite possible that he will crash into you at about forty miles an hour, knocking you off your feet. Or he may shoot right by in his inability to stop. If he is conditioned to sit when he gets to you, he will automatically slow down as he approaches. Repeat these techniques ten or fifteen times, or until he responds properly. Remember, all of this is done on-leash. At no time should you try it without the leash. The most important reason is safety. But another reason is for control, so that your dog can be guided if he starts veering left or right. To increase the distance for him to come, simply back up as he approaches you. Give him encouragement as he walks toward you. It helps to hold his attention and motivates him for future commands. "Okay, Pete, Come. Pete, Come. Okay. Good boy. Good fella." Once he gets to you, "Sit. Good boy."

Remember, never use the command *Come* in a harsh tone of voice and never reprimand the dog after he has obeyed the command. This carries over into the home as well as outdoors and during the training sessions. If the dog chews something in the living room and you call him in from the kitchen in order to scold or correct him, you will be destroying the value of this command.

Going into the *sit* position after coming when called. *Top:* After the command is given, pull the leash, using both hands, one after the other. *Bottom:* Because you've pulled in the entire leash, the dog has no choice but to sit when he gets to you. Pull up on the leash once he is at your feet and give the command "Sit." Praise him lavishly for this.

In your everyday usage of these commands you will reinforce the training if you execute the techniques properly.

CUSTOMIZED TRAINING

FOR THE HIGH-ENERGY/OUTGOING TEMPERAMENT

OWNER'S FRAME OF MIND   It's important to make sure the dog comes to you instead of everywhere else, despite all of his energy and his desire to run around. Your goal is to channel his energy so he loves coming to you. Conduct all training sessions with that idea in mind. You can make the dog's energy work for you by offering generous expressions of affection that are attached to your ability to take charge and control him.

The success of the command revolves around the idea that you must never call your dog to you in anger or with any implied threat. Never use your dog's name when you're yelling at him, because his name is an important part of the *Come When Called* command; and must always be associated with something pleasant. Always praise him lavishly when he comes to you; never chase him; and never call him in order to punish or scold him. If you maintain that frame of mind (and train him), you will definitely succeed.

BODY LANGUAGE   None. Simply stand there and use the leash properly. A high-energy/outgoing dog will have enough body language for both of you.

TONE OF VOICE   Use a happy but firm tone. Always indicate to the dog through the tone of your voice that you are controlled, consistent, and demanding.

VOICE CORRECTION   When necessary, your voice corrections should be loud and quick, indicating a no-nonsense attitude.

LEASH CORRECTIONS   The use of the leash should communicate to the dog that he must settle down and obey your commands. The leash corrections should be strong when needed.

WHERE TO TRAIN   A quiet, secluded location improves your ability to keep the dog concentrated on training. There should be no distractions.

FOR THE SHY TEMPERAMENT

OWNER'S FRAME OF MIND   *Come When Called* is the one command that every dog owner wants from his or her dog. The truth is that most dogs don't do it unless they are properly trained. Most people unrealistically expect a dog to drop everything (such as important sniffing and private investigations) to come. Few dogs, if any, are capable of or willing to do that. Shy dogs have the most difficult time with this command. They require a great deal of reassurance and coaxing.

Throughout the teaching process and whenever you command the dog to come when called, your frame of mind is exceedingly important. If you can communicate an enthusiastic, happy attitude to the dog when you call him, he will come to you. The success of the command revolves around the idea that you must never call your dog to you in anger or with any implied threat. This is especially important for a dog with a shy temperament. Because your dog's name is part of the spoken command, it must always be associated with something pleasant. Never use the dog's name in some unpleasant way or when correcting him. Always praise him lavishly when he comes to you; never chase him; and never call him in order to punish or scold him. If you maintain that frame of mind (and train him), you will succeed.

BODY LANGUAGE   Your body should communicate an upbeat enthusiasm with plenty of movement. Swing your arms. Run backward. Have a good time. Make no motions or gestures that can be interpreted by the dog as threatening. Make each training session as much fun for the shy dog as possible.

TONE OF VOICE   Your voice should be energetic and upbeat. The very sound of it should express praise and enthusiasm. Be happy, cheerful, fun-loving, and, most importantly, reassuring in your tone.

VOICE CORRECTION   None. Give lots of praise instead.

LEASH CORRECTION   Very little. Use the leash as a guide rather than as a correction tool.

WHERE TO TRAIN   Take advantage of the privacy of your home or backyard. Do not permit any distractions or spectators, not even in the hallway of your apartment.

FOR THE STRONG-WILLED TEMPERAMENT

OWNER'S FRAME OF MIND   If you give a strong-willed dog the opportunity, he will take advantage of you. Do not lose your patience. Remain firm about being in charge. A truly stubborn dog is going to test what you're made of. You must outthink, outwait, and outsmart a dog with a strong-willed temperament. It is not necessary, however, to be harsh. You simply must be more *stubborn* than your dog is. A stubborn dog can be taught to respond to this command very well, but it takes patience and a superior will.

The success of the command revolves around the idea that you must never call your dog to you in anger or with any implied threat. Never use your dog's name when you're yelling at him, because his name is an important part of the *Come When Called* command,

and must always be associated with something pleasant. Always praise him lavishly when he comes to you; never chase him; and never call him in order to punish or scold him. If you maintain that frame of mind (and train him), you will definitely succeed.

BODY LANGUAGE   Stand erect and be animated. Allow your body to express a firmness in purpose.

TONE OF VOICE   Definitely firm, indicating a no-nonsense attitude.

VOICE CORRECTION   Sharp, loud, and very consistent.

LEASH CORRECTION   Use a firm but quick tug of the leash. It must get the correction message across with as few jerks as possible.

WHERE TO TRAIN   Use a quiet area where there are no distractions for the dog.

FOR THE CALM/EASYGOING TEMPERAMENT

OWNER'S FRAME OF MIND   He will probably come to you on his schedule, not yours. Patience is important. Pack a lunch, bring a book to read. Have faith that eventually the dog will learn the command and obey it. Accept the idea that he is going to do this at his own pace.

The success of the command revolves around the idea that you must never call your dog to you in anger or with any implied threat. Never use your dog's name when you're yelling at him, because his name is an important part of the *Come When Called* command, and must always be associated with something pleasant. Always praise him lavishly when he comes to you; never chase him; and never call him in order to punish or scold him. If you maintain that frame of mind (and train him), you will definitely succeed.

BODY LANGUAGE   In order to stimulate the dog or energize him after giving the command, wave your arms, run backward, jump up and down, create excitement; such behavior may be necessary in order to motivate a dog with a calm/easygoing temperament. If the dog responds properly from the beginning without extreme movements, use your body in a very normal way.

TONE OF VOICE   Use a happy tone that energetically rewards the dog with praise and approval. Be enthusiastic.

VOICE CORRECTION   Use a firm, loud correction whenever the dog fails to pay attention. However, you must not confuse firmness with harshness. It is important that you not scare the dog.

LEASH CORRECTION   Give firm corrections. If the dog appears un-involved, give him a gentle correction and run backward as you pull him toward you. By making a game out of it, you may get him more involved. Not only will the dog be forced to come to you, but he may also enjoy the training sessions.

WHERE TO TRAIN   Use any location you like to train a calm/easy-going dog. Distractions help the learning process for dogs of this temperament. This is especially true as the training progresses. The sights and smells of new places and different people may actually motivate the dog to a greater involvement with the teaching process.

FOR THE AGGRESSIVE TEMPERAMENT

OWNER'S FRAME OF MIND   The dog may challenge you. Do the unexpected. Run backward; use a ball, a stick, or anything that is fun for him and you.

The success of the command revolves around the idea that you must never call your dog to you in anger or with any implied threat. Never use your dog's name when you're yelling at him, because his name is an important part of the *Come When Called* command, and must always be associated with something pleasant. Always praise him lavishly when he comes to you; never chase him; and never call him in order to punish or scold him. If you maintain that frame of mind (and train him), you will definitely succeed.

BODY LANGUAGE   Do nothing that is threatening. Bend down, run backward—use your body in ways that will motivate him.

TONE OF VOICE   Be loving, affectionate, and persuasive.

VOICE CORRECTION   When using "No" as a correction, be firm but nonthreatening.

LEASH CORRECTION   Administer a medium to firm jerk, depending on the dog's size and age.

WHERE TO TRAIN   Definitely in the privacy of your home or backyard. Do not permit any spectators to watch, and avoid distractions.

14.

GO TO YOUR PLACE

Unlike humans, a dog does not feel insulted if you put him in his place. As a matter of fact, it is a blessing for him to know where to be in order to stay out from underfoot. Even dogs can get frustrated by trying to please an indecisive and inconsistent person.

Although *Go to Your Place* is useful for people who live in a full-size house, it is manna from heaven for the city apartment-dweller. The average apartment has a bedroom, living room, and kitchen. When the apartment dweller is trying to prepare dinner for a small dinner party, the dog is usually driven mad trying to keep out of the way. If he settles at your feet in the kitchen, he is scolded and told to go into the living room. Once he settles in the living room, he has to dodge the dustmop and avoid being sucked up by the vacuum cleaner. By this time he has been yelled at seventeen times and he's just about ready to steal several caviar canapés (dogs love caviar), which will evoke a shrill hysterical scream from the belabored epicure. The dog is then locked in the bathroom for the evening until a guest uses it and passes out in fright. In the meantime, the dog is suffering from boredom and claustrophobia with a pinch of paranoia thrown in for good measure. Of course, the hosts are nervous and on edge and ready to give the dog to the first farmer who says he can use him to bite cows. Thus ends another potentially happy relationship between dog and owner. It's too bad, because all this can so easily be avoided with the command *Go to Your Place.*

DEFINITION OF *GO TO YOUR PLACE*

At your command the dog stops whatever he is doing and leaves wherever he is doing it, goes to a designated place, and stays there for an indefinite time.

BENEATH THE SURFACE OF THE TRAINING

The dog should have an out-of-the-way area designated as his little corner of the world. The area should be carefully selected so that once he's placed there, he is never in anyone's way or in danger of being forced to move. It is especially considerate of the owner to make sure that this area is not too removed from the activities of the family. Dogs get pleasure from merely watching the evening's entertainment. An added benefit of this command is that the dog will not beg for food after you have sat down to dinner.

One of the ways to enhance the training is to place your dog's toys, playthings, and bones in his designated area. He will feel quite at home and much more secure. Give him a small piece of carpet or an old cushion in order to make his area cozy and comfortable. Once all this is established, the dog will be in a much better frame of mind. It is very important for his well-being.

In a household where there is more than one animal, this designation of territory is very important. If there are two male dogs, for instance, there is a constant competition for territorial rights. In this situation, designate a place for each animal and never violate the established territorial rights of each dog. With a cat and a dog, never let the cat use the dog's area for anything. In the case of a male and a female dog, when the latter goes in heat there is very little that established territory can do so that they avoid contact. The dogs must be kept apart (assuming you don't want them to mate) in more practical ways. Outside of a mating situation, the animals will quickly learn to respect each other's territorial rights.

This command offers the owner a firm control over the animal's behavior at very important times. If a friend or neighbor enters the home and does not want to be annoyed with the dog's demand for attention, simply tell the dog to go to his place and that's the end of it.

It is helpful to understand that the dog will always go to his place on command if it is not made to seem like a punishment. Even though your motive is to get the dog out of mischief, always give the command in an upbeat way so that he does not feel that something bad is connected with going to his place. It is not to be equated with "Go to your room," an expression that many a parent has used on an errant child.

PROCEDURE AND TECHNIQUE FOR
GO TO YOUR PLACE

The first step in teaching this command is to select a permanent spot that will be used exclusively by the dog and be the one place he can go and never be in the way.

Starting at five feet. In teaching the lesson, use the standard six-foot leash and training collar. Because this is an action command, always use his name first. Start out five feet away from the designated place and say, "Pete, go to your place." Then commence to walk the dog to the spot. Once you get him there, give the command *Sit*. Praise him. Then give him the command *Down*, and finally *Stay*. Praise him. Leave him there as you walk six feet away. Do not leave his vision. He will probably stay, provided you're in the room. Assuming the dog has learned *Come When Called*, call him to you. Repeat this procedure fifteen times.

The command *Go to Your Place* should be given in a pleasant and gentle tone of voice. Even though learning is hard work for a dog, make him feel that this is a pleasant command, one he will enjoy. However, do not lose the firm, authoritative sound that you have developed. Just add a happy quality to it.

Once the dog willingly accompanies you to his place from five feet, try it at ten feet. Again, get his attention with "Pete, go to your place." Walk him to the spot. Place him in *Sit*. Place him in *Down* and then *Stay*. Walk six feet away, and after a few seconds call him. Repeat the whole thing several times. Don't be surprised if he starts leading you to his place once he's been doing it a few times. This is a happy experience for him. He gets a lot of praise and affection for doing it properly. Do not, however, become too lax during the training period. If he starts sniffing something on the way to his place, exercise firm leash control. Direct him to the exact location of his place. Nothing must stand in the way once you have given the command.

OTHER ROOMS   The next step is to teach him this command from other rooms. Using the six-foot leash, repeat the procedure, but this time from another room at a greater distance. Try it several times from every room in your apartment or house. You will actually be teaching him the path to his place from every part of your quarters, and it will be permanently printed in his brain. The toughest room for him will probably be the bedroom, because it is usually the farthest. But once he learns that, he will know the command perfectly. Once the dog knows this command on-leash, it is guaranteed that he'll be able to do it off-leash.

• • •

A word of caution. Do not give this command indiscriminately. Do not make it a family joke or something with which to impress friends and neighbors. Only use the command as it's needed. If he has to go to his place every five minutes it's going to make him crazy. Let him enjoy going to his place. Let him consider it his little haven when things get difficult. He will soon be going there without the command. He'll probably pick that area to stay for most of the day. That will be his little indoor doghouse, a home within a home.

CUSTOMIZED TRAINING

Because *Go to Your Place* is a relatively easy command to teach, especially to a dog who has already learned *Sit, Heel* and *Automatic Sit, Sit-Stay, Down* and *Down-Stay,* and *Come When Called,* we do not include customized training aids in this chapter. By now, you understand your dog's temperament and will intuitively make the proper adjustments for teaching *Go to Your Place.*

Now that you have successfully completed the last fourteen chapters, you may consider your dog obedience trained. Congratulations! Both you and your dog deserve a biscuit. Chapter 15 covers problem behavior and is, more or less, graduate work. With an obedience-trained dog, you may tackle his individual problems as outlined in the following chapter. The first fourteen chapters have given you a basis with which to work.

II.

After the
Obedience Course

Fortunately for us, dogs do not respond to Freudian analysis, pound-the-pillow therapy, or any other form of psychotherapy. If they did, there would probably be a stampede to dog "shrinks" and sniff-touch encounter-group studios. It would create a new set of expenses in an already costly pet market.

In this chapter we cover a great deal of territory in an attempt to give some useful information concerning the dozens of behavioral problems that can occur in dogs. We have selected the problems that come up most often. Many of these problems never arise because a successfully completed obedience course, such as the one in this book, was initiated. Others can be diminished in degree simply by going over various aspects of the obedience course. A well-trained and disciplined dog will not eat up the carpet, bark excessively, or bite. However, environmental factors beyond your control as well as inherited behavior sometimes play a part in the creation of those annoying or even destructive habits that dogs often acquire. For example, a family that goes to work every day and leaves the dog alone may come home to a ruined couch, never knowing that the phone rang continuously and put the dog into a mad frenzy. Incorrect discipline is the main cause of many problems and tends to worsen them as long as it is continued. Punishments, scolding, temper tantrums, and beatings all tend to create problems and make those that already exist worse.

Besides continual brush-ups on the obedience course, we suggest that you try to think through a dog's situation from *his* perspective. Like a psychologist, one can often solve a problem by understanding its cause. You would then be in a position to change or remove those factors that are upsetting the dog and making him behave the way he does. Teasing, roughhouse play, abuse from children, chaining, overexcitement, confinement in a small room are but a few of the factors that may be at the root of the problem.

Some dogs will not respond to the suggestions made in this chapter and will require the long, tedious kind of attention that only a professional trainer or a book specializing in problem behavior can provide. If you love your dog and want to keep him, it is best to take this final but effective step. A professional dog trainer not only has the technical facility to handle most dog problems, but is emotionally uninvolved, thus giving him the needed objectivity that underlies all good animal handling. It is like the difference between an aspirin and a doctor's prescription.

A wide variety of problems and their possible solutions are described in this section. Any dog owner can take these measures and experience good results with them. Some other problems, however, such as biting and other forms of aggressive behavior, cannot be solved by the average dog owner. These are problems that only a professional dog trainer or animal behaviorist can assess and resolve.

15.

PROBLEMS

BEGGING

 This is a problem that starts out in puppyhood as a cute stunt and winds up an obnoxious habit in mature life. There is nothing worse than a dog sitting next to you at the dinner table, looking up, and whining for food. Although barely tolerable when it's just a daily family dinner, it is completely unacceptable when you are entertaining guests. It can ruin an otherwise pleasant social occasion.

Obviously, this is a habit that is formed when the dog is very young. When you give the dog snacks and between-meal treats, you are on the way to teaching him to beg. He begins to expect food at any time of the day or night and never learns that his feeding times are the main meals of the day. He has learned that his eating area is anywhere that you are handling food. As in the section "Taking Food from the Table" (page 225), make it a firm rule never to feed him anywhere but in his bowl, in its regular place. Also, never give him anything except his own food, *at his regular feeding time only*.

In order to break him of his begging habit, start placing the leash and collar on him before dinner. Sit down to dinner and wait for him to make his move. The instant he starts begging from anyone, give him a firm corrective jerk (degree of firmness based on the dog's temperament) accompanied by a loud "No." Tell everyone at the table what you're doing so it doesn't upset them and ruin their meal. Alternatives to this method are use of the shake can accompanied with a firm "No" (based on the dog's temperament); the commands *Down* and *Stay*; and the command *Go to Your Place*. If you behave consistently, he will stop this habit in short order.

CARSICKNESS

There are only a few undeniable symptoms of carsickness—when the dog uncontrollably vomits, urinates, or defecates all over the car. Certainly, one possible reason for carsickness is feeding and watering before a long trip. With stop-and-go traffic, the dog gets nauseous and loses control one way or another. A good rule is never to feed or water a dog immediately before taking him anywhere in an automobile. And don't let the dog get overexcited before a trip. His running around will sometimes lead to the unpleasant physical sensations that cause carsickness.

If a dog is not really relaxed about riding in a car, he is going to have intense emotions that will induce carsickness. Therefore, it would be desirable to allow him to adjust slowly to riding in gradual stages. Open the door to the car and allow him to walk in by his own choice. Let him smell around and walk outside through the other door if he wishes. Let him sit in the car for a few minutes without your actually starting the engine. Let him claim the car as part of his territory before you drive off. Animals panic if they feel trapped in an unfamiliar situation. When you finally decide to give him his first ride, have him sit in the back seat while you hold on to his leash from the front seat. Drive a block and stop. Get out for a minute or two and then try it again. Repeat this process until you feel the dog is relaxed enough to continue without stopping.

It is also useful to convince the dog that riding in a car is fun. Try relating to the dog with cheerful enthusiasm just before entering the car. "Want to go for a ride? Come on, boy. Let's get in the car." This kind of entreaty does work in changing the dog's attitude about riding. If the dog is not emotionally upset, chances are he will not get carsick.

On the other hand, you do not want him to be uncontrollable. Maintain a firm control of the leash so that he does not jump around. Give him the command *Sit* and correct him if he does something wrong. The commands *Down* and *Stay* before driving off will undoubtedly help. The idea is to get him to ride in the back quietly and be a good passenger. Sometimes opening the window three or four inches is enough to satisfy him. It makes him feel less trapped and allows him to enjoy the fresh air and scenery. However, it is not a good idea to allow him to keep his head outside the window while the car is in motion. It can promote eye irritations.

For the purpose of safety and the prevention of carsickness, purchase a dog crate that is sized properly for your dog. Put the crate in the back of the car and place the dog inside. This will give him stability and a clear sense of boundaries. Another useful bit of canine travel equipment is the seat harness, designed especially for dogs. This too will help prevent carsickness. These items may be purchased in a pet-supply store or from a mail-order catalog for pet owners.

CHASING CARS, MOTORCYCLES, AND BICYCLES

When a dog chases after a moving vehicle he creates a clear and present danger, not only to his own life but to the occupants of the vehicle he is chasing. It is horrible enough to think about your dog getting under the wheels of a car or motorcycle, but what if the driver smashes into a pole or tree in an effort to avoid the offending animal? There have been situations where a driver was startled and made victim of a head-on collision with another car. For these reasons, vehicle chasing must be taken very seriously.

There are many possible reasons that a dog would behave this way in the face of terrible danger. One explanation is the instinct of the dog to be a running hunter. In his wild state, the dog (or wolf) must outrun his prey if he is to eat. This instinct is clearly demonstrated in greyhound racing, where a mechanical rabbit is used as bait. Another possible explanation is that the dog might have had a bad experience with a moving car such as a backfire, a near-miss by a passing vehicle, or having something tossed at him from a car window. Motor noises, exhaust fumes, or any number of factors may have conspired to create this troublesome reaction to moving vehicles. It is one of those rare situations where a knowledge of the cause offers little help in ending the problem.

What is needed here is to communicate to the dog that chasing cars, motorcycles, and bicycles displeases you and offers nothing but intense discomfort for his efforts. A strong training collar and training leash can be employed the next time the dog indulges his habit. Let him go to the end of his leash as he runs toward the moving vehicle. Then jerk for all you're worth, yanking him off his feet. As he reaches the end of the leash, shout "No." Then praise him. If the problem does not end, use a long length of rope in the same manner. Make sure it is a double thickness of strong rope so that he doesn't break it when he reaches the end. The longer the distance, the harder the impact when he reaches the end. You cannot allow yourself to be squeamish and hold back on that hard yank. It is absolutely certain that it will give the dog great discomfort. But compare that very temporary discomfort with the impact of a moving car.

CHEWING

Chewing is one of the most expensive and destructive problems any dog owner faces. We are talking about chewing furniture, curtains, draperies, appliances, baseboards, shoes, clothing, anything. Owners have lost hundreds and sometimes thousands of dollars through this kind of damage. Very often, chewing has been the cause of failure in owner-animal relations and has resulted in a parting of the ways. For the owner it ends in frustration, but for the dog it means an uncertain future. It's sad because there is no excuse for the problem, since it is easily solved.

There are several solutions. Some dogs will respond favorably to any one of the many sprays on the market. Just spray the items the dog likes to chew. Some sprays are unpleasant for the dog to smell, and others are unpleasant for him to taste. An alternative is to use alum, a powder that can be purchased inexpensively at any drugstore. Mix it with a small amount of water, make it into a paste, and smear it on the dog's favorite chewing items. The mixture tastes bitter and is extremely unpleasant for the animal. Although alum is not harmful if eaten, it should be used in small quantities. (Alum is used medicinally as an astringent and a styptic and could upset the dog if he swallowed a large quantity. However, that is not likely to happen owing to its unpleasant taste.) Tabasco or hot sauce is also effective.

A dog shut away behind a closed door and left alone will chew as a means of escape. He will gnaw away at the bottom of the door, the baseboards, or the wall itself. Because dogs are social creatures, it takes time for them to adjust to being left alone. During this period of adjustment they may become anxiety-ridden or frustrated and chew to alleviate their emotions.

If the dog's favorite chewing object is a couch cover or bolster or bed pillow, the mousetrap technique will certainly end the problem (see "Jumping on Furniture," page 217).

When the chewing problem pertains to a puppy, stay alert to which objects the animal is chewing and discourage it immediately, before it develops into an adult habit. Discourage him from going after wooden objects or anything at all that might resemble furniture, clothing, carpeting, curtains, or anything you value. A rawhide toy that he can call his own is the safest preventative you can employ to avoid a destructive behavior problem. Do not wait until it is too late and you have lost your valuable carpeting. A puppy's chewing problem is usually because of teething. When you leave the house, give the dog several ice cubes in his food bowl. The coldness will numb his gums and ease the pain. An alternative is to soak a washcloth in cold water and freeze it. This will serve the same purpose as the ice cubes. Many adult dogs chew when left alone because they are bored, frightened, nervous, or insecure about whether or not you will return. They do not do it to be spiteful. Punishment is counterproductive and changes nothing except to add to the dog's insecurity. If you can determine why he chews, you might be able to change the conditions of his environment and correct the problem. For example; take the phone off the hook if the bell frightens him; do not leave him alone for too long a period of time (have a friend look in on him); get him a cat for a playmate; leave plenty of rawhide toys or bones. With careful deliberation, almost every problem can be solved.

DOGFIGHTING

Although fighting is most common between two male dogs, it also occurs frequently between females or a female and a male. Dogfighting is sometimes so unpleasant that the joys of owning a dog are completely obscured. For those who own dogs in the city it is especially difficult because of the large dog population. You find yourself avoiding the dog's walk or dreading getting into an elevator for fear of having to cope with another dogfight.

Dogfights are based on the instinctive need to defend territory or establish rank, even in a nonexistent dog pack. The basis for most fights are the issues of dominant and subordinate status and territorial rights to wherever they happen to be at the time. If one dog enters another dog's yard or home, the possibility of a fight is great. A dog being walked on a leash will fight another dog to assert his territorial rights to the person holding the leash. This is often the cause of a fight between two dogs on leashes, even though they are not technically on their own territories.

Dogs who were never socialized with other dogs are likely candidates for dogfighting. Some dogs may have started fighting because they were attacked by another dog when they were very young. Another source of the problem may stem from puppyhood, where a dog might have been allowed to attack larger dogs in play. Older dogs often tolerate this behavior from puppies and young dogs. Such a dog easily becomes accustomed to challenging other dogs and grows up doing it on a regular basis.

If your dog gets into a fight, there are a couple of ways to stop it. (You must never place your hand near the dog's face. In the heat of battle a dog doesn't know whom he's biting.) If the dog is on-leash, administer a corrective jerk, say "No" in a firm tone of voice, turn around, say "Heel," and walk in the opposite direction. If that is not possible, pick him up off the ground by the leash, provided the dog is not a toy breed or too large for that maneuver. If the dog is off the leash, pull him up by the tail. Again, do this if the dog is not too big and do not place your hands near either dog's face. Try throwing a garment or blanket over the most aggressive dog's head. This breaks the intensity of the encounter long enough to get away from the situation.

Use the corrective jerk as effectively as you can. Maintain the collar high on the dog's neck so that he will feel the full impact of the jerk. When he is about to engage in a fight with another dog, give him a firm corrective jerk. When the collar is low on his neck, he hardly feels the tug of a correction. The assertion of your dominance over both dogs with body language and vocal power can break the intensity of their contact and get their attention. You can also try startling them by throwing objects close to them or dousing them with water. There is little else to be done.

The best you can do about dogfighting is take measures to prevent this troublesome behavior. It is easier to prevent or even stop a dogfight if your dog is obedience trained. The obedience course offered in *Good Dog, Bad Dog* is your first line of defense. A trained dog will respond to your commands to some degree, even when engaged with the enemy. Most dogfights can be averted by paying attention to the body language and behavior of your own dog around another. On occasion, two dogs will sniff each other and appear to be quite friendly. Suddenly, all hell breaks loose and you find yourself helplessly caught in the middle. Two dogs who are inclined to fight each other display raised hackles (fur standing on end), urinate, scrape their hind feet, bark, snarl, and growl. They also stare intensely at each other while attempting to look as large as possible, usually by standing sideways. Their tails become stiff, straight up or straight down. Leave the scene if you see any of these signs. An ounce of prevention is worth a pound of bandages.

EXCESSIVE BARKING

There are two aspects to the problem of excessive barking. The first is when the dog barks while the owner is at home, and that is usually caused by a doorbell ringing, noise outside the door, a stranger at the door, a desire for food, or a desire to go out. The second aspect is when the owner is not at home. The owner comes back from work or shopping and finds an angry note from a neighbor or landlord demanding that he stop the dog from barking or else face the legal consequences.

Solving the barking problem when the owner is at home is much easier than when the owner is not at home. By leaving the leash and training collar on the dog, you are prepared to deliver a corrective jerk and a firm "No" when the dog barks. Even rattling the shake can (how to use it is based on the dog's temperament) and saying "No" often works. But the corrective jerk is the most effective method.

If the dog barks excessively when no one is at home, the solution lies in the basic obedience course. There are many reasons why a dog will bark when he is left alone. He may be undisciplined; he may hear a lot of noises outside; he simply may want to have you walk through the door and play with him. Basic obedience lessons tend to calm him down, reassure him, and make him responsive. The more responsive the dog is to you, the more eager he is to please. If the dog has had no basic obedience lessons, this is the time to start. If he has had lessons, then simply go over three or four commands as a refresher. Run him through his paces and remind him of his training. Don't forget to praise him every time he performs properly.

If that doesn't work, then try leaving the house and waiting outside. Do everything you normally do when you leave. Follow the established routine. Do not lock the door. Be sure to leave his leash and collar on. Pretend to leave the house and do not stand so close to the door that the dog can smell you. He must be convinced that you have really left the house. When he starts to bark, run in, grab his leash, and execute a firm corrective jerk (use is based on the dog's temperament) accompanied by a firm "No!" If you do this three or four times with very firm corrections, he will understand exactly what you don't want him to do. Praise him afterward for having stopped barking. This is a problem that *must* be solved, because it can result in having to get rid of the dog or in finding yourself evicted from your house or apartment. A very firm corrective jerk is recommended if it's going to work. It's much more humane in the long run than having to get rid of the dog.

You may run into the problem of his not barking for an hour after you leave. One way to solve this is to wait out the hour outside the house on a weekend when you can spare the time, and use the corrective jerk as outlined above. But in either case the problem must be dealt with before it is too late.

In all these suggested methods you must always accompany your action with a firm "No" and then praise after he responds properly. In a short while you will only have to use a firm "No."

EXCESSIVE WETTING

Holding urine is one of the primary requisites for a domesticated pet. But many dogs release it in small quantities at the most peculiar moments and sometimes trail it all over the house. There are several explanations for this. It can be a symptom of sickness, disease, or injury to the kidneys and bladder. It doesn't hurt to have your dog checked by a veterinarian. Assuming the dog is in good health, wetting can be an indication of a very shy or timid dog. A dog of this temperament will piddle when he is punished or yelled at. He wets from fear or perhaps excitement. Urinating is an instinctual act of submission to the domination of another animal and is a direct parallel to excessive authority from the dog's master. When a male puppy is confronted with a mature dog of the same gender, a ritual takes place. They determine each other's sex by sniffing and then decide who will prevail in the situation. There is usually a brief physical encounter with the puppy or young dog losing the battle and indicating his submission by rolling over on his back and urinating: It is his way of acknowledging the older male's superiority. The identical interaction occurs between you and your dog when you punish him or yell at him and he urinates.

One way to cope with it is to be much more gentle than usual and to eliminate punishments and scoldings. Do not use threatening gestures or sudden movements. A limited water intake can help reduce the problem. If the problem of excessive wetting seems unsolvable, never greet the dog while he is in the house. If possible, keep the dog in the front or backyard in an enclosed area and greet him there. Weaning the dog away from his shy or timid responses to you will eventually end the problem.

FEAR OF CARS

Many dogs are afraid to ride in cars and run away the minute the car door is opened. Once forced inside, they generally whine, bark, or howl to be let out. Why? Perhaps they've had an unhappy experience with a car or they feel trapped inside or they are uncomfortable with this new and strange experience.

A car may have given your dog some trauma you know nothing about. One of the great causes of dog deaths is heat prostration. It usually happens when an owner, ignorant of the heat intolerance of a dog, locks the animal in a car while shopping. Even on the mildest day with the windows rolled down a few inches, the sun will immediately turn the car into an oven. The dog feels the intense heat and resulting oxygen shortage and panics when he finds that he can't get out. Eventually he will claw, scratch, and even hurl his body against the windows to get out. Often the result is a painful death. But it is possible that the owner appears in the very early stages of this nightmare and, without knowing it, rescues the dog. After an experience like that, it will be almost impossible to get the dog back into a car and the owner will never understand why. (Obviously, the windows of a car should always be open wide enough for good ventilation when locking a dog inside.) Heat prostration is only one of many traumas that a dog may have experienced while in a car by himself. Auto backfires, dogs in heat, teasing children, and gasoline fumes are but a few other possibilities.

Patience is the only solution. Make auto riding sound like fun. Turn it into a game. Get him into a cheerful mood with statements like "Who wants a ride in the car? Let's go in the car, boy." Make it seem like a treat. If he won't take the bait, then try coaxing him with a gentle tone of voice. Open the door on both sides and let him investigate on his own before you start up the engine. Once you get him inside on his own, let him sniff around and leave if he wishes. Do not force him to stay. It is important that the dog never feels trapped with no way out. A cornered animal soon panics and behaves irrationally. Once he sits down, close the doors gently and start up. Drive one block and stop and let him out. If he gets back in, then drive another block. If he refuses to get back into the car, then let it go for another day. Try it again and again until the dog is relaxed enough to drive several miles. Petting him, praising him, and sitting in the backseat with him for a few minutes will also help to reassure him that nothing bad is going to happen. Do this three or four times a day for a few days and the problem will be solved.

GOING INTO THE GARBAGE

Unless it has already happened to you, this problem seems to be one of those endearing little habits that make such good anecdotal material for people who enjoy talking about their dogs. In our opinion, this nasty little trait not only is disgusting but has all the potential for costing the owner a great deal of money. More than once a dog has ripped into the garbage sack and scattered trash all over the house. In addition, the little devil chewed up much of it and ingested such savories as eggshells and coffee grounds, among others. The dog then moved into the living room and threw up all over the two-hundred-year-old Persian rug. To come home to that is to experience the first emotions of *dogicide*. Of course, if the dog happens to split a few hollow chicken bones with his teeth and then swallows the jagged ends, you might come home to find a dead dog. Going into the garbage can be serious.

This problem arises whether you are home or away. Because of the powerful smell, animals are extremely attracted to this symphony of scents. Obviously, the easiest way to solve the problem is to simply not leave the garbage pail around, especially if you go out. But that doesn't really teach the dog anything. Set up a simulated situation. Place the leash and collar on the dog and purposely open the lid to the garbage pail. Walk away. The minute the dog sticks his nose in the pail, give him a firm corrective jerk (use is based on the dog's temperament) and a very loud "No." *Then praise him.* You may also try rattling the shake can if it's more convenient. (How to use it is based on the dog's temperament.) You should get good results if you repeat this technique four or five times.

In the event that you are leaving the house, sprinkle Tabasco sauce or hot Chinese mustard on top of the garbage. This is a self-teaching lesson that really works. An alternative is to use alum, a powder that can be purchased inexpensively at any drugstore. Mix it with a small amount of water into a paste, and smear it over the top of the garbage. The mixture tastes bitter and is extremely unpleasant. Although alum is not harmful if eaten, it should be used in small quantities. Alum is used medicinally as an astringent and a styptic and could upset the dog if swallowed in large quantities; however, that is not likely to happen owing to its unpleasant taste.

Some dogs will respond favorably to any one of the repellent sprays sold in pet-supply stores or mail-order catalogs for pet owners. Simply spray the garbage pails thoroughly. Some repellents are unpleasant for the dog to smell, while others are unpleasant for him to taste.

GROWLING

A growl is a menacing sound that comes from deep in the throat of a dog and should be taken as a warning to stop what you are doing or to come no closer. In most cases this warning should not be taken lightly. When dogs growl, they usually raise their upper lips into a snarl and bare their teeth. It is an indication that they may bite you.

Growling is an aggressive behavior, similar to biting, and with the same causes: poor breeding, lack of early socialization, environmental influences (negative experiences), and abusive human behavior. Most dogs growl as a response to punishment, to someone going near the food bowl, or to someone doing anything perceived as a threat. Growling is often the result of physical abuse or of excessive or abusive corrections. Using the hands for punishment (hitting, slapping, pointing) helps to create a growler.

Growling can be the beginning of a dog turning on its master. It is important to understand that dogs rarely turn unless they have been abused in some way, and this applies to all breeds. A puppy comes into the house, and the owners, in their ignorance or frustration, slap the dog for every false move. After ten or twelve weeks of being hit, a conditioned reflex is created and the dog flinches at every human movement. The dog grows up in fear and eventually fights back.

If a dog has grown up thinking of the human hand as an instrument of punishment, he will growl the minute a hand is used for anything to do with him. Some dogs will growl if you try to take something from their mouths or if you try to pet them.

Growling is also the result of spoiling the dog or never correcting him (in the proper way, of course) for anything. If he is allowed to get away with all manner of bad behavior, he is likely to growl when he finally is disciplined. From his perspective, his owner is turning on him, so he growls in anger or defense. If his behavior is effective in getting things his way, he continues until he becomes a bully.

If your dog is only a puppy between *seven weeks and six months old*, his growling (snarling and nipping, too) can be ended with corrections using vocal reprimands ("No") with or without rattling a shake can. Careful employment of the corrective jerk (use is based on the dog's temperament) can successfully solve this problem. Young dogs between the ages of *six and ten months old* can still be turned around with firm corrections. Of course, at this age growling is often accompanied by snarling, snapping, and shallow bites and must be dealt with quickly and effectively. But growling dogs *ten months and older* are extremely difficult to change. In fact, some cannot be changed. Once a dog is past ten months of age and has a growling, snarling, or biting problem, he can cause serious injuries and requires professional evaluation. If this problem has gone on for a year or two and you are terrorized by the dog, you have only two alternatives: call a professional dog trainer or find another home for you or the dog.

JUMPING ON FURNITURE

This is another undesirable characteristic of many dogs, young and old alike. It comes from poor discipline by an owner who allows the habit to develop. If the dog is allowed to sleep with his owner in the bed, it is very logical for him to assume that the chairs and sofas are merely an extension of the bed. Furniture is furniture and the dog makes no distinctions. Therefore, the question must be asked: Is the dog allowed to jump on the furniture or not?

There are several solutions to the problem. If the dog is still a puppy, the shake can is very effective. (How to use it is based on the dog's temperament.) Wait for the animal to jump on the furniture. The minute he does, shake the can and say "No" in a firm voice. Do not scare the young puppy. The shake can solves a multitude of problems, but do not forget to praise the dog immediately after each and every correction.

In the case of an older dog, apply the same technique by shaking the can as loudly or softly as necessary, depending on the age and temperament of the dog. Because the dog is older, it may take more shaking to get his attention. Once again, say "No" with a firm voice and then praise the animal after he responds.

In the event that the shake can method does not work, it is suggested you correct the dog with the leash and training collar. When you are home, leave the leash on until he jumps on the furniture. As he is doing so, give him a very firm corrective jerk (use is based on the dog's temperament) accompanied by a stern "No." As soon as he stops jumping, give him his praise. Remember, without the praise the correction is meaningless.

A very upsetting aspect to this problem is when the dog waits for you to leave the house before he jumps up on the sofa or on his favorite piece of furniture. (You can be sure he has one.) Do you come home and discover fur, saliva, or worse on your expensive bedspread or brocade slipcover? If so, it indicates that the dog waits for you to leave, commits his crime, and scoots off the minute he hears you coming.

One effective solution to this problem sounds awful, but in reality is painless. Set ten or fifteen small mousetraps on the couch or bed and cover them with five or six thicknesses of newspaper. Tape the paper thoroughly so that the dog cannot hurt himself. When you leave, the dog is probably doing to jump on the couch and set the traps off. The traps will hit the newspaper with a loud noise and startle him. This works almost every time. Repeat the technique until you come home to find that the traps have not been set off.

Another method for creating an aversion to furniture is to

spread aluminum foil on the surface of the furniture. The sound of it under your dog's paws is surprising and unpleasant to him, as is the slippery feeling.

Or you may string a piece of rope across the furniture like a barrier. You can even tie shake cans on it at ten-inch intervals. It might discourage the dog if he has to climb over or under the rope to get to his favorite resting place.

It is important to remember that dogs are taught to jump on furniture. If they are not allowed to do it at any time, then they usually won't start by themselves. Most people think it's cute to cradle a puppy in their arms and sit on the couch with it. There is no difference between a puppy sitting directly on the couch or sitting in your arms with you seated on the couch. That is the beginning of your problem and that's the time to nip it in the bud. Remember, it ceases to be cute when the dog is full-grown and the habit firmly established. Allowing the dog to sleep in your bed is also an open invitation to jump on the furniture. The choice is yours.

JUMPING ON PEOPLE

Almost any dog will jump on people if he is excited, happy, and untrained. This happens on the street and in the house when someone comes to visit. The animal usually wants to play and get some attention. The biggest problem connected with it is the behavior of the owner. If the puppy or the dog is not supposed to jump up on people, then that rule must apply in *every* situation. You cannot have the dog jump on you when you feel playful and then expect him not to do it when you are no longer in the mood—it is too confusing for him. Consistency is the only sure cure. In most cases where this problem exists, you will find that the owner encourages the dog to jump up once or twice a week. The rest of the time the owner does not like it and yells at the dog when he jumps. It is precisely because of this inconsistency that the dog jumps on anyone who pays the slightest attention to him. One must answer the question: Do you want him to jump on you or not?

If the answer is no, then a correction (the corrective jerk and a firm "No") will stop him in most cases, providing that you maintain that attitude. If you give in just once, you will destroy the training. If you teach a puppy not to jump by correcting him when he tries it, he will never do it unless you permit him that one time.

Puppies can be taught with the use of a shake can. (How to use it is based on the dog's temperament.) Whenever the puppy tries to jump or climb up on you or anyone else, shake the can vigorously and say "No" in a very firm tone of voice. Do not scare the little dog, simply command his attention and impress on him that his behavior is displeasing. Once you have made the correction and he responds properly, then give him affectionate praise. Do not bend over and pet him or he'll jump again. Tell him he's a good dog in a friendly voice. He will soon understand that he doesn't have to jump to get your love.

In the case of a grown dog who has been indulging in this behavior for a while, use a different technique that's based on the same principle. Arrange for a relative to have the dog on leash and training collar before you come home. When you walk in the door and the dog makes a jump, the person holding the leash gives him a corrective jerk (use is based on the dog's temperament) and a very firm "No." Assuming the dog has been obedience trained, he should be commanded to sit immediately following the correction. Give him his praise after he obeys the command. If the dog has not yet been obedience trained, then the corrective jerk must be done with vigor as you jerk to the right side. He may still try to jump after the first jerk. Simply do it again until he stops. If this process is repeated several times in one evening, you will be surprised at the results.

If the infraction occurs outside, do not merely pull the dog away. Give him a corrective jerk to the right and walk in the opposite direction. This jerk will cause the dog enough discomfort to discourage him from trying it again. Do it every time he jumps up, and you will solve the problem. But remember, if you or anyone else encourages the dog to jump up, this training will have no effect. You must ask everyone who comes in contact with the dog not to give the animal any invitations.

No cruel or excessively harsh techniques (that have been used in the past) are recommended, such as kneeing the dog in the chest or stepping on his toes. These painful techniques are not necessary if you remember to be consistent in your demands.

MOUNTING

A dog mounting a human is a serious problem. It is upsetting, and even dangerous in some situations. It can occur at any time during the life of a dog and usually involves the male of the species. Mounting is when a male dog jumps on a human, places his paws around some part of the human body (usually the leg), and goes through the motions of sexual intercourse. In rare instances, an aroused dog may mount a vertical object such as a piece of furniture. A dominant dog in the process of mounting, or one who is too intense to stop when ordered, may bite when attempts are made to stop him. It is especially dangerous for children who panic easily in this situation. The problem may begin soon after sexual maturity, but mounting has occurred in puppies of six months of age and even younger. Female dogs usually display no sexual behavior except during their estrous cycles (heat), but male dogs can become sexually aroused at any time. The first sexual stirrings of puberty make them active. Temperament can be a factor in creating a greater sex drive in some male dogs. Such dogs usually have dominant, aggressive temperaments.

If an unneutered male dog has never been mated and has little opportunity to release his pent-up energy in daily exercise, frustration may cause him to mount a person's leg. If he is constantly segregated from female dogs, he will probably develop strong human attachments, which can, at times, be sexual in nature. Often, nervous or excitable dogs are more easily aroused. Some dogs are stimulated by close contact with women who are menstruating. The habit of mounting is not simply embarrassing; it can lead to serious injuries. If a large dog attempts to mount a young child he can inflict mental and physical wounds. Any mounting behavior should be dealt with immediately. Sexual neutering (castration) is the most obvious answer. See a veterinarian. Another possible solution is to give a dog who mounts plenty of daily exercise, allowing him to work off his sexual energy.

Until these solutions are permanently effective, it is essential to correct the dog each and every time he mounts. Put his training collar and leash on him and wait for him to mount. The minute he tries it, administer a hard corrective jerk (use is based on the dog's temperament) and say "No" in a firm voice. Make the correction a tough one, and do not allow the dog to get very far before administering it. If the dog is permitted to mount with intensity, he may snap when you try to stop him. It is best to stop him as quickly as possible. A loud rattling of the shake can may be used effectively as an alternative to the corrective jerk. And this is one of the few circumstances where we recommend raising your knee to the dog's chest to knock him down. No matter which technique you use, it should be made very clear, as soon as possible, that mounting humans is totally unacceptable behavior.

NIPPING

All puppies have a teething problem, as do all infants. Because teething is painful, puppies bite or nip to ease the pressure of the incoming teeth. They will bite hands, fingers, toys, and furniture. Sometimes they are encouraged to bite if the owner makes a habit of placing his hand in the animal's mouth when playing. This is like teaching the dog to bite. There are several ways to ease the teething discomfort. One method is to soak a wash cloth in cold water and place it in the freezer. When it is frozen, give it to the dog to chew. The coldness will numb his gums and relieve the pain. Consequently, he will not bite as much. (This is just like the common practice of refrigerating babies' teething rings.)

Another approach to the problem is to give the puppy a rawhide or synthetic chew toy. It is not suggested that the dog be given an old discarded shoe or sock. You will be sorry later when the dog will not be able to distinguish between an old shoe and a new one. The rawhide toys may be used in conjunction with the frozen washcloth.

It is important to solve the nipping problem early in the dog's life because it can lead to a serious biting problem later. The puppy should always be discouraged from nipping at your fingers or anything else. It is better to substitute a rawhide toy for your fingers than to inflict a harsh punishment or scolding. All the yelling, hitting, or finger pointing in the world is not going to stop the dog's teeth from growing and giving him pain. And if you scare the dog when he is a young puppy, he may grow shy or aggressive and then you will have a biting problem that is much more difficult to solve.

RUNNING OUT OF THE HOUSE

This is a problem that could mean life or death for the dog. If he runs out the door and into the street he could be struck by a car, and good-bye dog. Most dog owners either have had this problem or are still experiencing it. Even if a dog has had some form of basic obedience course and has been taught the *Sit-Stay*, he will still attempt to run out the front door if given half a chance. The reason is simple. Going through the front door represents a happy experience to the dog. It is through that door that he is taken outside to play, to relieve himself, to see children and other animals. Obviously, he is primed at a second's notice to go dashing out to the never-never land of fun and games. He must be taught that he can go through the door only when given permission.

In order to break him of this habit, set up an artificial situation so that he can be corrected when he tries to run out. Put his training collar and training leash on and keep it in hand. Prearrange to have someone ring the doorbell. Place the dog in *Sit-Stay*. Tell the person to come in. The door should open and be left open. When the dog bolts for the door, give him an extremely firm corrective jerk (use is based on the dog's temperament), shout "No," and turn around and walk the other way. Then place him in *Sit-Stay* again. Every time the doorbell rings he should be placed in *Sit-Stay*. Repeat the procedure several times a day until he no longer tries to run out. It may take a few days, but it's well worth the effort.

When practicing, make sure you maintain absolute control of the dog. He may not respond properly at first, and if you do not keep a firm grip on the leash, he will run out. Do not lose the dog in the process of teaching him. Any time he makes a lunge for the door, give him a firm corrective jerk (use is based on the dog's temperament) and walk the other way. Praise the dog after each and every correction. Maintain a good relationship with him so that he doesn't think he is being punished. Test the dog's level of training by placing him in *Sit-Stay*. Then open the door and see if he'll remain in position. (At no time should you let go of the leash.) Once the dog is responding well, you can then answer the door yourself as the dog walks with you. Place him in *Sit-Stay* before opening the door and chances are he will no longer run out.

TAKING FOOD FROM THE TABLE

Stealing food from a set table or kitchen counter is not considered one of the more serious pet problems. As a matter of fact, almost every dog owner has at least one such favorite story about his little Princess. However, the habit is annoying and can cause considerable expense in view of the high cost of sirloin.

This problem is somewhat similar to that of begging, which is covered elsewhere in this chapter. There are two things necessary to cure the dog of this bad habit. First, never feed the dog anything from the table or kitchen countertops. Make this a hard-and-fast rule and do not allow anyone to violate it. This alone, after a while, will end the habit of your dog expecting a reward for "hanging around." Next, bait him. After placing the leash and collar on him, let him roam around as he pleases. Take a small quantity of freshly cooked food or food that you know appeals to him and leave it on a table or countertop. Step back and wait. When the dog goes for it, as he surely will, grab the leash and administer a firm corrective jerk (use is based on the dog's temperament) accompanied by a loud "No." Immediately afterward, praise him for obeying. Repeat this several times until he no longer tries to steal the food.

The use of the shake can is also very effective (how to use it is based on the dog's temperament). Say "No" and shake the can vigorously. This type of correction will startle him and help to end the annoying habit.

TALKING BACK

One of the cutest things a dog can do is bark at you after you give him a command. It is especially true in the case of a puppy. People fall to the ground in laughter and many an owner actually regards it as though it were a terrific trick that he has taught the dog. The problem is that it is all too often an expression of defiance and unwillingness to respond to commands. Experience has proven that it leads to aggressiveness, and the dog, in some cases, becomes a bully. Usually, when a dog is given a command it is for a good reason and therefore should not be disobeyed, ignored, or protested. As undemocratic as it sounds, the only correct relationship between a dog and his master is pure feudalism. Dogs are totally dependent on their masters for everything connected with their well-being, and a command is almost always in the best interests of the dog. Therefore, he must obey, and talking back is an indication of disobedience.

If your dog barks or howls at you aggressively or defiantly after you give him a command, he should be corrected. The corrective jerk with the leash and training collar accompanied by a firm "No" will end this behavior (its use is based on the dog's temperament). Don't forget to praise him immediately after the correction.

III.

100 Dog Breeds:

A Dictionary of

Training Behavior

The purpose of Part III is to provide you with information that pertains to training the various dog breeds. No two dogs are exactly alike and each breed has its own typical behavioral characteristics. The information in each entry tells you about the training challenges associated with each breed. Guidelines and advice are also offered. There is no information provided here about breed history, grooming requirements, show standards, height, weight, or the cost of puppies. (There are many fine books available with that information.) Rather, this Dictionary of Training Behavior assumes that you already have a dog, and is meant to help you train your dog based on behavioral information given for his breed. If your dog is not a purebred, you can still benefit from this section by looking at entries for the breeds that your dog resembles.

Each entry consists of three categories: Positive characteristics, Negative characteristics, and Specific training advice. The entries are based on adult examples of each breed. This information will be useful to those who would like to know what to expect from their dog once they begin training him.

Whether you have already purchased a dog or are about to do so, this section will be of considerable help. It explores the training demands unique to the specific breeds included in the section. A

German Shepherd Dog, for example, will pose different training questions from those of a Toy Poodle. These differences are the essence of this part of the book.

The Dictionary of Training Behavior is based on information gathered in the best way possible—from experience. It represents a synthesis of the firsthand experience that coauthor Matthew Margolis has gained in his capacity as owner-operator of the National Institute of Dog Training, Inc. in Los Angeles, California. He has trained many thousands of dogs representing every breed included here. And he has supervised the training of 25,000 dogs that have come through the obedience course at his training facility. Where a breed has been omitted, it is simply because he has had too little experience with it.

The dogs he has trained have come from every conceivable source. Many have been among the most expensive dogs from the best kennels. Others have come from pet shops, adoption agencies, shelters and pounds, private kennels, commercial kennels, and home litters.

Not all examples of each breed are alike, but when one trains hundreds of dogs of a particular breed, behavioral patterns become apparent. These patterns formulate the basis for the observations offered in the breed entries. The Dictionary of Training Behavior is not intended to praise one breed at the expense of another; after all, trainability is not the only important aspect of your dog's personality. But this is a training book, and this section will help you understand the training problems you are most likely to face with your particular breed. Your dog may not be *exactly* like the description of its breed; on the contrary, inconsistencies and contradictions are to be expected. Each dog has its own genetic background, particular environmental influences, factors of socialization, and *established* breed characteristics. You must compare your dog with its breed description and decide what to use and what to reject of the offered advice.

The authors have tried to make a fair appraisal of each dog's temperament *as it pertains to dog training*. This is based on observation and personal experience with many examples of the breeds described. The source of the dog and its early life are important factors if one is to make an accurate evaluation. A specific dog may come from a superior bloodline, and that certainly would be a factor in his behavioral characteristics. The opposite of this is also true: Some breeds are the victims of commercialization, which results in nonselective breeding. When a breed becomes very popular and there is a public demand for it, commercial breeders begin overproducing it without the slightest consideration for serious temperament problems or inherited medical problems. Reputable breeders are usually sophisticated in their knowledge of genetics and quite upstanding about selective breeding. They know better than to mate dogs who do not measure up to what is acceptable for their breeds. Unfortunately, there are many, many dogs who are uncharacteristic of their breeds and they are the result of commercial indifference or a mistaken devotion to a breed's appearance at the expense of behavior.

Thus, far too many examples of a particular breed exhibit traits uncharacteristic of the breed's traditional personality and temperament. That is why dog trainers often disagree with dog fanciers in their views of breed behavior. Every day they are asked to step in and deal with the sorrowful results of poor breeding. Dog trainers are usually the first to know about deviations from the normal characteristics of a breed. The authors believe that all dogs are good until proven otherwise.

Note: (AKC) next to the breed name means it is accepted for registration by the American Kennel Club. (UKC) next to the breed name means it is accepted for registration by the United Kennel Club.

AFGHAN HOUND (AKC, UKC)

Positive characteristics: Afghans are gentle yet bold dogs who love their families. They are beautiful, with a regal manner that has attracted many to the breed. These dogs have a quality of elegance and an air of royalty about them, like an old British colonial reflecting on days of Empire. Afghans are like expensive cars. They are often acquired as an element of conspicuous consumption; Afghan owners believe the breed has a touch of class about it. Over many centuries the breed has been identified with royalty; during the great days of the British Empire, Afghans were used for hunting the leopard. Despite their haughty, delicate look, they were first-rate hunters in the mountainous regions of Afghanistan. In the United States these aristocratic coursing hounds have been used primarily as show dogs and pets.

Negative characteristics: These are stubborn dogs and consequently offer much resistance to training. They lack motivation and are slow learners. It is extremely hard to train them. Where most breeds can begin training from eight to twelve weeks of age, Afghans will not respond to training until they are at least six or seven months old. By that time, housebreaking becomes extremely difficult. Housebreaking should begin early. Many owners have experienced some degree of success by exercising great patience.

The Afghan's tolerance for children is low. They can be aggressive bullies.

Specific training advice: Patience is absolutely essential. These dogs cannot be treated like any other breed. You must take your time throughout the training period. Give the dog lavish praise when he obeys a command.

Do not use a metal training collar because it will ruin the silken fur. Either a leather or nylon training collar is suggested. Do not work this breed for long periods, especially when teaching *Heel* and *Down*. Break up the training periods so there are more sessions for shorter periods of time.

Unless you are home a great deal and can walk this breed five or six times a day, you are going to have a terrible time housebreaking. An Afghan must be caught in the act of messing indoors before he can be taught to understand what you expect.

Members of this breed do not want to be left alone. They can be very destructive and chew valuable furniture and personal possessions. Because of their stubbornness, you will have to be extremely firm teaching the *Down* and *Down-Stay*. Despite the Afghan's great beauty and elegance, the training period is a battle of wills between human and dog.

AIREDALE TERRIER (AKC, UKC)

Positive characteristics: In a physical sense, these are probably the best of the terriers. They are tall, dignified animals with a rugged, beautiful stance. Airedales make excellent guard dogs. They are very protective of their homes and families and make a lot of noise whenever an intruder crosses the family threshold. They are fearless in any confrontation, and they never back down. An almost perfect family dog, Airedales respond to training very well because of their fine temperaments and quick responses. These remarkable dogs are wonderful in the country mostly because of their keen hunting abilities. On the other hand, they adapt well to city life and get along with children.

Negative characteristics: Like all terrier breeds, Airedales are very stubborn, strong-willed, and independent. Unless they are taught obedience with a firm hand, they are not enjoyable to have around. They get spoiled and try to dominate their households. They are diggers, chewers, barkers, and tend to jump on people. Some Airedale Terriers are dog fighters.

Specific training advice: Airedales are very good house pets. They are always responsive during training and are very alert. They are willing to please. Most problems can be avoided if training begins early, if the dog is taught what to do, and if he is made to obey and not allowed to ignore any commands. Give him lavish praise when he obeys a command. If you allow a year or a year and a half to go by before beginning training, you will have many difficult problems ahead of you.

AKBASH DOG

Positive characteristics: The Akbash has joined the ranks of those breeds being certified as Independence Dogs for wheelchair-bound owners. Few people know much about this Turkish breed because it is rare in North America. However, the certification as an Independence Dog is a good indication of its gentle nature. In addition to its excellent temperament and striking looks, it makes an excellent watchdog. Over the centuries it was bred to be a decision-making dog rather than one that obeyed blindly. These brilliant dogs are used to herd and guard flocks of sheep in Turkey.

Negative characteristics: Akbash dogs are very strong-willed, which makes them undesirable for easygoing families and owners who are inclined to be soft in matters of discipline. They are fighters and do not adapt to apartment living very well.

They also do not adapt well to change. This is a dominant breed that can be quite aloof, which is not to everyone's taste.

Specific training advice: These are highly trainable dogs, but you must be firm and consistent. You need patience, but they do train well. It will help to give an Akbash space and daily exercise to help him focus on the commands. Obviously, with such a strong-willed, independent breed, obedience training is a must. Akbash dogs can be good with children if they are introduced to the family when they are puppies. They will mature slowly with the kids, and they don't reach physical maturity until they are three years old.

AKITA (AKC, UKC)

Positive characteristics: The Akita is a formidable animal, a large, strong dog that can adapt to city as well as country life. The Akita's massive appearance and assertive personality make it an excellent watchdog. It is very playful and can take rigorous sessions with children. A prospective owner should research all the possible sources in search of a breeder that values good temperament. The Akita needs a very firm owner, although females are much easier to handle than males.

Negative characteristics: Many Akitas become one-family dogs and are very protective of that family. In a desire to encourage that protective instinct, some owners encourage growling and antisocial behavior. This breed has the potential to become aggressive as well as protective—the two qualities are very different and must not be confused. In fact, the best watchdogs are the friendliest ones. Dogs who are kept away from strangers, supposedly to make them suspicious of outsiders, cannot distinguish between a friendly guest and an intruder.

If breeders and owners socialize Akita puppies with many different kinds of people in many different situations, and provide many social opportunities with other dogs, the well-bred adult dog will be intelligent, playful, and protective without being aggressive.

Akitas are known to be dog fighters and must be socialized as young puppies to modify that characteristic. An adult dog's temperament should be evaluated by a professional trainer before a young child is introduced to the dog, especially in the dog's home. Akitas are hard to handle and require a firm, authoritative owner. They are notorious diggers, and engage in destructive chewing.

Although some people prefer a dog who relates only to his family, most will find it too difficult to deal with the dog's antisocial behavior. Early socialization is an important element in choosing or raising an Akita.

Specific training advice: The key to training this strong-willed, very stubborn breed is to begin training the puppy as soon as possible. Because the dog is so large, *Down* should be taught at a young age. *Heel* will be difficult because of the dog's strength. One of the most important commands for this breed is the *Come When Called.* With *Come When Called,* the owner can control the dog's very territorial instincts in the yard and redirect the dog's attention when he is initiating an aggressive action toward another dog. One must demand instant obedience with this breed and administer firm corrections. This firmness will pay off later.

Akitas are big and playful and love to jump on people. Where jumping might be tolerated in a smaller breed, it quickly becomes unmanageable and even dangerous in an animal this large and energetic. To prevent the problem, jumping must not be allowed from the very beginning, when the dog is a relatively small puppy.

ALASKAN MALAMUTE (AKC, UKC)

Positive characteristics: These dogs are like teddy bears. They are large, furry playmates and enjoy the roughhouse treatment of children. Children have been known to ride them like horses. Although it is not recommended, the breed can take a lot of punishment. These are cold-weather dogs who can stand being outside the house for many hours during the winter months. Their fur is so thick that they are capable of enduring the coldest temperature without feeling it. However, they adapt to apartment life very well. They do not require too much exercise and behave lethargically when indoors.

Negative characteristics: Malamutes are long-coated and shed a great deal. They are very stubborn and difficult to train. Many of them become aggressive. These dogs need the firm hand of a strong person. Many of them are diggers, chewers, and dog-fighters.

Specific training advice: Although a metal training collar is required for a firm correction, do not leave it on all the time. It will wear away the fur around the animal's neck.

Malamutes will housebreak satisfactorily if they are walked often and watched carefully during the training period. Obedience training must begin at an early age. These are stubborn dogs and not inclined to please their masters. They will constantly test you to see how much they can get away with. Give lavish praise when a command is obeyed.

If a Malamute is not trained properly he will become aggressive. He must not be hit, punished, or bombarded with "No." There have been several cases where Malamutes have become aggressive with their owners. It is not because this is a vicious breed, but rather because the owners believed a large dog requires harsh punishments.

Heel is one of the most important lessons for these dogs. They grow to ninety or one hundred pounds and can pull you down the street. Be firm and demanding with them at an early age. *Come When Called* off-leash presents a problem. At times a Malamute will refuse to respond. This command should be emphasized at all times.

Be very firm with a Malamute and make him obey as quickly as possible. Do not tolerate a refusal to respond to any command. Firm corrections are needed. The key to training this dog is to start when he is very young.

AMERICAN ESKIMO (MINIATURE, STANDARD) (UKC)

Positive characteristics: These are highly energized, attractive little white dogs. They are quick learners and make enjoyable family pets. Although they are small, they are good watchdogs. American Eskimos can live well in both the city and the country. They are clean animals. They are typical northern working dogs—alert, strong, and agile. The American Eskimo is admired for its thick, white coat and richly plumed tail. Its typical disposition is energetic and friendly, but conservative.

Negative characteristics: When bred badly, this dog can be strong-willed and aggressive, as well as shy. Hitting him will definitely turn him into a biter. Obtaining a puppy from a reputable breeder is of primary importance. Before bringing an American Eskimo into your home, whether it is a puppy or an older dog, have a professional trainer evaluate the dog's temperament.

These cute, bouncing little dogs love to jump on people, dig, and chew; they are excessive barkers; they have a tendency to be dogfighters; and they can be difficult to housebreak.

Specific training advice: Cuteness is the biggest problem because their owners let them get away with everything when they are puppies. That causes the development of aggressive and shy behavior patterns as they mature. Once these behavior patterns set in, it is very difficult to change them. They are very sensitive dogs and have a low tolerance for voice or leash corrections, especially after being spoiled. At the first instance of aggressive behavior, the owner should consult a professional dog trainer.

If training is begun at an early age and discipline maintained, this breed is pleasant to live with and take on vacations. Give him lots of exercise to help use up excess energy.

AMERICAN PIT BULL TERRIER (UKC)

Positive characteristics: Pit Bulls have a sweet, affectionate personality and are wonderful with children. They are playful, clownish, and quite vigorous. To know them is to love them. They thrive in the city or the country. Like most dogs they love to play ball and fetch sticks. The American Pit Bull Terrier is a remarkable companion animal.

Negative characteristics: Like most terrier breeds, they love to dig, chew, and jump on people. At times they are too exuberant and difficult to control unless they are obedience trained. Pit Bulls are highly territorial and have a tendency to be dogfighters unless discouraged from this behavior.

When American Pit Bull Terriers are not bred for good temperament, not socialized as puppies, or deliberately agitated to make them vicious, they are dangerous. Because of exploitive media coverage of several biting incidents and the behavior of various bad owners, attempts have been made to ban this breed in some communities through discriminatory breed legislation.

Unfortunately, this breed, and several others bearing a similar appearance, have been used in the illegal sport of dog-fighting and for the purpose of intimidation by criminals. They have misused the intelligence and strength of these dogs for wrongdoing and have caused harmful incidents to occur, which have been blown out of proportion in the media. The American Pit Bull Terrier is often mistaken for the American Staffordshire Terrier, the Staffordshire Bull Terrier, the Bull Terrier, the Boxer, the Bulldog, and various mongrelized versions of these breeds. Only dogs registered with the United Kennel Club can claim to be American Pit Bull Terriers.

Specific training advice: Pit Bulls like obedience training and hard work. They excel at it because they like to please. They are extremely exuberant dogs and require a firm hand and a great deal of exercise prior to each training session. Because of their stubborn temperament they require firm corrections and a no-nonsense attitude form their trainer. Never play tug-of-war or other aggressive games with them. Such game playing conditions them to use their teeth and promotes aggressive behavior. Aggressive Pit Bulls past the age of ten months must be evaluated by a professional dog trainer. Dogs acquired from a responsible breeder who has socialized the puppies will be easy to train.

AMERICAN STAFFORDSHIRE TERRIER (AKC)

Positive characteristics: The Am Staff is a very playful, outgoing breed. They are great athletes; they love to play ball and Frisbee, and they can take a lot of rough-and-tumble play with children. These are very alert, bright dogs. If the dog comes from a reputable breeder who has socialized the puppy well, it makes a great all-around pet and watchdog.

Negative characteristics: This breed is often aggressive to other dogs and to people if not properly socialized at an early age. If the dog does not get to meet many new people and other dogs in new and different situations, he is going to be aggressive and very territorial. That can be a big problem because this animal can be a formidable weapon in the wrong hands. The person holding the leash determines whether the American Staffordshire Terrier will be a loving family pet or something quite different.

These are energetic dogs. They often dig and chew destructively. They also love to jump on people and furniture.

Specific training advice: Am Staffs need *a lot* of exercise. Owners should begin obedience training at an early age and must be very firm in giving commands and corrections. *Down* may prove to be a tough one.

These are strong-willed dogs, but they are extremely intelligent, which makes them very responsive to training. However, owners must be consistent and maintain control. Playing tug-of-war and other aggressive games with this breed leads to aggressive behavior and biting.

AUSTRALIAN SHEPHERD (UKC)

Positive characteristics: These are brilliant working dogs. Their desire to please makes them highly trainable. They are very outgoing dogs, very agile. When they are socialized at a young age, they are friendly with people and love to play ball and Frisbee with children. Like all herding breeds, they have a naturally protective nature.

Negative characteristics: Australian Shepherds can be reserved with strangers, sometimes quite shy. And, if not socialized at a young age, they can also be aggressive. These drawbacks, in combination with their active natures, may make them a problem for elderly people. As a breed they can be chewers, diggers, and excessive barkers. They often like to mouth people or nip their hands, which should be stopped before it becomes an entrenched habit.

Specific training advice: Active dogs such as these must be trained or they will be too much to handle. Training must begin at a young age or it will be a difficult chore. Training should be given by a strong-willed person. Give lots of exercise to help work off that energy. Because of their abundant energy, they are easily distracted. Begin training in a quiet location and then bring them to busy, crowded areas. They love to jump up, and that must not be encouraged. Be consistent in your firmness or they will take advantage of you. These are incredible working dogs, and thorough obedience training can make them a pleasure to own as pets.

BASENJI (AKC, UKC)

Positive characteristics: Basenjis are good-tempered, loving, and affectionate animals. They are highly individualistic dogs who tend to attach themselves devotedly and loyally to one person. Adapting to city life very well, they make excellent apartment dogs. These are quiet dogs who never bark. They are responsive to training and indicate a willingness to please.

Results are the best if training begins at a young age. These enjoyable animals are distinguished by their almost human-looking faces. They are good with children and can take the rigors of child's play if they are raised with children. Because this is not a nervous breed, Basenjis can be left alone for many hours and still maintain their even temperaments.

Negative characteristics: Since they are stubborn dogs, we do not recommend them for elderly people. Once they decide to do something you will have to match their obstinacy with your firm authority every inch of the way. They like to chew, dig, and sit on furniture. Because they are "barkless," they make poor watchdogs.

Specific training advice: Because of their stubbornness, be sure to give each command properly. Be very firm and let them know who is boss. Give lavish praise after the dog obeys a command.

BASSET HOUND (AKC, UKC)

Positive characteristics: Bassets are very good with children and make excellent house pets. Because they are not very active, they never run wild through the house. Don't expect excitement with a Basset; his lethargic demeanor joined with his droopy face is considered part of his charm. This breed has come into its own since advertising agencies discovered the dogs' amusing appeal and started making salesmen out of them on TV commercials. Bassets are ideal apartment pets. They enjoy a normal life span (twelve to fifteen years) and have gentle, sweet temperaments. Bassets respond very well to training, even past the training period of the average dog.

Negative characteristics: Basset Hounds are diggers and chewers. Housebreaking is sometimes a problem, but that can be overcome if training begins early. Many Bassets are picky eaters.

Specific training advice: Pay attention to the long, floppy ears when administering the corrective jerk. They sometimes tangle in the training collar and leash, which can be very painful for the dog. In some cases the training collar is not recommended. Whether or not to use it would be determined by the temperament of the dog. Use a soft nylon collar instead.

In *Heel,* your dog is going to have difficulty keeping up with you. Bassets walk much more slowly than other breeds and have trouble keeping up a brisk pace. It also takes them longer to go into the *Sit* than it does other breeds. You should make allowances. The *Stay* will be the easiest command. Maybe it's because Bassets don't like getting up too often.

They respond more to praise and affection than correction. Give them lavish praise when they obey a command. It is recommended that the corrective jerk be administered gently and not too often. You will get better results from a loving, gentle tone than from firm discipline. The *Down* and *Come When Called* are good commands for them. These lovable animals are endearing and can make training sessions a delightful experience. Most professional trainers enjoy working with Basset Hounds.

BEAGLE (AKC, UKC)

Positive characteristics: Beagles adjust well to apartment life or country life. These sweet little dogs look like stuffed toys and are very good with children. They are usually gentle and playful, with pleasing personalities. They are hardy eaters with a good life span (twelve to fifteen years).

Negative characteristics: Because this is a stubborn breed, many owners try to use force to get their way. The consequences are many. Most important is that the dogs become aggressive and nasty if mistreated. They have been known to become aggressive with their families, growl, bite children, and get into dogfights. They love to dig and chew, they have a tendency to bark excessively, and there could be a housebreaking problem if you don't start training at a young age. Much of this can be avoided if one exercises patience and a minimum of discipline. Force will only bring out the worst in a Beagle. The key to its training is to maintain an attitude of teaching as opposed to one of harsh discipline.

Specific training advice: Start training early to avoid the negative aspects described above. Even though they are stubborn, Beagles are easy to teach at a young age. Take care not to catch their ears when administering the corrective jerk. A metal training collar is not recommended if you are going to teach a puppy. Use nylon or leather. An older Beagle can tolerate a very fine metal training collar.

Be firm but not harsh. Most of the basic commands will be relatively easy to teach. However, Beagles offer resistance to the *Down* command. Give them lavish praise.

When training these dogs, select a location that offers few, if any, distractions. You must command a Beagle's attention more than most breeds.

BEARDED COLLIE (AKC, UKC)

Positive characteristics: Lots of hair, lots of fun, lots of energy make this breed ideally suited for the rigors of children. This wonderful midsize dog is good for city or country life. Beardies learn quickly, and they make excellent watchdogs.

Negative characteristics: Some bright dogs are stubborn and strong-willed, and the Beardie falls into that category. They love to dig and chew, they have a tendency to bark excessively, and there could be a housebreaking problem if training isn't started at a young age.

Specific training advice: The energy of animals like this needs to be released regularly if they are going to do their best in training and in social situations. They love to jump on people, and they should be stopped from the very beginning. Beardies develop the best relationships with their families when they begin training very early.

They are very easily distracted, so train in a quiet place at first and then bring them out to more distractions when they are confident with the commands. With strong-willed dogs, one tends to use a firm hand, but when Beardies are trained with an overly firm hand, they can become aggressive; if they are trained with too gentle a hand, they ignore it completely. They can be difficult dogs to handle. This is a lot of dog. If you must err, lean toward being too gentle. But do not let a Beardie get away with too much.

BEDLINGTON TERRIER (AKC, UKC)

Positive characteristics: Bedlington Terriers are unusual-looking dogs with their curly coats and topknots creating the appearance of a lamb. Despite their aggressive tendency toward other dogs, they are lovable pets and make fine companion animals. They are excellent with considerate children and adjust well to family life, providing there are no other animals living with them. Bedlingtons are easygoing when indoors unless aroused by a dog or cat. They are very alert watchdogs.

Negative characteristics: Like all terriers, the Bedlington has a stubborn quality. Whether this is negative depends on each owner's point of view. They are aggressive toward other dogs, and they are chewers and diggers.

Specific training advice: Because these dogs are stubborn and strong-willed, you must be firm in all corrections. Exercise patience during the training period and give the dog plenty of time to learn each command before initiating any corrections.

Bedlingtons will test you quite often, so you mustn't be afraid to correct them. They are very sturdy little dogs and can take any reasonable correction. The trick is not to overjerk them.

BELGIAN SHEEPDOG (AKC, UKC)

Positive characteristics: The Belgian Sheepdog is a high-energy breed that excels at obedience training, tracking, protection work, and search-and-rescue work. They are athletic animals who make good sled dogs and good herding dogs. They are lovable, obedient, and gentle with their friends and family. These solid black dogs were bred for herding and guarding and are alert watchdogs by nature. This breed thrives best in a rural setting.

Negative characteristics: They have too much energy for elderly people or apartment living. Some poorly bred specimens may have aggressive tendencies. Belgian Sheepdogs have a reputation for being very clever at getting loose and escaping from fenced-in areas. They also have a reputation for excessive barking and chewing.

Specific training advice: Training is essential because of their great energy and great curiosity. They must be trained early and well. Exercise them vigorously, especially before training sessions. This breed is easily distracted and must be taught in a quiet area at first. Be patient and the results will be great. Obedience training is a mental and physical challenge and another way for them to exercise: They love it and excel in obedience competition.

BERNESE MOUNTAIN DOG (AKC, UKC)

Positive characteristics: These are wonderful house and apartment dogs and are very good with children. These ancient Swiss aristocrats are extremely gentle and have even temperaments. Bernese Mountain Dogs are all-weather animals. They are very loyal and focus their affections exclusively on their own families.

Negative characteristics: The large size of this dog makes him difficult to handle during the teaching process. Bernese tend to jump on people and engage in destructive chewing. These problems must be dealt with at an early age.

Specific training advice: This is a very sensitive breed. Be patient and gentle in all training commands. Too many hard corrections will make the dog jerk-shy.

If using a metal training collar, do not leave it on the animal for long periods of time. It can wear away the long fur around the neck.

BICHON FRISE (AKC, UKC)

Positive characteristics: These fluffy white bundles of energy are great pets. They love to play and can take reasonable rough-housing from children. Bichons enjoy training because they love to please people. Although they need an outlet for their energy, Bichons adapt well to the city as well as the country.

Negative characteristics: Teaching others how to pronounce Bichon Frise may be the hardest problem the owner faces (Bee·*shon* Free·*zay*). The breed has become so popular in recent years that many Bichons are not being bred selectively. Poorly bred Bichons may show shyness or snappiness. The search for a reliable breeder will be worthwhile.

Bichons tend to be destructive chewers, very yappy, and excessive barkers.

Specific training advice: To train a Bichon one must be firm and consistent, not because Bichons are strong or stubborn, which they are not, but because they are so cute. Owners love Bichons on laps and furniture and can be charmed out of training commands with alarming ease.

Housebreaking can be difficult. Territorial marking instincts are particularly strong in Bichons. The best remedies are an early decision on whether to housebreak or paper train, and early obedience training. Project your future life-style into the decision.

Start the training in a quiet area. Bichons have a tendency to get distracted. They are high-energy dogs. The combination makes them easily distracted by anything that moves, including people, cars, and other animals. Once they seem to understand what is expected of them, try the lessons in a busy area.

BLACK AND TAN COONHOUND (AKC, UKC)

Positive characteristics: Black and Tans are affectionate. They enjoy the country much more than the city. They are very responsive to training and have excellent appetites.

Negative characteristics: These dogs are not well suited to city life. Like many of the hound breeds, they do not adapt well to the restrictions of a small apartment. You must be on top of them all the time. Their attention span in the city is poor, owing to their inclination to wander, both mentally and physically.

Specific training advice: As is true of many hounds, Black and Tans abound in energy and require a great deal of exercise. There is nothing like a good long run to make them more responsive to training. A good daily exercise program will help them work off their nervous energy and make them easier to live with in the city.

BLOODHOUND (AKC, UKC)

Positive characteristics: These are great, fun-loving dogs. They are very loyal and remarkably docile. And, of course, they are highly proficient tracking dogs. The breed is lovable and somewhat seductive. For the right people, these are wonderful companion animals.

Negative characteristics: Some Bloodhounds are shy. Because they are easygoing animals, they need patient, loving owners. They have been known to bark and they do have some skin and eye problems. Their aloof, reserved disposition is sometimes mistaken for arrogance.

Specific training advice: Bloodhounds are very strong-willed in their own laid-back fashion. They require a firm owner with a firm hand. Yet they're very sensitive. Be authoritative and consistent without being harsh. Patience is necessary when training this breed because Bloodhounds are lethargic, strong-willed, slow to respond to commands and corrections, and physically strong. *Heel* is a very important command to teach as soon as possible. Use a nylon training collar to avoid hurting the long ears—a metal collar could damage them.

BORZOI (RUSSIAN WOLFHOUND) (AKC, UKC)

Positive characteristics: These are marvelous, elegant-looking dogs. Thin and lanky, they move with great speed and dash. Many city-dwellers consider them status symbols and very chic to own. Borzois are regal in stature. In most instances, they are purchased for reasons of ornamentation, or perhaps ostentation. These tall beauties are easygoing and capable of staying put for many hours in the position in which they were placed. Because they are not too active, they make excellent city pets. They are quiet, dignified animals who are very willing to please. In their natural habitat Borzois are hunters, and for that reason are very well suited to country living.

Negative characteristics: Borzois are not especially suitable for children. They can be aggressive if pushed too hard. They do not respond well to rough treatment. Like cats, they are aloof animals. Picking a puppy with an easygoing temperament is the key to having a successful relationship with a dog of this breed.

Specific training advice: One need not administer too many firm corrections. Giving them a great deal of praise whenever they respond properly will get better results than overcorrection.

Be gentle with the leash because Borzois resist constant jerking. Show them what to do and they will do it.

BOSTON TERRIER (AKC, UKC)

Positive characteristics: The Boston Terrier is one of the very few purebreds originating in the United States. Like most Yankees, they were developed from English stock. They are a cross between the Bulldog and the English Terrier. In existence only since the Civil War, they have firmly secured a place for themselves in the world of purebred dogs. Though very strong, Boston Terriers are small in size. They range from fifteen to twenty-five pounds.

These unusual-looking animals were used for many years as the advertising symbol for Buster Brown shoes: *"I'm Buster Brown, I live in a shoe. This is my dog Tige, he lives there, too."* Many children grew up with the Boston Terrier in mind as the ideal child's dog because of this ad. Bostons are lovable animals and are wonderful for children. They are gentle but rugged dogs. They make excellent pets for elderly people, too. For those who are looking for a small, lively dog who does not require too much exercise, this is it.

Negative characteristics: Like most Terrier breeds, the Boston manifests a stubborn, aggressive streak. Bostons are also extremely sensitive.

Specific training advice: These dogs have a difficult time being housebroken. They must be watched carefully and walked frequently. Because of their stubbornness, you must be firm and constant in making them obey. Take your time with each command and give them lavish praise whenever they respond correctly.

BOUVIER DES FLANDRES (AKC, UKC)

Positive characteristics: These large, shaggy animals are fine guard dogs and make excellent house pets. They are open with children and adore family life. Bouviers are eager to please and learn quickly. They respond to training better than most breeds. They are in a class with the German Shepherd Dog and the Standard Poodle as ideal domestic pets. They have pleasing personalities and are exceptionally gentle and loving.

Negative characteristics: Examples of this breed can be born with shy or aggressive temperaments due to nonselective breeding, which comes about through commercialization of the breed.

Specific training advice: They engage in destructive digging and chewing. They also tend to jump on people. These large dogs are strong on the leash and like to pull. This will make teaching *Heel* more difficult. These dogs are a lot to handle if they are not trained properly. However, if you show them what to do, they will do it.

BOXER (AKC, UKC)

Positive characteristics: Part of the great appeal of this breed is its wonderful facial formation. The sloping jowls and wrinkled cheeks create the most fascinating and heartwarming expressions. These dogs have such open, expressive features that you can tell what they are about to do before they do it. They are excellent dogs for children. They are powerful and can survive a child's play with ease. Once they have been trained, they respond very quickly when a command is given.

Negative characteristics: The temperaments of Boxers vary from responsive to nervous to aggressive—it all depends on the bloodlines of the individual animal. Be sure of the breeder and the progenitors of the dog before making a purchase. This is one of the breeds that has been hurt by commercialization and inbreeding. Don't be afraid to ask questions or to ask to meet the puppy's dam and sire. Boxers chew excessively.

Specific training advice: Boxers are sensitive to corrections. They are also stubborn, which makes training difficult. The younger the dog, the better he will respond to obedience training. Once they reach six months or more, they are going to be set in their ways and offer great resistance to training. *Down* will be the most difficult command to get across. They do not want to respond to it. Take your time with this command and spread it out over a long period.

Housebreaking will not be difficult if it is started at a very early age. Boxers love to jump as a release for their great energy.

BRIARD (AKC, UKC)

Positive characteristics: Briards make excellent watchdogs. They are large, strong, and very assertive. For many admirers, the dog's tremendous energy and rare and unusual appearance are assets. They require a lot of exercise. When trained properly, the Briard can perform quite well in obedience work.

Negative characteristics: This breed can be shy as well as aggressive, which makes the choice of breeders and breeding stock a primary consideration. Briards are dogfighters but can be aggressive to people as well. Some people may find owning a male difficult when the male's desire to dominate is coupled with the breed's strength and strong-willed behavior. If children are to live with a Briard, the dog must be introduced to the household and the children as a puppy. Do not bring an older Briard into a house with younger children, and have the dog evaluated by a professional trainer, especially if it is an older dog.

This is a mouthy breed. Chewing is a major problem. Digging is also a problem and Briards can be excessive barkers due to overdeveloped territorial instincts.

Specific training advice: Briards are stubborn and strong-willed in training. They will test their owners every day. If the Briard owner makes himself or herself number one in the house— the boss—and makes all the commands strong, firm, and consistent, the dog will be happy and a joy to live with. Briards need a lot of exercise.

Beginning obedience training at a young age is essential. Be sure *Heel* is learned well to keep the dog from pulling you down the street. *Come When Called* will be the most difficult command, but *Down* will be a challenge. Start young. When older Briards are taught *Down* they will bully the owner and may even try to growl and bite. The younger the dog is when it's trained, the more control the owner has, and the easier the Briard is to live with.

BRITTANY SPANIEL (AKC, UKC)

Positive characteristics: Brittanys are as delightful as they are beautiful. These are lovable dogs who enjoy working in obedience training. Children can give them all the exercise they need, running and playing. They do surprisingly well in the city for active dogs. If properly socialized with humans and dogs, they get along well with other dogs.

Negative characteristics: When not properly socialized, Brittanys tend to be shy and quite sensitive. Their hunting instincts give them a tendency to wander. They are destructive chewers.

Specific training advice: Brittanys are easily distracted and quite sensitive. Be easy with the use of your voice and leash corrections. Teaching *Stay* will probably require added training time. The more praise you give these dogs, the better their responses will be to the training. Brittanys do not have many training problems. They enjoy training sessions and make the trainer look good.

BULLDOG (AKC)

Positive characteristics: Until 1835, this breed, like so many others in England, was used in blood sports—bull baiting in particular—and it created a tough, ferocious animal. However, since their sporting days ended, Bulldogs have been bred for their stately physiques and sweet natures. There is probably not a gentler and more even-tempered dog in existence. Although the current specimens look nothing like their athletic progenitors, the original stamina, intelligence, and courage remain. These stocky dogs with their pushed-in faces, flapping jowls, and barrel-shaped bodies will snort out their love and affection or scare the pants off any potential attacker. Bulldogs are wonderful with children because of their very playful spirits. They can take all the punishment a child can dish out. Although they are delightful to watch in the country, they also make wonderful apartment dogs. They respond to training very well.

Negative characteristics: Most people pass up this breed because they do not like its physical appearance. The Bulldog looks mean (even though he isn't) and difficult to manage (which he is not). They do slobber, and for the fastidious housekeeper this is problematic. They also have a bit of a breathing problem because of their short noses, set far back on the face; they must be watched carefully in hot weather.

Although this breed is the national dog of England, it does not possess the table manners of the very proper English people. Bulldogs are sloppy eaters and make the most intriguing sounds at dinnertime. If not trained early they can become unmanageable by virtue of their great strength and tenaciousness.

Specific training advice: Because of their physical strength, Bulldogs are capable of taking the firmest correction. However, they are sensitive in nature and should not be overjerked. Bulldogs can be very stubborn and must be dealt with in a firm manner. Training should begin early. When it does, you will find them very willing students who will respond to vocal corrections and praise. They respond so well to training that it is almost effortless to teach them a new command. Once they understand that they must respond to you, they will, and then training is a pleasurable occasion.

BULLMASTIFF (AKC, UKC)

Positive characteristics: Bullmastiffs are solid-looking animals who combine size, strength, and even temperaments. They are, in their own way, beautiful dogs. They were originally bred in England as a nonvicious attack dog for controlling poachers on large estates.

However, these are easygoing dogs and make excellent pets for elderly people. Regardless of their size, they are easy to handle. They are good with children and adapt very well to apartment life. They are also very good in the country. Members of this breed make fine guard dogs. They are gentle, alert, and very responsive to training. When kept indoors they are lethargic and sleep much of the time.

Negative characteristics: Because they are so large, they can be a problem if they become too protective as guard dogs. They are also clumsy; you wouldn't want one in a china shop. Feeding these large, hungry animals can be expensive.

Specific training advice: Training should begin when the dog is very young. Bullmastiffs will perform all commands rather slowly, especially *Sit.* This slow response time should not be confused with stubbornness or lack of responsiveness. If some Bullmastiffs are stubborn, this can be overcome in early training before it develops into a mature characteristic. The hardest command will be *Down,* because of the animal's sheer size.

But here, too, if the training begins early in the dog's life it will not be a major problem.

BULL TERRIER (AKC, UKC)

Positive characteristics: It is now accepted that the Bull Terrier was created by mating a Bulldog with the now-extinct White English Terrier. This breed also has its origins in the blood sports of England, although this heritage has no relationship to the illegal organized dogfights that take place clandestinely today.

To those who know this breed, these dogs are friendly, affectionate, and good-natured. And certainly to those who own them or have owned them, they are beautiful. These lively dogs are marvelous with children and are well-suited to apartment life. Because they are so frisky, they make excellent country dogs.

Negative characteristics: Not everyone has the right personality and life-style to own a Bull Terrier; be sure to learn more about the breed on a firsthand basis before deciding this is the dog for you. They are stubborn, like all terriers, but for many fanciers that is interpreted as independence and is therefore considered a positive characteristic.

Bull Terriers were originally bred for pit fighting when that was a gentleman's sport in nineteenth-century England. The instinct to fight still remains to some degree, even though the sport does not. These animals make excellent guard dogs. However, once they are trained for that purpose they can become dangerous if not handled properly, and that's something to consider before becoming involved with this breed.

Specific training advice: Although these dogs are willing to learn, they still have the stubborn streak that is characteristic of all the terriers. They will resist learning each command you try to teach. This stubbornness can only be overcome with patience, firmness, and consistency. Take each command slowly, but let the dog know who is boss in the situation.

CAIRN TERRIER (AKC, UKC)

Positive characteristics: These mighty little dogs were developed in Scotland and, despite their small size, were bred as hunters. Cairns have sporting instincts and are effective vermin killers. It was a Cairn Terrier that appeared in the motion picture *The Wizard of Oz* as Dorothy's dog, Toto. They are lovable and very devoted animals. They relate well to children and elderly people. Cairn Terriers adapt well to both country and city life and make excellent house pets.

Negative characteristics: This is a small, feisty breed that is very excitable. This is not necessarily a negative characteristic, unless you are looking for a dog who is calm and relaxed. Cairns are very yappy and because of their high-energy activity, they may not be suitable for an elderly person. Cairn Terriers like to jump on people. They are also destructive chewers. Some of them are aggressive toward other dogs.

Specific training advice: As with almost all terrier breeds, Cairns have that aggressive, stubborn quality that makes them tough, scrappy little animals. You must be firm. Two months of age is the perfect time to start their training. Housebreaking could be difficult for some examples of this breed. Do not over-jerk any dog who is very young. Be gentle and patient.

CANAAN DOG (AKC)

Positive characteristics: These Israeli citizens are very devoted to their families and their homes. They are loyal, intelligent, and very territorial.

Negative characteristics: Canaan Dogs need to be socialized at a young age because they are naturally aloof and do not like to be touched by strangers. They can be excessive barkers and at times do it indiscriminately. They like to dig holes.

Specific training advice: Canaan Dogs are strong-willed yet very sensitive. Patience and early training are the keys to success.

CARDIGAN WELSH CORGI (AKC, UKC)

Positive characteristics: The Cardigan Welsh Corgi is similar in many ways to the Pembroke Welsh Corgi, except that it is somewhat larger, bigger boned, has longer ears, and is born with a long, full tail. The easiest way to distinguish the Cardigan from the Pembroke is the tail. The Cardigan is the more reserved of the two breeds, and does well in the country or in the city. Cardigans are sturdy animals, able to take rough-and-tumble play, yet still serve as good companions for elderly people, children, and those living in small apartments. They also make good watchdogs. These are lively, well-behaved, loyal, and affectionate animals.

Negative characteristics: Corgis were bred to herd cattle, and the way for a small dog to persuade a large cow to move is to nip at its feet. Many Cardigans take charge of their human herds in the same manner. Shyness or biting behavior can sometimes appear in poorly bred Cardigans.

They have a tendency to be strong-willed. Their long bodies may cause some back problems; they love to chew and dig.

Specific training advice: Begin housebreaking at a young age to avoid serious problems. *Down* could be the most difficult command to teach.

CAVALIER KING CHARLES SPANIEL (AKC, UKC)

Positive characteristics: The Cavalier King Charles Spaniel is a delicate, retiring pet when sitting regally in its home. Once outdoors, its true nature as a miniature bird dog comes to the surface. Behind its seemingly sad face is an energetic animal filled with zest for anything that flies or moves in the bushes. It is a delightful companion animal that craves human handling and affection. It is an ideal breed for either city or country life. Cavaliers are easy to travel with from one place to another. They are small- to medium-sized lap dogs who are devoted to their owners and are especially fond of calm, thoughtful children. They are easily trained.

Negative characteristics: Cavaliers are very sensitive, which is not to everyone's taste. Some cannot tolerate overly vigorous play of young, exuberant children.

This breed only shows serious problems if it is babied too much or carried around too much. If they are not properly socialized or if they are spoiled, they may become shy with people or dogs. They snore and sometimes wheeze. They also have difficulty with housebreaking. This breed requires more attention than most and has little tolerance for being left alone.

Specific training advice: Housebreaking could be a problem. Start early. These little dogs have a tremendous desire to please, so teach them the fundamentals of each command carefully and praise them when they get it right. They respond poorly to any harsh training or housebreaking correction. Because of their sensitivity, they must be corrected gently. Do not use a harsh tone of voice or firm leash correction with this breed. Use a nylon training collar and lightweight leash—they do not require anything heavier. *Heel* will be a problem if they have been carried around too much.

CHIHUAHUA (AKC, UKC)

Positive characteristics: The most obvious feature of this very special breed is its size. These dogs are ideal for those who want as little dog as possible in their lives without giving up the notion entirely. They are tiny creatures with "apple-domed" heads, and they range from one to six pounds.

The smaller Chihuahuas can fit into a jacket pocket or a handbag. These frail creatures were introduced to the United States by Xavier Cugat and his Latin American orchestra. In most of his films, the popular band leader held a Chihuahua in his arms during his musical numbers. This helped make the breed fashionable. They may be the best house pets for elderly people because of their size and ability to be easily controlled.

Negative characteristics: Probably the most negative aspect of this breed is learning to spell Chihuahua. Because these tiny animals are so pampered and spoiled (they are carried every-where), they become insecure and frightened of anything un-familiar. This causes them to withdraw from everyone but their owners. Dogs very often express their fears through aggressiveness, and that is sometimes the case with Chihuahuas. These dogs are excessive barkers. They also like to jump on your bed, which is a problem for many people.

Specific training advice: Housebreaking is a big problem—it should begin as soon as possible. Chihuahuas must be socialized at an early age by exposing them to many people. Do not carry them everywhere as though they were helpless babies. This makes them unsocial and unwilling to accept training. Many owners of this breed believe there is no need to train these dogs because they are so small. This is a mistake.

CHINESE SHAR-PEI (AKC, UKC)

Positive characteristics: The changeable, varying wrinkles of the Chinese Shar-pei became the symbol of wealth and privilege in the decade of the 1980s. For those who can afford it, responsible Chinese Shar-pei breeders produce a unique breed of dog. In addition to their value as status symbols, these dogs are loyal companions to family and friends. If you enjoy a dog with a dominant personality, this is the right breed for you. They enjoy the company of humans.

Negative characteristics: Be cautious when purchasing a Chinese Shar-pei. The lure of the high price tag has brought many less reputable breeders into the market. A significantly large number of Shar-pei puppies are unusually aggressive or shy. Shar-peis also have serious medical problems associated with their skin and eyes. Have all puppies and grown dogs evaluated by a professional dog trainer before making a purchase, especially if the dog is to live with a child. It is not the best breed for children.

Specific training advice: Acclimate the puppy to the leash at a young age and do it very gently. If the dog's temperament is not extreme, training will be easy. However, a shy or aggressive Shar-pei will make the obedience training very difficult. Determine your dog's temperament. If it is shy, be very gentle and loving in your training. If it is aggressive, you will need the services of a professional dog trainer.

CHOW CHOW (AKC, UKC)

Positive characteristics: Originating in China, the Chow Chow has gained wide appeal throughout the Western world and is universally accepted as a fine watchdog. Faithful to Chinese traditions, these dogs quickly develop deep-rooted loyalties and strong protective emotions about their families. Because of these qualities, they make ideal guard and companion dogs. When groomed properly, they are among the most striking and beautiful creatures in the dog world. Chows also respond very well to training. If you've owned one, fifteen years later you will want another.

Negative characteristics: Because these dogs are very aggressive, they are not ideal for everyone. Unless you match their aggressiveness with equal firmness, they will end up dominating the household. These are remote and aloof animals who do not need or desire any undue expressions of emotion or play. Their blue-black tongues and facial scowls do not always endear them to the average pet owner. They are not ideal for those who are purchasing their first dog. They require a true "dog person" to own them—a strong, firm individual who has owned several dogs before. Due to commercialization and lack of selective breeding, many examples of this breed are excessively aggressive. Be very cautious of Chows around young children. When considering such a dog, have him evaluated by a professional dog trainer. Try to learn as much as possible about his family tree, especially his parents.

Specific training advice: Chows require training at a young age, when you have complete control of them. They are very responsive dogs and can learn anything you teach them. However, they are stubborn and require a strong, firm hand.

COCKER SPANIEL (AKC, UKC)

Positive characteristics: Cocker Spaniels are sturdy animals, capable of taking strong correction. If trained at an early age, they will respond quickly to any command they have been taught. They can heel perfectly and lie down almost the instant the command is given. They are excellent with children and adapt to apartment life very well. Although they are rambunctious dogs, they can be handled easily by elderly people if they are trained. They are ideal for people who want a dog who is not too big and not too small.

Negative characteristics: Due to excessive breeding, many Cocker Spaniels have become aggressive. In addition, if they are hit they can become growlers, biters, dog fighters, and generally hostile. It is not because of the breed, but rather the breeding. Spaniels have appeared in English history as far back as the twelfth century and have developed a large popularity in the United States. The Cocker Spaniel is a subdivision of the land spaniel group, and is identified as one of the smallest of the spaniels, which accounts for its great popularity in this country. It is this popularity that has led to its massive breeding, much to the detriment of the breed. The best advice is to exercise caution and selectivity before purchasing one. Investigate the puppy's pedigree. If possible, examine his parents; ask a lot of questions; try to evaluate the temperament of his progenitors. This investigation is necessary because only a well-bred specimen will respond favorably to training.

Specific training advice: Cocker Spaniels have long ears. Avoid entangling them in the choke collar and leash when administering the corrective jerk.

These mischievous dogs will jump on furniture, take food from the table, and jump on people. These are problems that must be solved in puppyhood or they will remain throughout the life of the dog. If you allow the puppy to sit on your lap, he may eventually jump up on people. If you let him sleep on the bed, he will jump on the furniture.

When giving Cockers commands, make sure they are forced to respond. If you give in at the beginning, they can never be relied upon to obey. *Go to Your Place* is very useful for Cockers because they tend to get into mischief, and this will give you a tool for control. *Down-Stay* is useful, too. *Down-Stay* will also help in the car. They do not travel well as a rule; excitement or nervousness makes them jump from seat to seat. *Down-Stay* makes them stop.

When Cockers are excited and their energy is high, they can have wetting problems. However, this same behavior can be caused by excessive discipline or hitting, in which case it would be referred to as submissive wetting. The problem is the same as when the dog wets from excitement, but the cause is different.

Hitting this breed can cause more behavioral damage than with other breeds. The result will be a nasty animal. Housebreaking is usually when hitting begins, and with Cocker Spaniels that's the beginning of an aggressive temperament. Most of the negative characteristics mentioned here can be avoided if you exercise self-control and avoid hitting or abusing the dog in any way.

Cocker Spaniels are hunters and as such are best in the kennel of an estate. However, if yours is a house pet he must be obedience trained as a puppy so that you may both enjoy fifteen or more years of pleasant relations.

COLLIE (AKC, UKC)

Positive characteristics: The Collie's public image comes from the many years of television's favorite dog, Lassie. Most Collies live up to this reputation for beautiful temperament. Because of the *Lassie* TV series, we tend to think of the Collie as a free spirit, roaming the countryside, running and walking great distances. However, the Collie is also an excellent city dog, adaptive to apartment living if given adequate exercise by its owner. They do require outdoor activity and exercise. They are seen in two varieties, rough-coated and smooth-coated. Lassie was rough-coated.

Collies are easygoing and get comfortable in one area and stay there. They respond to training very well. They are wonderful with children and develop lasting relationships. So far, the breeding of Collies has been very responsible, producing a stable, even-tempered, responsive animal. Because they are not too high-spirited and are not hard to handle, they make excellent pets for elderly people.

Negative characteristics: Collies are stubborn dogs. This opinion, however, is based on experience in training older Collies. They are more willing students when they are puppies. They have sensitive personalities even though they are quite stubborn. Therefore, early motivational training and patience when training helps a great deal. They tend to be barkers.

Specific training advice: You must not leave a metal training collar on the dog for any great length of time. It will wear away the fur around his neck. A nylon training collar is preferable.

Some Collies develop bad chewing habits when they are left alone. Make sure you are very patient with these dogs and never abuse them. You will create complex behavioral problems if you are too harsh or if you overjerk. If the dog is too frisky and outgoing before a training session, simply calm him down in a soothing manner. You must use a soft touch.

DACHSHUND (SMOOTH, LONGHAIRED, WIREHAIRED) (AKC, UKC)

Positive characteristics: These dogs are among the most even-tempered animals in existence. They are very good with children, and especially good with elderly people. Dachshunds, no matter what kind, are ideally suited to apartment living. Their eating habits are good and they live a long time. Very few people can resist their frisky, gentle manner.

Negative characteristics: Dachshunds are one of those breeds that have great difficulty making the transition from paper training to housebreaking. If you begin with paper training, then you should stay with that technique. If, ultimately, you want the dog to go outside, then begin housebreaking from the start. Some Dachshunds are aggressive.

Specific training advice: Do not use any type of training collar. Dachshunds have tender necks and can be hurt very easily, which is true of most small breeds. An ordinary leather collar will do the job.

If you begin training a Dachshund as young as seven weeks old, then work slowly. They need a lot of praise and affection. Do not use "No" too often. Small dogs can be frightened very easily, causing behavioral complications that are not inherent to their natures.

Exercise patience when teaching the *Sit.* Because of the irregular shape of a Dachshund's body, it takes him longer to sit properly. He will be very slow getting into position. Dachshunds also have trouble heeling properly. Their legs are very short, so they walk slower than the average dog. Consequently, they will not be able to keep up if you walk too quickly. You will probably have more problems with them lagging behind than pulling ahead.

Be patient teaching *Stay* and *Down.* They are eager to please, but it takes them longer to respond to a new command than is usual with other dogs. They need a lot of praise. Dachshunds respond to *Come When Called* better than most commands, owing to their great desire for affection. Be sure to give them a lot of praise when they respond to this command.

DALMATIAN (AKC, UKC)

Positive characteristics: The owner who enjoys exercise will love these dogs because they were bred to run as carriage dogs. These spotted beauties make ideal pets in the city and the country. They are obedient, responsive to training, and wonderful with children. They are capable of taking the pounding of a child's play. They possess keen memories and are endowed with a willingness to please.

Negative characteristics: Dalmatians are very stubborn dogs. They love to chew and dig destructively, but vigorous exercise and obedience training can help eliminate these problems. Occasionally a puppy is born with a shy temperament. Before purchasing a puppy, it is a good idea to check for deafness. If you obtain a puppy from a reputable breeder, your chances of avoiding deafness or shyness are much better. Before making a purchase, investigate the qualities of the prospective pet's dam and sire.

Specific training advice: Despite their stubbornness, they are responsive to training and desire to please. They will require a slow, firm approach to training. You will have to be a little more forceful because of their excitability and nervousness. These dogs require a strong, firm hand. When training this breed, use a nylon collar for its very sensitive neck.

DANDIE DINMONT TERRIER (AKC, UKC)

Positive characteristics: Once a favorite hunting dog in Scotland and England, Dandie Dinmonts retain all the qualities of an excellent family dog. Very yappy, they make good watchdogs. They are good for elderly people and thoughtful children, and are ideal for apartment life.

Negative characteristics: Like most terriers, they tend to be stubborn and unyielding once they make up their minds about something. Sometimes their yapping is a nuisance. They tend to dig and chew.

Specific training advice: These dogs can become stubborn if they are not trained at an early age. Seven weeks of age is not too early to start training. Do not overjerk any dog who is very young. Be gentle and patient.

DOBERMAN PINSCHER (AKC, UKC)

Positive characteristics: This breed is endowed with a tremendous willingness to please. Dobermans make formidable adversaries as guard dogs but are also fine companions who do very well with children. Contrary to their bad press, it is not true that they are vicious curs who will turn on their masters. It is only when beaten or abused that members of this breed have turned their strength and biting power on their owners. Socialization during the first weeks of puppyhood is the key to maintaining a Doberman's good temperament.

These dogs have never endeared themselves to anyone who has met them in the execution of their watchdog duties. However, they offer a unique combination of love and protection to their families. In training, they will respond to a basic obedience course better, quicker, and with more grace than almost any other breed. Dobermans have been bred and trained in many ways for various purposes. For example, the companion Doberman is ideal as a house pet and as a psychological deterrent against would-be assailants. There are also highly trained protective Dobermans, guard Dobermans, and attack Dobermans. As a unique member of the dog world, the Doberman has proven himself to be a loyal, faithful, and affectionate companion.

Negative characteristics: The overly aggressive and hypersensitive behavior found in some examples of this breed are the results of poor breeding and lack of early socialization. Negative traits are common in Dobermans that have been bred from a line of high-strung and nervous dogs. It is important to examine a Doberman's pedigree before making a purchase. Seeing the dam and sire will help. If the dog is extremely sensitive, he will require extra handling around strangers, in cars, and in new environments. Because of his protective nature, he can be regarded as ferocious if he senses an impending attack either to himself or to any member of his family. This, however, is usually regarded as a positive trait.

Doberman Pinschers are notorious barkers and destructive chewers and diggers. Exercise is crucial. When they do not get adequate exercise they may spin around and suck their flanks as a displacement activity to relieve their nervousness. It is very important to know why you want this breed. Be absolutely clear about the dog's tasks. They will greatly affect the kind of Doberman to purchase, because some are bred as companion animals and some are bred as protection dogs.

Specific training advice: It is important to know your Doberman's temperament. Is he easygoing, friendly, unafraid of noises, crowded areas, other people? If so, he can be trained in exactly the same way you would train most other breeds. A highly sensitive Doberman should be in the hands of a professional dog trainer.

The only difference in technique for the even-tempered Doberman is that the corrective jerk should not be too firm. These dogs are quick to learn and will understand in five minutes what it may take thirty minutes for other breeds to learn. This is important if they are to keep their good temperaments. They must never be made to feel that they are being punished. Maintain a light touch. Because of their extreme sensitivity, they must not be shouted at or handled with abusive authority.

These dogs will not want to stay in the *sit* position for too long. Use a longer leash and keep praising the dog every moment he stays in position.

Down and *Down-Stay* will require a little more time than usual for this breed. They must be introduced to these commands very gently.

With this breed, conduct shorter but more frequent training sessions—two or three times a day is ideal. Dobermans must not be rushed into each command. If this time span is observed, the results will be truly rewarding. It must be emphasized that affection and praise are quite necessary. However, a firm "No" must always be applied with each correction. Dobermans will respond to it better than most dogs. They must be taught that you are the boss and totally in control of the situation. If you are afraid of them, they will know it immediately and use it against you.

The guidelines for Dobermans are:

1. Do not abuse them.
2. Do not pamper them.
3. Make them feel that they are part of the family.
4. Do not display fear because they will react to it.
5. Treat them with kindness, praise, and affection.

ENGLISH SETTER (AKC, UKC)

Positive characteristics: English Setters are easygoing to the point of lethargy. Unlike most other hunting breeds, they are ideally suited to elderly people because of their sedate temperaments. They adjust to apartment life very well. These dogs are wonderful with children. In fact, they are so gentle they will let you do almost anything to them without ever complaining or acting aggressively.

Negative characteristics: These are strong-willed dogs. And they can develop destructive chewing problems if left alone. Their stubbornness takes the form of resistance rather than uncontrollable obstinacy. Instead of pulling on a leash, they will simply walk slowly. Instead of going into *Sit,* they will lie down. When called, they will come slowly instead of giving the immediate response a command demands.

Specific training advice: The basic obedience commands must be handled with great diligence, more so than with other breeds. Extra patience is required and also extra firmness.

English Setters must be made to obey each command. For example, if your dog refuses to heel, you might go so far as to get on the ground and call to him, backing up a little as he comes, all the while praising him and giving him confidence. This gets the dog moving, but at the same time gives him the opportunity to feel at ease about it. Strong-arm tactics with this breed will bring nothing but disappointment.

The *Down* and *Down-Stay* will be very difficult to teach— the dog will fight you every inch of the way. In this case the training sessions should be broken up into shorter sessions and spread over a longer period of time.

English Setters do not respond quickly to *Come When Called.* With most English Setters a slow response is to be expected. These dogs will rebel at browbeating. Therefore, they should be trained as puppies while they are still carefree, playful, and energetic. One of the best ways to keep them out of mischief is to give them a place that is exclusively their own in the apartment or house. (See Chapter 14, "*Go to Your Place.*")

There are many years of rewarding pleasure ahead if the city dweller begins an obedience program when this member of the hunting breeds is a puppy.

ENGLISH SPRINGER SPANIEL (AKC, UKC)

Positive characteristics: English Springer Spaniels are good city dogs and good country dogs. They make excellent pets for children and elderly people. They adjust well to apartment life, are easy to get along with, are well suited to training, and adapt easily to most situations. Beauty and utility are combined in this even-tempered breed.

Negative characteristics: Well-bred English Springers respond well to training, but unfortunately there are too many poorly bred specimens around. Poorly bred Springers can become aggressive, and if they are hit they can become growlers, biters, dogfighters, and generally hostile. This breed, like the Cocker, has become so popular that many puppies have been bred for profit at the sacrifice of quality. The well-bred Springer's characteristics show few negative qualities. Be cautious and investigate the puppy's pedigree. If possible, evaluate the temperament of the dog's parents.

Specific training advice: Because English Springers are difficult to housebreak, begin as soon as possible.

Be careful of the dog's long ears when administering the corrective jerk. Do not catch them in the training collar and leash.

During all training, but specifically for *Heel,* be alert to the tendency to wander away and become distracted by other animals, as is characteristic of all hunting dogs. If you bear down on *Heel,* you will not have problems with the other commands. *Go to Your Place* is also important for this breed. *Down-Stay* is another important command. These commands give you tools for greater control and make it easier for the dog to please you.

Among the behavioral problems are digging, chewing, excessive barking, jumping on people, and jumping up on the furniture.

Vigorous obedience training at an early age is the key to enjoying the many pleasant aspects of this breed.

FILA BRASILEIRO

Positive characteristics: Part Mastiff, part Bloodhound, these hundred-pound beauties serve as a visual deterrent against intruders and other wrongdoers. Fila Brasileiros are naturally good watchdogs. In their homeland of Brazil, ranchers use them for protection, to hunt jaguar, and for scent tracking. They are devoted to their owners, self-assured, and totally fearless.

Negative characteristics: This breed is not for everyone. New people must be introduced to the dog by the owners because of its natural aversion to strangers. They are usually very aggressive, which is a serious problem when dogs are as large and as strong as these.

Specific training advice: This dog must be socialized during puppyhood or it will be dangerous. Early obedience training is a necessity or it will prove to be too difficult to handle.

FINNISH SPITZ (AKC)

Positive characteristics: Finnish Spitz are very intelligent, alert dogs. In their native Finland they are still used for bird hunting. They are lively and playful with children and do especially well in the country. Some adapt well to the city, too. The Finnish Spitz makes an alert, vigilant watchdog. They are characteristically happy dogs and make fine companion animals.

Negative characteristics: A Finnish Spitz may be very difficult to live with if his owner is not firm, or if the apartment is too small. Spitzes sometimes bark excessively. Barking is a unique aspect of their hunting style. After scenting a bird to a tree they bark continuously until the hunter shoots. The more the dog barks (or yodels) the more intrigued becomes the bird, who sits there mesmerized. However, what is a positive quality in the field is a negative behavior in the home.

Specific training advice: The very dominant personality of the Finnish Spitz causes him to resist training. He will test everyone unless someone in the family establishes him or herself as the person in charge. Easygoing people may find his strong-willed personality too difficult to train. A very patient person with a strong personality is required to train these dogs. Exercise and space to run in goes a long way toward helping to train these dogs successfully.

FOX TERRIER (WIRE AND SMOOTH) (AKC, UKC)

Positive characteristics: These small dogs, among the most popular in the world, are very sturdy and respond to training very well. They are capable of accepting a correction without being ruffled. Fox Terriers are adaptable to the city and are very well suited for long walks. Once they have been trained they do not pull on the leash, are easy to control, and do not get skittish. Although they are spirited animals, they are very good for children and elderly people. They are compact and travel easily. Their outstanding characteristics are their out-goingness and their desire for love and affection.

Negative characteristics: These are high-energy dogs. Some can be excessive barkers. Some are aggressive to people or other dogs if they are not socialized or if they are mistreated.

Specific training advice: Because these dogs are small and affectionate, they can become spoiled if overindulged. Owners tend to pamper them to the point where training is useless. Refrain from spoiling your dog, or he will become stubborn and strong-willed. You must maintain discipline, especially during the training period. Corrections must be firm but not severe. A strong vocal correction with a gentle corrective jerk will do the job. Chewing and housebreaking are the most difficult problems to solve. Begin training at an early age; seven weeks is not too soon.

GERMAN SHEPHERD DOG (AKC, UKC)

Positive characteristics: There are no dogs more willing to learn and to respond to all phases of training than German Shepherd Dogs. They represent everything a good all-around dog should be. They have set the standard as guide dogs for the blind, for guard work, for drug detection, bomb detection, search and rescue, as therapy dogs, and, at the same time, make truly fine house pets. Anyone can own a German Shepherd Dog. They are wonderful with children and elderly people. They are good in the city and the country. They are healthy eaters and live to a ripe old age. They can adapt to any environment.

Negative characteristics: Because they are so popular, a medical problem has developed over the years because of irresponsible breeding practices: Hip dysplasia, a hereditary disease, seems to attack Shepherds more than other large breeds. This disease, in oversimplified terms, is a congenital dislocation of the hip socket and often cannot be detected until the animal is past eight months old. Before purchasing a German Shepherd Dog, it is important to discuss the animal's bloodlines with the breeder. If there is any evidence of hip dysplasia in the animal's background, *do not buy it.* There is nothing more heartbreaking than living with a dog for eight or ten months only to have to put him down or have him undergo major surgery because of this painful and crippling illness. This is a grim consideration in choosing a German Shepherd Dog.

There are many stories about Shepherds turning on their owners. Aggressiveness can be an inherited quality in this animal. But because of the Shepherd's high level of trainability, his inherited aggressiveness can usually be brought under control. But no animal will remain even-tempered if he is yelled at, hit, or beaten, and this remains true for Shepherds, Dobermans, Collies, or Dachshunds. It is important to understand that some animals have been made ferocious purposely by foolish owners.

Specific training advice: This breed will have chewing and digging problems if not corrected at an early age. Give these animals every chance to learn, reward them with praise, make training a lot of fun, and you will have no problems with the obedience course in the first part of this book.

GERMAN SHORTHAIRED POINTER (AKC, UKC)

Positive characteristics: Members of this breed are very lovable and capable of giving great warmth and affection. They are friendly and exceptionally good with children. Powerful dogs such as these are very good in the country because they have a desire to run and need a great deal of exercise. If they are kept in the country and get the proper amount of exercise they will be very responsive to training. They make excellent companions.

Negative characteristics: German Shorthaired Pointers are high-strung animals. Characteristically, they have high-energy/outgoing temperaments. Unless they are given sufficient daily exercise it is impossible to keep them in an apartment. Their desire to jump, combined with an accumulation of energy, results in total chaos. They will jump on furniture, jump on people, steal food from the table, get into the garbage, and chew anything, whether it's nailed down or not.

They can also be stubborn dogs with very strong wills. If the owner is not truly firm, his or her animal will be a constant source of trouble. This breed requires a great deal of authority. If the owner spoils the dog, he or she will regret it for the rest of the dog's life. German Shorthaired Pointers must be trained as soon as possible. If the owner waits too long to begin training, it may be too late. Strict training can begin in the seventh week of puppyhood.

Specific training advice: Use a good strong training collar and a six-foot leather leash. When executing a corrective jerk, be certain the leash does not get caught in the dog's long flapping ears. It can cause him great pain and make him aggressive.

Because these are hunting dogs, they are not as attentive as other breeds. They are constantly indulging their keen sense of smell and must be forced to pay attention to commands. In the *Heel*, try to keep the dog's attention by talking to him. The more you capture his attention, the more responsive he will be.

These dogs should be worked exceptionally hard in *Stay*, since they are not too good at it and will remain in *Stay* for only a short time. It is especially important in the city, where there are so many distractions to lead them into trouble or danger. They should never be allowed off-leash in the city. Their greatest difficulty is with the command *Come When Called*.

Because these are hunting dogs, they must be made to obey absolutely. The more obedience training they are given, the more responsive they will be in the city. One of the best ways to keep them out of mischief indoors is to give them a place that is exclusively their own in the apartment or house. (See Chapter 14, "*Go to Your Place*.")

Hunting dogs must be obedience trained more vigorously than other breeds if they are going to share a house or an apartment with a family. No-nonsense obedience training at an early age is the key to enjoying the many pleasant aspects of this breed.

GOLDEN RETRIEVER (AKC, UKC)

Positive characteristics: Goldens are among the most loyal, bright, and attractive breeds to be found, which explains their great popularity. Their expressive faces often reflect the comedies and tragedies occurring in the lives of their families. Their intelligence level makes them superior guide dogs, and they are among the top successful breeds in obedience competition.

They are equally at home hiking in the mountains or lying happily couch-side in an apartment. The one prerequisite for any Golden is to share the day with his or her owner. This is not a backyard breed.

Negative characteristics: Golden puppies are very active, though no more than any other sporting dog. Obedience training and exercise will channel this excess energy into appropriate activities and help the dog avoid punishment and scoldings. This breed is very sensitive and does not tolerate being hit or yelled at.

Goldens, being retrievers, have an inborn "need" to carry and mouth things and will resort to chewing if bored. Providing interesting toys and establishing a program of *prevention,* instead of correction, will get most Goldens through adolescence with the furniture intact. They do have a tendency to dig, as well.

Specific training advice: Gently begin leash breaking at the earliest age possible. Use motivation techniques instead of force to teach commands, which means "Command, Correction, Praise." Once the command is learned, enforce its execution firmly and follow up with sincere praise.

In almost all the basic commands, Golden Retrievers have a tendency to inch up after obeying. That is an infraction of the rules, and if a dog is allowed to get away with it he will become less and less responsive. When giving the command *Sit,* make sure the dog stays for a short period of time without moving. When executing *Heel,* do not let him walk ahead. The same applies to *Down* and *Down-Stay. Come When Called* may be a problem in the city. Remember, Goldens are hunters. Do not give this command in the city without a leash. It is dangerous.

One of the best ways to keep these dogs out of mischief is to give them a place that is exclusively their own in the apartment or house. (See Chapter 14, *"Go to Your Place."*)

Hunting breeds are not usually considered city dogs. However, because of their beauty and many other attributes, Goldens are desired by many city dwellers. It is therefore recommended that an intense training program for urban dogs be initiated as soon as possible.

Goldens are born opportunists. They are very bright. If required to perform consistently, they develop good behavior habits. But if they know they can get away with murder when they flash those big brown eyes at you, they will.

GORDON SETTER (AKC, UKC)

Positive characteristics: These gentle, friendly dogs are very good with children. Their need to run and exercise in open spaces makes them ideal country dogs. For the fancier, they are stylish, special, and regal looking. This intelligent breed, with its handsome black and tan coat, has a bearing of strength and dignity.

Negative characteristics: Gordon Setters have strong-willed temperaments. One of the reasons they are not seen in the city very often is the difficulty they have adjusting to apartment life. Although they are not the largest of breeds, they behave as though they were and require a firm, strong hand from their owners.

Specific training advice: Exercise care in administering the corrective jerk. The long ears can get caught in the training collar and leash. Housebreaking should begin immediately.

In administering corrections, the first jerk should be quite firm; don't apply five or six mild jerks. The more you jerk, the more a Gordon will rebel. One hard jerk will be enough to let him know who's boss.

Do not let a Gordon off-leash in the city. Like other hunting dogs, Gordons become distracted by squirrels, pigeons, and other animals and refuse to come when called. Their response to this command is unreliable even with a leash.

In an apartment, Gordons manifest many annoying problems such as chewing, jumping on furniture, and going into the garbage. This is precisely why an early start with obedience training is important. Problems that arise in puppyhood are difficult to end as the dog matures. This breed should never be fed from the table. Once you start, you will have a canine dinner guest for the rest of his life, and a Gordon can be a large nuisance. One of the best ways to keep him out of mischief is to give him a place that is exclusively his own in the apartment or house. (See Chapter 14, *"Go to Your Place."*)

If the Gordon Setter is to be enjoyed as a pet rather than as the hunter he was meant to be, it is definitely advisable to begin obedience training at an early age. Seven weeks of age is not too soon.

GREAT DANE (AKC, UKC)

Positive characteristics: Great Danes have many positive characteristics. These are fine city and country dogs. Despite their size, they adapt well to apartment living. Because of their size, they are lethargic; a small apartment does not represent a stifling existence to them. They are wonderful with children. Their largeness is often overwhelming when they run and jump, but their bounciness is always in the spirit of play. These are easygoing dogs with gentle natures. Great Danes can be used for guard work if trained for it professionally.

Negative characteristics: There are some physical problems with this breed. Some specimens develop a swelling or soreness around the knees. Because they are big-boned animals, they sometimes develop bone disorders and severe calluses. Consult a veterinarian for more details.

The medical history of the animal and his progenitors should be investigated before making a purchase. They are large eaters; one cannot be economy-minded and own a Great Dane.

Specific training advice: Great Danes should be housebroken and obedience trained as soon as possible. They are very sensitive dogs and require gentle handling. Too much jerking will make them shy and skittish. They should be exposed to traffic, noise, and strangers as young puppies.

These dogs are leaners. For whatever the reason, they like to lean on those closest to them. This can be a problem when a Dane weighs 150 pounds. Decide early whether your dog is to be allowed this habit or not. Once you indulge it, he is going to be stubborn about breaking the habit. The same applies to jumping on the furniture. It's cute when a Dane is a puppy but very disturbing when he reaches full size. *Sit* is a difficult command for any extra large breed and will be performed slowly and with some difficulty. This must not be mistaken for stubbornness. These are wonderful dogs to own and offer few training problems.

GREAT PYRENEES (AKC, UKC)

Positive characteristics: Even though Great Pyrenees are very big, they do not require a lot of exercise or extra living space. They adapt quite well to city or country living. These animals appear so regal and calm that their very strong protective responses may come as a surprise. Firmly entrenched territorial instincts are the source of their protective behavior.

Negative characteristics: Great Pyrenees must be socialized at a young age with lots of people and dogs. If they are not, they develop a fear/aggressive personality and their size and strength make them too difficult to handle. If they are kept in the yard most of the time they may become aggressive in the house and with all strangers. Only a well-socialized and loved dog can become a good, useful watchdog.

Digging and chewing are the most difficult behavior problems Great Pyrenees have, but a full obedience course will help this. Because of their natural instinct toward protection, they can develop an excessive barking problem but only if they are kept outdoors all the time. They are stubborn, strong-willed dogs.

The dog should be raised with children from puppyhood if he is to live with children. Have the dog evaluated by a professional trainer. Young children should not be around a dog two years or older unless they have been raised together. Great Pyrenees can be aggressive toward other dogs.

Specific training advice: Begin training as early as possible. Seven weeks is not too soon. Males are more difficult to train than are females—some people may have a hard time handling a male. Great Pyrenees take longer to mature physically than do other breeds. Do not confuse size with maturity. These are lethargic dogs and will execute commands slowly. You must be patient but firm. They may growl in defiance of your commands. You must not permit a Great Pyrenees to bully you.

These are very strong dogs and must be trained at an early age. They require a firm hand when training. *Come When Called* and *Down* are the two hardest commands for the dog to learn because of his stubbornness. Use a lot of praise; these dogs need to be motivated in training. Learning *Heel* will be a problem due to the breed's size and strength. *Sit* is a difficult command for any extra large breed and will be performed slowly and with some difficulty. This must not be mistaken for stubbornness. Great Pyrenees mature slowly, and that influences their rate of learning. The breed works slowly, so work at a more leisurely pace and be firm.

Train indoors as much as possible so that your dog learns to obey you there as well as outdoors. Dogs purchased from reputable breeders are more easily trained. Taking dogs of this breed to a training class will help socialize them. Research all breeding sources before obtaining this breed.

GREYHOUND (AKC, UKC)

Positive characteristics: The look and the elegance of the Greyhound make them appealing. Greyhound owners take great pleasure in mentioning that this breed is the fastest in the world. Outside the racetrack they are not too common, which is another source of pride for the Greyhound owner. Their truly distinctive gait gives them an aristocratic air. They prance while they take their daily constitutional. That agility allows them to respond to commands very quickly. They adapt to country life best because there is an absence of noise and distraction. They are much more responsive when it's peaceful and quiet.

Negative characteristics: These timid, high-strung animals are not suitable for elderly people or children. They have high-energy/outgoing temperaments and are nervous. They do not fare well in the city with its traffic noises. Because of their high spirits, they do not make the ideal family dog—they are simply too nervous.

Specific training advice: Training should begin quite early in the dog's life. Gentleness is required. They cannot be jolted with too many firm corrections. The best way to train this breed is to show them what to do and give them a good reason for doing it. They cannot take constant harassments such as "No," "Bad dog," or "Shame." Do not expect the same kind of response that you would get from a German Shepherd Dog or even a Beagle. Greyhounds require tender loving care.

IRISH SETTER (AKC, UKC)

Positive characteristics: Temperamentally, these dogs are affectionate and loving, gentle and sweet-natured. Excellent hunters, they are ideal country residents. Irish Setters have good appetites and adjust very well to family life.

Negative characteristics: They are strong-willed and require firmness in all training matters. It is important to administer strong corrections when they ignore commands; otherwise they tend to do as they please. They are not convenient for elderly people. Training must begin as early as possible to avoid problems later. If these dogs are not trained properly they can literally ruin an apartment. It starts with messing in the middle of a good carpet and ends with chewing expensive furniture to sawdust. However, an Irish Setter can adjust to apartment life if given an obedience course from the minute he first enters the household.

Specific training advice: Irish Setters have extremely long ears that can get caught in the leash and training collar when a corrective jerk is administered. Be cautious.

Housebreaking should begin as soon as possible. The dog must be watched carefully until the housebreaking is completed.

The correction "No" does not work effectively unless the dog has come to associate it with a firm corrective jerk. Throughout most of the training period the corrective jerk should be administered firmly but not excessively. Too many corrections will make the dog jerk-shy. Next to housebreaking, walking in *Heel* is the biggest problem. One minute your Irish Setter will walk in perfect heel, and the next minute jerk your arm out running to play with another dog. Irish Setters are very easily distracted and will use force to get what they want. It is important that heeling be strictly enforced. Never allow one infraction of this rule without adminstering a corrective jerk.

Never allow this breed off-leash in the city. Irish Setters have been known to run off and never return. City life imposes a limitation on much-needed exercise and creates a great deal of pent-up energy that can be destructive. For this reason alone these dogs should not be allowed off-leash in the city. One of the best ways to keep them out of mischief indoors is to give them a place that is exclusively their own in the apartment or house. (See Chapter 14, *"Go to Your Place."*) Digging and chewing up landscaping are also common problems.

IRISH WOLFHOUND (AKC, UKC)

Positive characteristics: Rugged, playful, and protective, Irish Wolfhounds are very good with children and make ideal house pets. They are at their best in the country where they can run and play hard. It is difficult to resist their sweet, gentle natures and affectionate personalities. In the city they are lethargic for the most part and sleep a great deal, adjusting to apartment life quite easily.

Negative characteristics: The very size of these dogs can discourage the city dweller from owning one. They are among the largest dogs in existence and require a great deal of food, so if economy is a consideration, you should think twice before buying one.

Specific training advice: Irish Wolfhounds require a very firm hand. Because they are so large, you cannot equivocate or back down from a command. If they get out of hand it could lead to serious problems. It would be impossible to handle a thirty-four-inch, 175-pound Irish Wolfhound who suddenly became aggressive. That is why early training is absolutely necessary. Although this breed responds well to training, it does so at a slower pace than others. *Sit* is a difficult command for any extra large breed and will be performed slowly and with some difficulty. This must not be mistaken for stubbornness. Irish Wolfhounds will lope to you on *Come When Called* rather than run swiftly. In fact, they may take longer on all commands, but don't confuse their leisurely response time with stubbornness or unresponsiveness.

If the dog is to be handled by a family member who is not strong or powerful, it is essential that training take place while the dog is still small and manageable. Firmness is important.

When using the corrective jerk, snap the leash hard. If you emphasize the "No" simultaneously, you will eventually be able to achieve the same corrective results without the jerk—the vocal correction will suffice.

JACK RUSSELL TERRIER

Positive characteristics: Jack Russells love people and people love them. They are entertaining, funny, bright, athletic dogs. They have enormous energy.

Negative characteristics: Some of these terriers can be aggressive toward other dogs, and a few even demonstrate aggression toward people. They are so active that living in a city environment may not always be successful. Like most terriers, they love to dig and chew.

Specific training advice: The owner must be prepared for the training difficulties involved with Jack Russells. They must be trained at an early age, with a firm hand—one cannot be too soft. Regular, enjoyable exercise is essential and will help the dog meet expectations—they do require a tremendous amount of exercise. Housebreaking may be a problem. They love to dig and chew, as do other terrier breeds. They often jump on people and must be corrected for that early in the game. If not corrected at an early age they can become aggressive toward other dogs and some people.

KEESHOND (AKC, UKC)

Positive characteristics: These lively and intelligent animals make ideal companions; they have no desire to leave their masters' sides. They are furry in appearance, with wolflike coats. Keeshonds are very loving and affectionate. They are even-tempered and responsive to training. These rugged dogs get along very well with children and make ideal family pets.

Negative characteristics: They have strong-willed tempera-ments but are not excessively stubborn. They are easily dis-tracted, especially by other dogs.

Specific training advice: Remove the training collar immedi-ately after each training session. It will wear away the fur around the neck.

Because they are so easily distracted, they must be trained in a quiet, secluded area. These are high-energy dogs. They love to dig and chew.

Apply the basic training techniques, give a Keeshond a lot of praise and affection, show him what to do, and he will re-spond beautifully to the training.

KERRY BLUE TERRIER (AKC, UKC)

Positive characteristics: Kerry Blue Terriers represent a par-adox that exists in the world of purebred dogs. These rare and elegantly groomed creatures, seldom seen out of the show ring, come from circumstances far less stylish than the dog show. Originating in the mountainous regions of County Kerry, Ire-land, Kerry Blues were used for sheep and cattle herding, re-trieving, and for killing rats, badgers, and rabbits. Yet today they are true expressions of status and elegance when seen in a large city.

They make excellent companions and house pets. They

enjoy all the roughhouse play of children. Strong and protective, they make fine guard dogs.

Negative characteristics: They have extremely strong-willed temperaments and are among the most stubborn of all the terriers. Kerry Blues are also aggressive toward other dogs. They are dog fighters and require a very strong hand. Only those who are willing to be firm at all times should consider this animal. Under no circumstances should this breed be indulged. They take great advantage of those who spoil them.

Specific training advice: This is one of those breeds that must wear a training collar, even after the training session. You must use the training collar firmly on every command. A Kerry Blue can take firm corrections and must be made to understand that you mean business.

Teaching *Down* will present the biggest problem. They do not want to respond to this command. Extra patience and extra time will be required. Spread the lessons out for this command—twice a day for a week is not excessive. Give as many lessons as necessary for the dog to learn the command and to respond to it properly. Be patient and firm. Select a training site that has no distractions—it will make the task that much easier for you and the dog.

KOMONDOR (AKC)

Positive characteristics: The long ropelike coat of the Komondor is remarkable, especially on such a large dog. The average person has never seen a Komondor, so the dog draws considerable attention when out in public. These are very bright animals with strong territorial instincts and a desire to protect those they claim as their family.

Negative characteristics: Strong-willed and independent, this breed can and will test its owner's resolve at every opportunity. The adult Komondor can be very aggressive with strangers he meets on his own territory. The breed must be thoroughly socialized with people and other dogs beginning in the early stages of puppyhood. If the dog is to live with children, he must be introduced to the family at an early age and be raised with those children. Other dogs inspire aggression in Komondors; they chew and dig destructively; they can be excessive barkers if kept outside all the time. This breed is not for the mild-mannered person.

Specific training advice: A large, strong breed such as this requires an extremely firm, consistent hand. This is a very energetic breed that requires regular vigorous exercise. In addition to socializing Komondor puppies early, obedience training should also begin at a young age. Without this early work the dog will be unable to protect his family because of indiscriminate aggressive behavior to all strangers and all other dogs.

The commands will be difficult to teach, although females will be much easier to handle than males. Because these dogs are so bright they bore easily. Short, positive training sessions accomplish more because they help the animal focus on the command just long enough to learn it, but not long enough to tire of it.

KUVASZ (AKC, UKC)

Positive characteristics: This rare Hungarian breed is often confused with the Great Pyrenees. They are both large, white, handsome dogs. Kuvaszok (the plural of Kuvasz) do well in a city or country environment providing they are exercised frequently. Their territorial instincts make them very good watch-dogs.

Negative characteristics: If a Kuvasz is the result of a careful breeding program and is socialized in the early weeks of life with many people and dogs in many situations, the dog will not be fear/aggressive. However, a dog who has not been bred selectively and then properly socialized will show the negative characteristics of a fear/aggressive dog. The genetically rooted territorial instinct can be developed into a positive protective ability if the dog is constantly introduced to a variety of people and is treated with affection. The Kuvasz is often aggressive toward other dogs.

Digging and barking will be a problem if the dog is left out all day and night. An indoor/outdoor life-style is far more successful. Kuvaszok have a life span of ten to twelve years. If the dog is to live with children he must be introduced to the household as a puppy and be raised with the children. If an older dog is to be introduced to younger kids, he should be evaluated by a professional trainer. It is important to purchase this breed from a reliable source.

Specific training advice: These are large, strong dogs who need a firm hand. They may be too difficult for some people to handle. Because they grow into very strong animals, obedience training must begin at a young age. This is especially important for the commands *Heel* and *Down*. Males are more difficult to train than females—they may growl in defiance of your commands. They must not be permitted to bully you. Kuvaszok must be trained at an early age. Train them indoors as much as possible so that they learn to obey you there as well as outdoors. Taking dogs of this breed to a training class will help socialize them. *Sit* is a difficult command for any extra large breed and is performed slowly and with some difficulty. This must not be mistaken for stubbornness. Research all sources before making a purchase. Buy from someone who can show you the bloodlines in a pedigree and how they affect the puppy in question.

LABRADOR RETRIEVER (AKC, UKC)

Positive characteristics: Because of their keen hunting instincts, these dogs generally do better in the country. They adjust perfectly to family life and are very tolerant and patient with children. Labradors are being used more and more as guide dogs for the blind, and that speaks highly of their ability to be trained. That ability is good for all types of training, including basic obedience and guard work. Because they respond to human beings so well, they take to training more easily than do many other breeds.

They are among the most intelligent of the breeds and enjoy a long life span.

Negative characteristics: Dogs of this breed require a great deal of exercise, which can be a problem for those living in city apartments. A Lab would have to be vigorously exercised at least two or three times a week if kept in the city. Like all hunting breeds, Labradors are not ideal for elderly folks. They are too energetic and physically demanding and they require a firm, strong hand.

Specific training advice: When executing the corrective jerk, be certain the leash does not get caught in the dog's long, flapping ears. This can cause him great pain and make him aggressive.

Be certain your dog obeys all commands the first time with no delays; otherwise he will take advantage of you and obey only when he feels like it. Make great demands of the dog and enforce all commands. Do not allow him off-leash in the city.

Obedience training must be initiated in puppyhood to avoid the characteristic mischief a Labrador Retriever can create in an apartment situation.

Like most hunting breeds, Labrador Retrievers are high-energy dogs. They tend to dig, chew, and jump on people. The more training they receive, the happier everyone, especially the Lab, will be.

LHASA APSO (AKC, UKC)

Positive characteristics: The Lhasa Apso presents a rare combination of good qualities in a dog. It is small, hardy, rugged, frisky, intelligent, and very beautiful. Lhasas are not lap dogs, even though they have become extremely fashionable in city apartments. They are elegant animals found among the fashionable and the wealthy.

These Tibetan dogs are loving and affectionate. Despite their small size, they are not fragile, as are so many of the toy breeds. They can take a great deal of roughhouse play and for that reason are wonderful for children. These versatile dogs are very responsive to training and are completely portable. They can be taken anywhere, including long trips, with a minimum of inconvenience. Lhasa Apsos are even-tempered and fare well in the city.

Negative characteristics: If they are hit or overjerked when corrected, they will become aggressive and growl, snarl, or even bite. If they are hit, they will bite whenever anyone tries to touch them. Anything that gives the dog pain will make him aggressive.

Due to commercialization and the lack of selective breeding in numerous instances, many examples of this breed are very aggressive. Careful selection of a breeder and a puppy are essential for a happy, successful outcome. Sometimes babying the dog too much and carrying him everywhere cause aggressive behavior.

Specific training advice: Housebreaking is the greatest problem for the breed. Decide as soon as possible whether to housebreak or paper train your dog, and stay with that method.

If training begins at a young age and with a good deal of love and affection, you will have no problems. A Lhasa Apso must never be hit or corrected severely. If you are going to train a Lhasa Apso who is one year old or older, you must exercise great patience and take your time in teaching each command.

MALTESE (AKC, UKC)

Positive characteristics: Of all the toy breeds, the Maltese is one of the brightest, the most responsive, and the most beautiful. Its long, flat, silken coat is of the purest white fluffy fur. Looking like delicate porcelain figurines, these graceful dogs prance from room to room with mercurial speed. Their tiny appearance is misleading, however. They are sturdy dogs with great stamina and hearty appetites. They are clean, refined, and faithful. They are wonderful for elderly people and ideally suited to apartment life. These beautiful creatures are famous for their sweet temperaments and make ideal companion animals.

Negative characteristics: This lap dog tends to be pampered and spoiled. Consequently, it can become insecure and totally dependent on its owner. Because Maltese tend to follow their owners around the house and are underfoot much of the time, they can get stepped on quite easily. They are very yappy and bark at the slightest disturbance.

Specific training advice: Never use a training collar with this breed—it is too delicate.

Housebreaking will be the biggest training problem. Because Maltese are so small, they are usually paper trained. However, after a while they tend to have many accidents. If you change to housebreaking once the dog has been paper trained, you will experience great difficulty. The only answer is to keep a watchful eye on the animal no matter which technique you use, and continue to implement the training until the problem is resolved. The best answer is to select one kind of training and remain consistent with it.

MANCHESTER TERRIER (STANDARD AND TOY) (AKC)

Positive characteristics: Both the Standard and the Toy Manchester Terrier are good companions for more retiring people. They are the perfect size for an apartment and make good small watchdogs. Their size and temperament are perfect for travel.

Negative characteristics: If not properly socialized they can become fear/aggressive and growl menacingly at strangers and other dogs. The Standards are often aggressive toward other dogs. Both varieties must be socialized at a young age. Manchester Terriers can be excessive barkers and chewers.

Specific training advice: The Toys could have a housebreaking problem. Decide early whether to housebreak or paper train and stick to the chosen method. Start off with a nylon training collar for both varieties. If a metal training collar becomes necessary, introduce it gradually. Teaching *Stay* could be a problem for some. Manchester Terriers can be aggressive toward other dogs.

MASTIFF (AKC, UKC)

Positive characteristics: The Mastiff is a sweet, lovable dog. The newly initiated Mastiff lover is sometimes surprised to find such a big, warm heart in such an imposing dog. Despite their size, Mastiffs adjust beautifully to apartment life. These are great dogs to play and have fun with. They love the company of children and are fine family dogs.

Negative characteristics: Big dogs eat big dinners. Expenses for food and care will be higher than they would be for a smaller dog. Because of the Mastiff's size and strength, obedience training is necessary. Unfortunately, these wonderful dogs do not live as long as dogs of other breeds. Their life span is approximately eight to ten years.

Specific training advice: It will be much easier to train a 20-pound puppy than a strong, well-built, 160-pound dog. Teach *Heel* immediately to keep them walking with you rather than in the opposite direction. *Down* is much more difficult to teach to a large dog, so begin early. *Sit* is a difficult command for any extra large breed and will be performed slowly and with some difficulty. This must not be mistaken for stubbornness.

The Mastiff thinks slowly and therefore requires patience

during training. His slow responses must be forgiven and tolerated. He loves praise and responds well to encouragement. The Mastiff loves to learn.

MINIATURE PINSCHER (AKC, UKC)

Positive characteristics: Miniature Pinschers are very alert, outgoing, feisty little dogs. They are good obedience workers who enjoy working for you and for praise. Their size and temperament make them well suited to the city and to traveling. Though small, they make good watchdogs.

Negative characteristics: Housebreaking is often a problem, as it is with most toy breeds. Individual dogs can be snappy to people outside the family if they have been babied and carried around too much. Too much pampering can also lead to excessive barking and yapping.

Miniature Pinschers do not have much tolerance for pulling and roughhousing, so they may not be good with young children. If the dog is to live with children, bring him into the household as a puppy and raise the puppy and child together. Introducing a child to a Miniature Pinscher over two years old is not a good idea.

Specific training advice: Do not be misled by the Miniature Pinscher's small size. Toy breeds definitely need obedience training. A dog who can stand on his own four feet, even if he's small, is a more successful companion than one who expects to be carried everywhere. Consider teaching the commands *Sit, Stay,* and *Down* on a table. It puts you on the same level with the dog and makes your size less overpowering. Begin the training with a nylon training collar, then carefully make the transition to a metal one to allow the dog's neck to adjust. If the dog is carried around too much he will have trouble with leash breaking and walking on-leash. Housebreaking problems should be dealt with as soon as possible. The decision to paper train or housebreak must be made very early. If the owners work all day, paper training may be the best choice. Do one or the other, but stick with the method you've chosen.

NEAPOLITAN MASTIFF

Positive characteristics: The Mastiff features give the Neapolitan the appearance of a formidable watchdog. The breed does not disappoint in this area. Its innate characteristics make it a very good watchdog. Neapolitan Mastiffs are incredibly strong. They love their families. They are elegant in movement and appearance, very bright, and require fairly little maintenance.

Negative characteristics: Neapolitan Mastiffs have a tendency to be one-owner dogs, which can be seen as a positive or a negative quality depending on one's viewpoint. If they have been carefully socialized at a very young age and if they live with their families in the country, that loyalty could be a positive factor. But if they are expected to love everybody and meet strangers constantly in a city, it could be a problem. They are very aggressive on their territory, which, in their minds, could include the sidewalk or the elevator. Because of their tendency to be aggressive toward people outside the family and their natural strength, serious problems are possible.

Specific training advice: In addition to its size and strength, this is a very dominant breed. Individuals must be trained with a very firm hand beginning at a young age. The owner/trainer must be the leader at all times. Neapolitan Mastiffs must be socialized as young puppies or training will be difficult. Training these dogs requires great strength and stamina. They are just too big and powerful for trainers who are mild-mannered and frail. Socialization is all-important.

NEWFOUNDLAND (AKC, UKC)

Positive characteristics: These outgoing dogs are among the finest-tempered, most responsive dogs alive. They are lovable, affectionate, and very good with children. They will tolerate the abuse that children notoriously dish out—they will rarely react with anger or snappishness to overexuberant children. Newfoundlands love to play. They are wonderful family dogs and they thrive in the country. In the city they adjust to apartment life with no difficulty because they are lethargic indoors. Most oversized dogs would rather spend the day sleeping or staying put instead of running and jumping like many of the smaller, more restless breeds. For this reason they make excellent pets for elderly people. A Newfoundland is companion, guard, playmate, and loyal friend combined in one magnificent dog.

Negative characteristics: These are very large dogs and require large amounts of food. They are not for the economy-minded. Although well suited for city living, they are not practical in a tiny apartment. Newfoundlands, like all giant breeds, have a shorter life span than other breeds.

Specific training advice: You cannot be hard on a Newfoundland when training him. This dog is very sensitive and will become shy and skittish if jerked excessively. Although the dog's great size demands a metal training collar for training, it should be removed immediately after each session. The collar will wear the fur away from long-haired dogs.

When teaching *Heel* or any basic command, take the time to show this breed what to do even if it takes a lot of repetition. It is better to repeat the training process than to administer too many corrective jerks. Because the dog is so large does not necessarily mean he requires hard correction. Easy correction is suggested because of this breed's great sensitivity. *Sit* is a difficult command for such a large dog and will be executed slowly. Newfs have a slow response time, which should not be confused with stubbornness or lack of responsiveness. They are very willing to please and hard corrections are unnecessary with them.

NORWEGIAN ELKHOUND (AKC, UKC)

Positive characteristics: Because they are inclined to bark a great deal, these animals are very good watchdogs. They love the roughhouse play of children and make excellent house pets in both city and country. They have good appetites, live between twelve and fifteen years, and are even-tempered.

Negative characteristics: These excitable dogs run and play very hard and consequently are not recommended for elderly people. They have strong-willed temperaments and require a firm hand to control their tendency to take advantage of owners, especially owners who allow them to get away with the slightest disobedience. If they are hit they will become aggressive or shy.

Specific training advice: They respond very well to training. Housebreaking will offer few problems. However, if left alone, they will develop chewing problems or will chase around the apartment doing damage. Digging can also be a serious problem. Strenuous exercise before leaving these high-spirited dogs alone may help.

Teaching the proper commands will not be difficult. Authority and firmness should be the rule. Distractions are the biggest problem.

OLD ENGLISH SHEEPDOG (AKC, UKC)

Positive characteristics: This breed has become popular because of its unique furry appearance. These dogs seem to be stuffed animals come to life. Television advertising has recognized the visual appeal of the breed and uses it in many commercials.

Old English have good temperaments and are ideal with children. Although they are irresistible as puppies, they become even more appealing as adults and add a woolly beauty to any household. Like many other breeds, they adjust well to city and country life. Because they are so strong, they can take the roughhouse play of children without getting hurt. These sturdy dogs can take a good strong correction and will offer few problems in an apartment.

Negative characteristics: Because of commercialized breeding practices, Old English Sheepdogs are sometimes nervous, aggressive, and stubborn. If they have been hit they are capable of having bad tempers and can become biters. In some cases both bad breeding and bad handling have conspired to create a very bad example. Because these dogs have become so popular, many are bred unselectively without regard to temperament or medical problems. The only safeguard is to become familiar with the animal's parents and grandparents. Do not hesitate to ask questions about the dog's bloodline. In reference to the animal's handling, it is common sense to realize that an abused dog is eventually going to strike back out of fear and distrust, so never hit your dog. These excitable dogs are too difficult for those who are not strong and physically capable of handling their size and strength. They are not recommended for elderly people.

Specific training advice: This is a stubborn breed and requires firm handling. Housebreaking must begin as soon as the dog enters his new home. Obedience training should begin when the puppy is at least three or four months of age. Old English Sheepdogs mature later than most other breeds, which makes training very important. Although a metal training collar is necessary, remove it immediately after each session; otherwise, it will rub away some of the hair around the neck.

Almost every command in the obedience course will result in a struggle between you and the dog. This is especially true when teaching *Down* and *Heel.* These two commands should be emphasized. Old English Sheepdogs should not be allowed off-leash in the city or in any area with auto traffic.

These dogs tend to chew, dig, and jump on people and furniture.

PAPILLON (AKC, UKC)

Positive characteristics: The delicate, elegant Papillon is a regal dog, perfect for the city. Papillons love people as much as people love them, especially elderly people. These dogs love to travel.

Learning obedience commands is fun for them; their love for obedience work is apparent.

Negative characteristics: A poorly bred example of this breed can be shy or aggressive. They are not good with young children unless they are raised with the child from puppyhood. As with other toy breeds, if the Papillon is carried around excessively, it will have a tendency to become snappy and aggressive. The delightful Papillon temperament can be ruined if the owner is too permissive and indulgent.

Specific training advice: To avoid problems, decide in early puppyhood whether to housebreak or paper train, keeping in mind your work schedule and the dog's gender. Males have trouble with paper training because of hind-leg lifting when urinating. Using a table when teaching commands such as *Sit*, *Stay*, and *Down* is less threatening for such a small dog. A nylon training collar is better for the fur. Make a slow transition to a metal one, and only if it's necessary.

If you make a Papillon a lap dog, he will always be on your bed or on your furniture. This is more a person problem than a dog problem.

PEKINGESE (AKC, UKC)

Positive characteristics: These unusual-looking dogs make excellent house pets, and are very well suited to apartment living. They are good with considerate children, though they are best for elderly people. They are wonderful companion animals offering warmth and solace when needed.

Negative characteristics: They have a strong stubborn streak and can be very noisy when a doorbell rings.

Specific training advice: Gentleness is the keynote to training this breed. You must never use a training collar. Pekingese are very willing to learn, but they are sensitive and should not be jerked too hard. If you take the time to teach them the basic commands, you will always have a responsive, disciplined pet.

Because of the Pekingese's size, paper training is recommended. Decide early whether to paper train or housebreak.

If you make them lap dogs they will always be on your bed or on your furniture. This is a person problem rather than a dog problem.

PEMBROKE WELSH CORGI (AKC, UKC)

Positive characteristics: The Pembroke Welsh Corgi is born without a tail. Those born with tails have it docked (surgically shortened). Pembrokes are distinguished from Cardigan Welsh Corgis by the absence of the tail in the Pembroke. Both breeds do well on country farms or in city apartments, but the Pembroke does well in castles, too: It is the favorite breed of the royal family of England. Pembrokes are quite sturdy and enjoy the rough-and-tumble play of children. They are excellent companions for just about anyone. Behaviorally, Pembrokes are a bit more animated and more easily excitable than Cardigans.

Negative characteristics: Some Pembrokes are known to nip at the heels of their human families. This is natural, because they were bred to herd cattle and nipped at the cows' heels to herd them. Shyness or biting behavior can sometimes be a problem. This breed has a tendency to be strong-willed. Their long bodies may cause some back problems, and they love to chew and dig.

Specific training advice: Begin housebreaking at a young age to avoid problems. *Down* could be the most difficult command to teach.

PHARAOH HOUND (AKC, UKC)

Positive characteristics: The rare, aristocratic, and elegant Pharaoh Hound is a very down-to-earth dog who gets along with single owners, couples, senior citizens, and other animals such as cats and small dogs. Although very energetic, it adapts well to apartment living.

Negative characteristics: Pharaoh Hounds have a tendency to be shy and skittish. This characteristic can be accentuated by keeping the puppy away from social contacts with people and other animals, or it can be lessened by early socialization. When these dogs live in a household with other dogs, or when they live in pairs, as they often do, they tend to relate to one another rather than to new people. In addition to people and animals, they need to be socialized around noises to prevent sensitivity to loud or foreign sounds. Due to their extreme sensitivity, they are not recommended for very young children.

Specific training advice: At the start of training, work them in a quiet area because they are very easily distracted. Pharaoh Hounds are sensitive and require a gentle hand in training, but will learn if owners are patient. Use the leash in a gentle manner and do not jerk it excessively. Use your voice firmly but not harshly. *Stay* will be the most difficult command to teach— it is the command that you will have to work the hardest on.

Pharaoh Hounds like to lie on furniture, so you must decide as soon as possible whether that is acceptable. This is more an owner problem than a dog problem. Do not allow puppies on the furniture if you think it is going to bother you later. Pharaoh Hounds are known to be escape artists, so if they are kept in the backyard, reinforce the fences. Make sure all the gates are closed or get some type of self-closing gate. Keeping these dogs alone in the yard for long periods can lead to excessive barking.

POMERANIAN (AKC, UKC)

Positive characteristics: Furry, fluffy little Pomeranians make wonderful traveling companions. They are good watchdogs and especially nice for the city. This versatile breed is gentle enough for elderly people yet hardy enough for children. They enjoy working in obedience.

Negative characteristics: Pomeranians have a tendency to be excessive barkers. Because they are so irresistible they are often spoiled to the point of shyness and aggressiveness. Carrying a Pomeranian around in one's arms too much or babying him too much could make him aggressive toward strangers and everybody else. They might even be aggressive toward children if not properly socialized. They certainly cannot take the rough-house play of a toddler. Socialize a Pomeranian in early puppyhood with people, other dogs, and children. All the wonderful Pom traits shine through if they are socialized and not spoiled.

Specific training advice: In anticipation of some housebreaking difficulties, decide early whether you want to paper train or housebreak. Choose the plan that best suits your life-style and stick to it. Paper training may not be a good choice for a male dog because of hind-leg lifting when urinating. A pampered dog will wind up sleeping in your bed or jumping on your furniture or on everybody else's furniture—more a people problem than a dog problem.

The earlier training begins, the more well-mannered the dog is going to be and the easier it will be to visit other homes and to travel with him. *Sit*, *Stay*, and *Down* should be taught on a table to avoid intimidating such a little dog with your size. The table gives you eye-to-eye contact.

At the beginning of training, use a nylon training collar. Slowly change to a metal one, if necessary. A dog that is used to walking on his own four feet will housebreak well. Poms should walk around like other dogs; don't get into the habit of carrying a Pom everywhere.

POODLE (STANDARD AND MINIATURE) (AKC, UKC)

Positive characteristics: Although this breed originated in Germany, it is considered the national dog of France. In France it is called *Caniche*. There is little difference between the Standard and the Miniature Poodle except size. The Standard Poodle is fifteen inches or more at the shoulder and the Miniature is between ten and fifteen inches at the shoulder. An oversized Standard is informally called the Royal Standard.

These dogs are intelligent, frisky, dignified, and very elegant-looking.

The Poodle is one of the most popular breeds in America. Poodles are extremely intelligent dogs, brilliant in training, and very eager to please their owners. They are good family dogs and get along well with children and with other dogs. Many people own more than one. City life appeals to this breed. There is no dog more cosmopolitan-looking than a poodle. They bring the boulevards of Paris with them no matter where they go.

Negative characteristics: Because many owners primp and pamper them so much, they can get spoiled. Careful puppy selection from a reliable breeder is recommended when a breed is as popular as the Poodle.

Specific training advice: Housebreaking, barking, and jumping on people are their primary training problems. However, these are highly intelligent dogs and if you show them what to do, they will do it. Problem behavior must be corrected at an early age.

POODLE (TOY) (AKC, UKC)

Positive characteristics: The most obvious factor here is size. The Toy Poodle is the smallest variety of all the Poodles. For many potential dog owners, size is the most important consideration. As the name implies, these are tiny animals and measure under ten inches at the shoulder.

Toy Poodles are very affectionate dogs and are excellent with elderly people. They are also good with children, but only the larger varieties are more capable of enduring roughhouse play. These dogs are very gentle, loving animals and set the standard for house pets. They are among the best pets available.

Negative characteristics: They are usually spoiled by their owners and become stubborn and yappy. They will bark at the least disturbance and insist that things be done the way they want them. This only happens when they are treated like human babies. Because they are so popular, careful puppy selection is important to avoid being victimized by the commercializers of the breed.

Specific training advice: Housebreaking is the number-one problem. Decide as soon as possible whether the dog is to be paper trained or housebroken. Many owners tend to carry Toy Poodles around, which can turn the dogs into insecure barkers with shy-aggressive behavior. They will always be on the furniture and on the bed if allowed; however, that is a person problem rather than a dog problem.

These animals require discipline and should be obliged to obey all commands. If they are indulged like spoiled children they will never be trainable. The key to training Toy Poodles is to treat them like animals, not children. However, you must not use a training collar on Toy Poodles. They are too delicate for that equipment.

PUG (AKC, UKC)

Positive characteristics: Can a dog with a pushed-in face, small, brutish body, and loose lines of flesh around the shoulders be considered beautiful? Ask any Pug owner. Pugs do not require cuddling and have adapted to various working tasks not expected of a toy breed. It is interesting to know that the Pug is essentially a miniaturized Mastiff. These dogs are affectionate in a quiet, dignified way. They are good in a brace (two together) because they tend to get along with other dogs; many owners keep two. They adapt very well to the city and make wonderful family pets.

Negative characteristics: Pugs suffer from shortness of breath that often sounds like asthma. Because of their breathing difficulties, Pugs cannot be left alone in a closed car, even with the windows slightly open, or they will suffocate. If you have occasion to travel frequently, this is not the dog for you. Pugs have a tendency to overeat if allowed, and they snore.

Specific training advice: Never use a training collar with this breed. Because of the breathing problem, training sessions must be very short. No lesson should last longer than five minutes and the dog must not be jerked much. You may give two five-minute lessons within a one-hour period.

Do not train these dogs where there are distractions. The objective is to try to avoid as many corrections as possible. Be gentle and patient.

PULI (AKC, UKC)

Positive characteristics: Sometimes known as the Hungarian Puli, this breed offers an unusual feature. There are many persons who desire a dog who can tolerate a lot of roughhouse play, but at the same time they do not want an oversized animal. These dogs fill that need. They are medium-sized dogs and are not fragile. Dog and child can play for hours without hurting each other. Pulis are very responsive to training and make wonderful watchdogs. They are very protective of their families and demonstrate proper aggressiveness when necessary. Apartment life offers no hardship or difficulty for the Puli. They do not run around wildly or need excessive exercise.

Negative characteristics: Pulis can be too aggressive, almost to the point of violence. They are nervous and high-strung animals and are not recommended for elderly people. Occasionally you will find a Puli who is not good with children. The best way to purchase one is to deal with a reputable breeder and investigate the animal's bloodline for behavioral traits.

When not from good bloodlines, Pulis are difficult dogs to own.

Specific training advice: Even a well-bred Puli is going to be stubborn. If the animal comes from poor bloodlines, he may prove to be too nasty to live with. Training must start early in life. Techniques of fear and punishment will irreparably damage the Puli's personality; if a Puli is hit he will become aggressive, and perhaps a biter as well. Pulis tend to chew, bark excessively, and dig.

RHODESIAN RIDGEBACK (AKC, UKC)

Positive characteristics: Members of this large, powerful breed function very well in guard work. They are tough and make excellent guard dogs. They are aggressive, but not in a vicious sense.

Ridgebacks are very intelligent dogs. They play and exercise hard; they are well suited to either the country or the city.

Negative characteristics: These dogs are strong-willed and require a robust handler. It takes a strong, firm individual to command one. A Ridgeback will take advantage of any owner who does not enforce discipline or allows poor responses to each command. He can be very stubborn.

Specific training advice: They tend to chew and dig. Because of their stubborn behavior, you must exercise patience when teaching the basic obedience commands. However, make them obey every command given. Once they have been trained, do not allow them to disobey. Firm corrections are the only way to achieve success. They must be made to obey the first time, every time.

When they walk, they must be made to walk by your side, rather than pull ahead as they tend to do. Ridgebacks are aggressive toward other dogs. This problem must be dealt with the minute it happens. The basic obedience course will help. The key to their training is complete control at all times.

ROTTWEILER (AKC, UKC)

Positive characteristics: These animals are among the finest guard dogs in the world. They have been bred especially for this work and have proven to be extremely effective. Family life suits them. These dogs are responsive to training and highly tolerant of correction. If you need a very obedient dog and a good protector, then this is definitely the breed to buy. In addition, these powerful animals are majestic in carriage and beautiful in appearance.

Negative characteristics: Overly aggressive behavior has become a great problem in this breed because of commercialization and nonselective breeding in numerous instances. Quality breeding is essential.

Rottweilers are stubborn dogs. They require a strong, dominant hand to maintain control. The stubbornness is the same as that of some of the hunting breeds. Select a puppy carefully from a reputable breeder to insure a good example of the breed.

Specific training advice: Begin obedience training at a young age. If the dog is past one year of age and shows signs of aggression, you *must* seek professional help. Rottweilers have a tendency to be dogfighters, diggers, and chewers. Exercise is very important for this breed.

Because of this breed's stubbornness, you are going to have to work very hard teaching each command. But the end result is well worth the trouble. Rottweilers are very responsive to training and have the potential to obey perfectly. Getting through their stubbornness is the problem—they will fight you on each command when learning. When being taught *Heel*, they will try to pull your arm out of its socket. The only answer is a firm correction each time the dog fails to respond to your command.

ST. BERNARD (AKC, UKC)

Positive characteristics: St. Bernards are the greatest bundles of fun in the world. These gentle dogs are phenomenal with children. They are excellent for the country. They can endure the coldest temperatures for many hours. Despite their great size, they can be surprisingly happy in an apartment. They are very responsive to obedience training. They want to please and can take a firm correction with no negative reaction. St. Bernards are loving, affectionate, and passive enough for elderly people to handle. They are not nervous or high-strung. They have a wonderful lethargic manner.

Negative characteristics: Select a puppy carefully from a reliable breeder. This breed has become so popular that it has become the victim of nonselective breeding and commercialization. When examples of this breed do not have the true St. Bernard temperament they can be extremely aggressive.

St. Bernards slobber; saliva constantly gathers at the corners of their mouths. This can be unappealing depending on your tolerance for the more earthy qualities of dogs. It could also be costly if you have fine furniture and carpeting.

Specific training advice: Teach each command as outlined and a Saint will respond very well. Some Saints are more outgoing than others. The more lethargic the animal, the less willing he will be to please. He may be slow to sit or respond slowly to other commands, but don't confuse this leisurely response with stubbornness or unresponsiveness. When selecting a puppy, try to choose the most outgoing of the litter: He will respond best to obedience training. No matter which puppy you get, you will find him easy to housebreak. These are very clean animals. Do not overjerk in your corrections. One firm correction should suffice for these willing pupils.

SALUKI (AKC, UKC)

Positive characteristics: Salukis are even-tempered animals and make excellent house pets in the city or country. These are very quiet, exotic dogs.

Negative characteristics: Because they are independent and aloof, they are not good family dogs. They usually appeal more to rugged individuals who are private in their life-styles. These dogs are not extroverted and consequently appeal most to a few special types of people. It is hard for the average family to relate to this exclusive, reserved animal.

Specific training advice: Salukis respond to training but not as well as other breeds because they are nervous and high-strung. Noises make them skittish. It is not advisable to train them near busy streets or noisy environments. A peaceful country setting is the optimum training place. Because of his nervousness, you must reassure a Saluki with affection and praise whenever he responds properly. Give lavish praise when he obeys a command. Do not hold back with your approval.

SAMOYED (AKC, UKC)

Positive characteristics: Samoyeds are among the most beautiful dogs in the world. They have pure white fur broken only by a black nose and dark almond-shaped eyes. They are good country dogs, especially in the winter. Their thick fur coats allow them to endure the coldest of climates. They respond well to training and are excellent with children. These rugged dogs weigh between fifty and sixty pounds and easily take the punishment of a child's play. They are easygoing dogs and respond well to the city because they do not require too much exercise.

Negative characteristics: Samoyeds have strong-willed temperaments. They completely rebel against being left alone. This may account for their chewing problems. If they live outdoors most of the time they become excessive barkers. Housebreaking is difficult. They are destructive chewers and diggers. Punishment is no answer for these problems. (See Chapter 15, "Problems.")

Specific training advice: You must use a metal training collar because of the need for firm correction. However, remove it immediately after each training session—the metal collar can wear the fur away. A leather or nylon training collar is a good alternative.

Teaching the commands will be a battle between you and the dog. Eventually a Samoyed will do what you want him to, but it will be a fight to reach that level of training. The main training problem will be housebreaking. If you are very patient with them, Samoyeds ultimately respond well to training, but you must be very firm if you are ever to get to that point. These dogs require the authority of a strong person during the training process; they are extremely stubborn.

SCHNAUZER (GIANT) (AKC, UKC)

Positive characteristics: Giant Schnauzers are one of the three varieties of Schnauzers. The Standard and Miniature are almost identical to the Giant except in size. Giant Schnauzers originated in Bavaria, where they were developed from the Standard variety and worked with cattle. Since then, they have been highly successful as guard dogs in Germany. These are fine guard dogs who adjust well to country or city life.

Negative characteristics: The Giant Schnauzer is a very independent dog and is sometimes regarded as stubborn. Select a puppy carefully from a reliable breeder. This breed has become so popular that it has become a victim of nonselective breeding and commercialization. When examples of this breed do not have the true Giant Schnauzer temperament they can be extremely aggressive.

Specific training advice: Adjust your teaching efforts to the temperament of your dog. If he is hypersensitive, you must not be as hard on him as you normally would be. If he is extra stubborn, you must be extra firm. These are strong-willed, aggressive dogs and they can be dogfighters. Giant Schnauzers are exceptional animals to work with, and they will respond to training with ease and competence.

SCHNAUZER (STANDARD AND MINIATURE) (AKC, UKC)

Positive characteristics: Both Standard and Miniature Schnauzers respond very well to training. Except for size, there is little difference between the two. They accept correction well. Schnauzers are marvelous family dogs. They are outgoing and affectionate, with great tolerance for the rigors of a child's play.

These rugged animals are wonderful in the city. They are endowed with enormous energy and assertive playfulness. They can be left alone for many hours without becoming lonely or bored. They are responsive to affection and eager to please. The more affection you give these dogs, the more they will respond to you. Schnauzers are fearless and perceptive guard dogs.

Negative characteristics: Schnauzers are stubborn. When they make up their minds to do something it is difficult to stop them. They are strong-willed animals.

Specific training advice: Schnauzers require patience. Too much authority works against the training. You must show them what to do with patience and affection.

The toughest command to teach this breed will be *Down*. Make sure your dog knows *Sit*, *Stay*, and *Heel* before you teach *Down*. However, Schnauzers do respond to the other commands very well with no hesitation. Be firm with your corrections, but add a lot of praise immediately afterward.

SCOTTISH TERRIER (AKC, UKC)

Positive characteristics: These are very affectionate dogs who make excellent companion animals and house pets. They adjust well to both city and country life. Their compact size and even temperament makes them ideal for children and elderly people.

Negative characteristics: Scottish Terriers do not like being left alone, which creates problems for people who must go to work every day. They also can have a difficult time being house-broken. These dogs have the typical terrier stubbornness.

Specific training advice: Extra time and patience will be required during the housebreaking period. These are stubborn dogs, and they can be excessive chewers. They tend to dig, and if confined too much or improperly they become excessive barkers. Many become dogfighters. Training a Scottie can be a lot of work, but if you are patient you will be rewarded with great results.

SEALYHAM TERRIER (AKC, UKC)

Positive characteristics: It is hard to believe that the elegant dog we see in the show ring—the one with the beautiful white fur—was originally bred to kill vermin. The Sealyham originated in Wales and is named after the estate of its first breeder. Developed from an obscure ancestry, Sealyhams became proficient at exterminating badgers, otters, and foxes. It is, no doubt, these beginnings that created the Sealyham's instinct for guard work. They are excellent watchdogs and very perceptive in determining friend from foe.

In the home they are second to none as loving, loyal pets. They respond to training very well and have a great willingness to please. Sealyhams make excellent pets for children. They have a great fondness for play and enough physical stamina

324 100 DOG BREEDS

for the rough treatment of children. The Sealyham is a unique breed, not seen too commonly.

Negative characteristics: Like most terriers, they are stubborn. These small dogs also bark at any disturbance and have a great deal of energy, which is only a negative for those who desire a calm, easygoing dog.

Specific training advice: They tend to chew and dig. The most difficult command to teach them is *Down*—it will require extra effort, patience, and much praise. Reinforce every command you teach with great affection. If you merely apply the corrective jerk when things do not go well, you are going to have a terrible fight on your hands. Like most terrier breeds, Sealyhams will test you to see how much they can get away with. Be firm. Use a training collar, but remove the collar immediately after training sessions; otherwise the fur will wear away at the neck.

SHETLAND SHEEPDOG (AKC, UKC)

Positive characteristics: Reminiscent of the larger rough-coated Collie, Shetland Sheepdogs are loving, affectionate dogs. They are excellent with elderly people and fine with children because they are neither excitable nor aggressive. They are extremely gentle dogs. Shelties are ideal for small apartments. They take up very little space and are fairly docile. However, the peace and quiet of a rural environment better suits their sensitive temperament. They are very intelligent dogs with pleasing pesonalities.

Negative characteristics: Shetland Sheepdogs can be nervous, hypertense animals tending toward shyness when not bred from good bloodlines. They require extra love and affection. These are not dogs to roughhouse with. They are sensitive and reserved with strangers.

Specific training advice: Because of their sensitivity, Shelties require tender loving care, especially during the training period. Do not use any form of training collar. Be gentle in all corrections; this applies to every command you teach them. This does not mean you shouldn't be firm when giving commands. Simply use a soft touch when making corrections and be sure to lavish them with praise.

Shelties should be trained slowly. Take more time in teaching each command than in looking for immediate results. Otherwise, you will end up with a very shy animal.

SHIBA INU

Positive characteristics: This breed originated in Japan and is quickly gaining popularity here. A beautiful animal, it resembles a plush fox, although some claim it looks more like a miniature Akita. This small spitzlike dog is compact, attractive, clever, and possessed of a charming personality. Shibas are very intelligent dogs. They thrive as both city or country dogs. Typical of most northern breeds, the sturdy Shiba can tolerate most temperature extremes. Those who have owned them claim their behavior is similar to that of a cat. They are clean, controlling, aloof with strangers, and quite independent. They will even walk on tabletops and counters in the fashion of a housecat.

Negative characteristics: The Shiba tends to have an aggressive temperament due to its dominant nature. However, it is often the female Shiba Inu that is aggressive toward other dogs. Because they were originally bred for hunting they are highly observant and easily enticed into the chase for any prey animal that makes itself available. They are very likely to run away if allowed off-leash outdoors.

Specific training advice: This is a very sensitive breed, so the degree of correction must be adjusted accordingly. These are strong-willed dogs who require very firm handling, but if the corrections are too strong they will react poorly and become snappy. Be firm, patient, and consistent. The trainer must balance these elements and accept the reality that these are difficult dogs to train. Early socialization during puppyhood is of significant help to the training process. Any early signs of aggression must be taken seriously and corrected immediately.

SHIH TZU (AKC, UKC)

Positive characteristics: These dogs can quite literally serve as toys for careful, well-behaved children. They love to play and run around. They are also excellent for elderly people. The Shih Tzu is a very elegant-looking dog, though it can behave like an uninhibited clown. Despite its size, it can be enjoyed in the country, where it will run and play vigorously. It does well in the city, too. These warm and even-tempered animals are very responsive to training and are completely portable. Shih Tzus are the perfect traveling companions because they cause no inconvenience. They are intelligent animals with pleasing personalities.

Negative characteristics: Shih Tzus are difficult to housebreak.

Specific training advice: The selection of a good Shih Tzu puppy is the key to happiness. Many families tend to baby them too much and turn them into total lapdogs—they sleep in the bed and lounge about the furniture. As a result of being pampered, they often become aggressive or bark excessively.

You must choose whether to housebreak or paper train, then stay with your choice. During paper training you will find that from time to time Shih Tzus may forget to use the paper. When that happens you must go back over the training and reinforce what has already been taught. Never use a training collar on these delicate animals.

SIBERIAN HUSKY (AKC)

Positive characteristics: These remarkably intelligent and gentle animals have the unique ability to adjust to any climate and any set of living circumstances. Siberians are dense-coated dogs capable of enduring the severest cold weather or the hottest temperatures. They are a joy to behold in the country, especially in the snow, and yet live remarkably happy lives in the city.

They are naturally gentle and friendly, rendering them useless as watchdogs but distinctive as warm, loving companions. These north-country beauties are almost human in personality and engage in deep, meaningful relationships. They make superb pets for children. Sturdy and playful, they not only endure the rough play of children, they demand it. These dogs will go out of their way to sniff around a child, even a stranger, and entice him into playing. To hear the wolf howl, or "singing," of a Siberian Husky is to be irresistibly drawn to him for life.

Negative characteristics: These dogs sometimes develop into very picky eaters. If they do not have the company of another animal to eat with, or do not like what they are being served, they will go without food to the point of near starvation. Huskies are extremely stubborn and hardheaded about having things their own way. For this reason they are not recommended for elderly people or for permissive people. Because they are so friendly they are useless for guard work and cannot be relied on as watchdogs.

Siberian Huskies are independent, curious, and very high-spirited. Consequently, they cannot be trusted off-leash. They will run with great bursts of energy, not realizing how far from home they have gotten. They are often lost when allowed off the leash, and it may require a search party to find them.

If not trained with firmness and discipline, a Husky will pull your arm from its socket to get to another animal on the street or perhaps to some prospective playmate. Huskies also do not tolerate being left alone for long periods of time. When this happens, they will chew anything they can get to, including baseboards, curtains, and any number of household appliances. They are easily bored. They are notorious diggers. Sometimes adding another animal in the home prevents their destructive behavior. Another dog or even a cat helps to alleviate their boredom.

Specific training advice: A metal training collar is the only effective equipment for administering a correction. Bred for pulling heavy sleds, the collar and neck muscles of a Husky are well developed, and he will feel only the firmest correction. However, the metal collar must be removed immediately after each session because it tends to wear away the fur around the neck.

Occasionally an individual Husky has a hard time being

housebroken. Huskies demand constant attention and many walks during the housebreaking period.

These dogs learn quickly and respond beautifully to training. However, they retain their independence and cannot be relied upon to obey every command even after the most arduous training program. Because they are easily distracted, they should be trained in a quiet, secluded area. They require frequent brush-up lessons to remind them who is boss and what is expected of them. They will test your authority every chance they can. Because they are so lovable and endearing, they will use all their wiles to avoid obeying a command and to get their own way. Firmness and authority are the key to controlling these dogs.

You must not allow yourself to indulge them when they violate their training. This is the hardest thing about owning a Husky. They will run, jump, or sing to distract you, and they too often succeed.

SILKY TERRIER (AKC, UKC)

Positive characteristics: Silkys are very loving, affectionate, and outgoing dogs. They are true lap dogs, even though they have been used in their native Australia as workers to hunt rats and snakes. These compact animals are completely portable and travel well. They are also wonderful pets for small apartments. Silkys are small but very sturdy and capable of taking a great deal of abuse from children. They are ideal as an all-around family pet.

Negative characteristics: Like most terriers, they have a stubborn disposition. Housebreaking will be problematic.

Specific training advice: Do not use a training collar; use a leather or nylon collar and leash. These dogs can be excitable and consequently will be distracted very easily. Try to keep their attention. In the early phase of training use a quiet street or the privacy of your home. Once your dog learns the commands, you can work him outside where there are noises and strange people. His stubbornness must be met with firmness when he disobeys. Train him at an early age.

SKYE TERRIER (AKC, UKC)

Positive characteristics: This is an uncommon and interesting-looking breed, making for good conversation with people on the street who have never seen one. Skye Terriers adapt as well to the city as to the country, providing they receive a proper amount of exercise. For a small breed, they are good watchdogs. Like most terriers they are excellent hunters and adept at mousing.

Negative characteristics: Sometimes these terriers are shy or aggressive to people and to dogs if they have not been properly socialized. They can be territorial. Terriers dig and chew, and the Skye Terrier is no exception. Also, they are excessive barkers. They do not relate well to those outside their families. This is not a breed for everybody.

Specific training advice: The Skye Terrier is a very strong-willed breed and requires a strong, firm, and consistent hand. *Come When Called* and *Down* will be difficult commands to teach.

SOFT-COATED WHEATEN TERRIER (AKC, UKC)

Positive characteristics: Like many terriers, Soft-Coated Wheaten Terriers are very energetic, bright, and playful. They can be great with kids if the breeding is good. The Wheaten, at about thirty-five pounds, is a good size for both city and country life. Although they look and feel like big cuddly teddy bears, they are very alert and make excellent watchdogs.

Negative characteristics: When the breeding is poor or the dog has not been properly socialized at a young age, the Wheaten can be fear/aggressive. As young puppies, Wheatens need to meet new people and dogs in many different surroundings. If this breed is kept outdoors all the time it develops fear/aggressive problems.

Wheatens have a common terrier personality trait: stubbornness coupled with a high energy level. Wheatens are also fond of barking, chewing furniture, destroying landscaping, digging, and jumping, and they can be dogfighters.

Specific training advice: This breed and its owners can benefit greatly from firm consistent training begun at an early age. Wheatens are energetic and intelligent, which should not be confused with their stubbornness. They are very bright and hard-working dogs when they want to be. All the commands will be difficult to teach, especially *Come When Called, Heel,* and *Down.* If a cute, cuddly Wheaten convinces you that he is a lap dog at a young age, you will have a hard time getting him out of your bed for the rest of his life. Decide early what you will tolerate and stick to your decision.

STAFFORDSHIRE BULL TERRIER (AKC, UKC)

Positive characteristics: These are sweet, lovable, medium-sized dogs, wonderful for the city or the country. They love to play, fetch, and retrieve, and still have boundless energy to spare. They are good dogs for children.

Negative characteristics: Due to bad press, bad owners, and poor breeding, many communities want to ban this breed. Staffordshire Bull Terriers are inherently no worse than any other powerful breed. Statistically, they have been involved in very few biting incidents. However, a criminal, someone in the dog-fighting business, or someone seeking a macho image can misuse the intelligence and strength of this breed to suit his own warped needs. How suitable Staffs are as pets depends on the breeder, the breeding, and the character of the owner.

Like all terriers, they have a tendency to be dogfighters; they love to dig, to chew, and to jump on people. They are physically strong. This breed is not for weak or passive people.

Specific training advice: Staffordshires are good obedience dogs—they like to work. They are exuberant and require a lot of exercise. Never play tug-of-war or other aggressive games with them. Such game playing conditions them to pull and use their teeth. People who have a good attitude toward this breed can really enjoy a Staffordshire Bull Terrier.

VIZSLA (AKC, UKC)

Positive characteristics: These natives of Hungary are very good with children. They make wonderful house pets and are also good in the country. They adapt very well to apartment life. Appetite is never a problem (except during illness), and their life span is from twelve to fifteen years. Sweet-natured and affectionate, the Vizsla is well suited to training and responds without too much correction.

Negative characteristics: Like other hunting breeds, Vizslas are stubborn. Occasionally, due to poor breeding, they develop a problem of nervous wetting—poor breeding has created many nervous Vizslas. Although they are good apartment dogs, there is one qualification: If training does not begin at a very young age they develop chewing problems and cause much destruction. Even a trained Vizsla will chew up an apartment if he is not exercised regularly. Chewing is caused by confinement, and exercise combined with obedience training is the only answer.

Specific training advice: Vizslas tend to be diggers. Administering the corrective jerk is crucial with this breed. But be careful—their ears are very long and get tangled in the training collar and leash, which can be very painful for the animal.

The Vizsla is a very excitable animal and will cross in front of you or jump on you when learning to heel. Emphasize *Heel* and do not let him pull you. He will respond to an authoritative voice. Because he craves affection in large doses, he will work very hard to please you. The trick is to know when to withhold affection and when to give it as a reward for responding properly to a command.

With this breed, emphasize the *Sit-Stay* and *Down-Stay.* Vizslas tend to demand attention from anyone who enters the house. They also like to run out the door the minute it is opened. By emphasizing the *Stay* command, you will be able to maintain greater control over them. *Go to Your Place* is another important command.

The plains of Hungary are the natural habitat of this great hunting breed. Keeping one as a house pet demands that obedience training begin at a very early age if the dog is to live successfully in a domestic situation.

WEIMARANER (AKC, UKC)

Positive characteristics: There is a great ambivalence in most Weimaraner owners. They are stubbornly loyal and absolutely devoted to these "Gray Ghosts," despite the many difficulties involved in owning one.

Weimaraners are excellent companions for children. They have a tremendous tolerance for the rough-and-tumble treatment usually meted out by small children. They will endure a child's eye gouging, ear pulling, back sitting, and tail yanking. Because of their need for exercise, they will run a great deal and can be a joy to behold in the country. The more exercise they get, the better they are to live with.

These German hunting dogs are strong and lively and can be used effectively for guard work. They can be trained to growl, bark, or bite on command. Protective of their families by nature, they adapt to this work very well. However, guard work can be accomplished only with expert training. Weimaraners are even-tempered.

Negative characteristics: Weimaraners embody all the negative characteristics of the hunting breeds. They are stubborn and strong-willed and try to get away with everything possible. At times they do not obey commands. They will wander off if given the chance. If their pent-up energy is not released in some positive form, they are capable of destroying entire apartments.

If they understand that their human leader does not operate with great authority, they will take liberties, such as pulling him or her down the street. Because Weimaraners are so lovable, it is hard to avoid babying them.

Weimaraners are dogfighters. They are not recommended for elderly people. They require a firm, strong hand and will respond to nothing else. Chewing problems are common in this breed. They are notorious for destroying, in some instances, thousands of dollars' worth of furniture and personal possessions. Their chewing will try every ounce of patience you possess, and without great patience it can be a difficult struggle, if not impossible, to train a Weimaraner. Unless these dogs are forced to respond to obedience training through patience and authority, they will be difficult to own.

Specific training advice: Their long ears get tangled in the training collar and leash, so be cautious when administering the corrective jerk. This is critical, because Weimaraners require very firm corrections. Without firm corrections, they will take advantage of the owner and make a simple walk a living nightmare. They need to be handled with authority. These dogs will always test their owners to determine how much they can get away with. When administering a corrective jerk be firm. Continue to deliver firm corrections, especially when teaching *Heel. Sit-Stay* and *Down-Stay* will be very useful commands when control is needed, as it often is.

Weimaraners can be pests, demanding attention and affection when the situation does not call for it. That's when *Stay* commands are very handy. Weimaraners should never be taken off-leash in the city. They are completely untrustworthy and will chase the first animal they see, which could cause an accident.

They are excessive diggers and can completely destroy a yard or lawn. One of the best ways to keep a Weimaraner out of mischief is to give him a place that is exclusively his own in the apartment or house. (See Chapter 14, *"Go to Your Place."*)

Owners who declare their great pleasure with and love of the breed are legion. But Weimaraners can be tolerable house pets only if they are trained at a very early age.

WEST HIGHLAND WHITE TERRIER (AKC, UKC)

Positive characteristics: Many dog fanciers consider the Westie the best of all the terrier breeds. These little dogs are surely the model for those fancy stuffed dogs sold at exclusive toy stores. They are among the best dogs for apartment living. They are compact yet rugged, highly intelligent, and faithful to the end. Westies, with their marvelous temperaments, are ideal for children. They are gentle, responsive, and beautiful.

Negative characteristics: This is a small, feisty breed and very excitable. Those are not necessarily negative characteristics, unless you are looking for a dog who is calm and relaxed. Westies are yappy, especially when the doorbell rings, and because of their highly charged activity levels, they may not be suitable for elderly people. These terriers like to jump on people and chew. Some of them are aggressive toward other dogs. In some instances they are difficult to housebreak. Start at an early age and decide on housebreaking or paper training and stay with one method.

Specific training advice: Because of their energy they require exercise, especially before each training session. But they are intelligent, easy-to-train dogs. You merely have to show them what to do and they will do it.

WHIPPET (AKC, UKC)

Positive characteristics: These are racing dogs much like the Greyhound, only smaller. They are affectionate, intelligent animals capable of running thirty-five miles an hour. Although they are geared for high-speed racing, they make very good house pets. They will sit indoors in a quiet, graceful manner and add dignity and beauty to any room. Because they bark at strangers, they make good watchdogs. They are gentle in nature, however.

Negative characteristics: Whippets are fragile. They are very sensitive to loud noises and get skittish on the street. They are not recommended for children.

Specific training advice: It is almost impossible to teach a Whippet commands while outdoors. The outdoor noises are too frightening to them. They must be trained indoors, with no distractions. Be sure these dogs have been taught to obey each command before trying them outside.

Do not use a metal training collar. We suggest a nylon or leather training collar, and at that you should not be too hard with your corrections. Training will require patience. If you are too hard on Whippets they will not trust you and will become very nervous. One problem is that they are often babied and not allowed outside, which results in a very nervous, frightened dog. It is advisable to take a Whippet outside frequently as a small puppy and get him used to strange noises.

YORKSHIRE TERRIER (AKC, UKC)

Positive characteristics: Yorkies are very often kept as decorative lapdogs and serve their families as the quintessential companion animal with no function other than raising the status of their owners. Nevertheless, Yorkshire Terriers are wonderful pets for considerate children and elderly people. Because they are terriers they are sturdy animals with lots of spunk. They are equally at home in the country and the city. Yorkshire Terriers are extremely intelligent.

Negative characteristics: They are difficult to housebreak and have the same stubborn behavior found in other terrier breeds. Many owners keep their Yorkies indoors to avoid extra grooming, and this can hamper their need to be adequately socialized.

Specific training advice: Yorkies are aggressive and yappy. The most difficult command to teach is *Heel.* They dart from side to side and back and forth when being walked. You must be firm, demanding, and patient when teaching this command.

It is recommended that you housebreak these dogs right at the start. Although they have difficulty being housebroken, they are even less reliable if paper trained. They still have mishaps long after the training has ceased. During the housebreaking period they bear constant watching and many walks.

Do not use a training collar; they are too delicate. Because Yorkies are stubborn, begin training at an early age. Be firm and patient. Most corrections should be vocal. Do not overjerk. Because these dogs are so small and precocious, their owners tend to spoil them.

INDEX

Scolding, urinating as response to, 213

Scottish Terrier, 322–23

Sealyham Terrier, 323–24

Seat harnesses, 205

Shake cans, 45–46, 73

in housebreaking, 63

Shake cans (*cont'd*)

jumping on furniture and, 217–18

in paper training, 56–57

Shar-pei, Chinese, 264–65

Shetland Sheepdog, 324–25

Shiba Inu, 325–26

Shih Tzu, 326–27

Shy dogs, 41. *See also* Fear/aggressive dogs

body language and, 16, 17, 19

Come When Called command and, 189–90

correction of, 30, 35, 86

Down command and, 148, 149, 151, 154, 160, 172–73

fear or submission wetting by, 27, 212–13

Heel command and, 115, 120–21

housebreaking of, 27

shake cans and, 46

Sit command and, 101

Sit-Stay command and, 139–40

temperament of, 33–35

Siberian Husky, 327–29

Silky Terrier, 329–30

Sit command, 90–106. *See also* Automatic Sit *command*

after coming when called, 185–88

customized training for, 98–106

definition of, 90

dog's name before, 92

food technique for, 96–98

placing technique for, 95–96

procedures and techniques for, 91–98

pushing technique for, 93–96

reasoning behind, 91

small dog technique for, 98

Sit-Stay command, 129–44

and backing away as dog remains in *Stay*, 134–35

customized training for, 138–44

definition of, 129

pivoting technique for, 131

to prevent running out of house, 224–25

procedure and technique for, 131–38

reasoning behind, 129–30

and secret of teaching *Stay*, 131–34

as temporary position, 145

voice command and hand signal for, 131

and walking around both sides of dog as he remains in *Stay*, 135–36

and walking behind dog as he remains in *Stay*, 136–37

Six-foot leather leashes, 44–45

Skye Terrier, 330

Sliding leash technique, for *Down* command, 156–58

Small dogs

body language and, 16, 19

Down command and, 160

Sit command and, 98

Soft-Coated Wheaten Terrier, 331

Spaniel
  Brittany, 256
  Cocker, 266–68
  English Springer, 276–77
Spiked collars, 43
Spoiled dogs, growling by, 216–17
Sprays, repellent, 207, 215
Staffordshire Bull Terrier, 332
Staring into dog's eyes, 17
Stay. See also Down-Stay *command;*
  Sit-Stay *command*
  as command vs. correction, 177–80
Strong-willed dogs
  body language and, 16, 18–19
  Come When Called command and,
    190–91
  correction of, 87
  Down command and, 149, 151,
    154, 156, 158, 160, 173–74
  Heel command and, 121
  Sit command and, 102–3
  Sit-Stay command and, 140–41
  temperament of, 35–36
Submission. *See* Dominance and sub-
  mission
Sweep technique, for *Down* com-
  mand, 151–54, 160

Tabasco sauce, 207, 215
Table, taking food from, 225
Table scraps, 65
Table technique, for *Down* command,
  160
Talking back, 36, 38, 226
Teething, 208, 223
Temperament, 11, 27, 29–39. *See
  also* Aggressive dogs; Calm/
  easygoing dogs; High-energy/

outgoing dogs; Shy dogs; Strong-
  willed dogs
aggressive, 37–40
breed characteristics and, 229–32
calm/easygoing, 36–37
combination of qualities in, 31–
  32
defined, 30–32
high-energy/outgoing, 32–33
responsive dogs and, 40–41
shy, 33–35
strong-willed, 35–36
Terriers, 31. *See also specific terriers*
Territoriality, 39, 46, 50
  dogfighting and, 209
  Go to Your Place command and,
    195–96
Touching your dog, 18
Toy breeds. *See also specific toy
  breeds*
  collars and leashes for, 45
Toys, rawhide, 208, 223
Training. *See also* Basic obedience
  course; *specific topics*
  myths about, 7–8
  proper frame of mind for, 5
  reasons for, 5–7
  suitable area for, 13
  temperament and, 30
  when to begin, 9
  who should participate in, 9
Training collars. *See* Collars, jeweled
  training
Training sessions
  breaks in, 94
  corrective jerk in, 94–95
  for *Down* command, 147–48
  ending of, 127